Empire of Conspiracy

Empire
of Conspiracy

*The Culture of Paranoia in
Postwar America*

Timothy Melley

Cornell University Press   Ithaca and London

Excerpts from the following titles appear by permission of their publishers and authors: *Bodily Harm* by Margaret Atwood. Copyright © 1981 by O.W. Toad, Ltd. Reprinted with the permission of Simon & Schuster and Phoebe Larmore; *Catch-22* by Joseph Heller. Copyright © 1955, 1961 by Joseph Heller. Copyright renewed © 1989 by Joseph Heller. Reprinted with the permission of Simon & Schuster and Donadio & Olson, Inc.; *Gravity's Rainbow* by Thomas Pynchon. Copyright © 1973 by Thomas Pynchon. Used by permission of Viking Penguin, a division of Penguin Putnam, Inc., and Melanie Jackson Agency, L.L.C.; *Libra* by Don DeLillo. Copyright © 1988 by Don DeLillo. Used by permission of Viking Penguin, a division of Penguin Putnam, Inc., and the Wallace Literary Agency, Inc.; *One Flew Over the Cuckoo's Nest* by Ken Kesey. Copyright © 1962, 1990 by Ken Kesey. Used by permission of Viking Penguin, a division of Penguin Putnam Inc., and Sterling Lord Literistic, Inc.; *The Shadow Knows* by Diane Johnson. Copyright © 1974 by Diane Johnson. Reprinted with permission of Alfred A. Knopf, Inc. and Sterling Lord Literistic, Inc.; "The White Album" from *The White Album* by Joan Didion. Copyright © 1979 by Joan Didion. Reprinted by permission of Farrar, Straus & Giroux and the author. Special thanks to Grove Press and Little Brown, who did not charge for the scholarly use of excerpts from their titles.

First published 2000 by Cornell University Press
First printing, Cornell Paperbacks, 2000

Printed in the United States of America

Librarians: A CIP catalog record for this book is available from the Library of Congress.

Cornell University Press strives to use environmentally responsible suppliers and materials to the fullest extent possible in the publishing of its books. Such materials include vegetable-based, low-VOC inks and acid-free papers that are recycled, totally chlorine-free, or partly composed of nonwood fibers. Books that bear the logo of the FSC (Forest Stewardship Council) use paper taken from forests that have been inspected and certified as meeting the highest standards for environmental and social responsibility. For further information, visit our website at www.cornellpress.cornell.edu.

Cloth printing   10 9 8 7 6 5 4 3 2 1
Paperback printing   10 9 8 7 6 5 4 3 2 1

FSC FSC Trademark © 1996 Forest Stewardship Council A.C.
SW-COC-098

Contents

Preface

Conspiracy theory has a long history in the United States. It has animated our political culture from the early Republican period to the present, at times powerfully swaying popular opinion. But its influence has never been greater than now. Since 1950, an extraordinary number of writers have used expressions of paranoia and conspiracy theory to represent the influence of postwar technologies, social organizations, and communication systems on human beings. Writers as different as William S. Burroughs and Margaret Atwood, Thomas Pynchon and Joan Didion, and Kathy Acker and Don DeLillo have depicted individuals nervous about the ways large organizations might be controlling their lives, influencing their actions, or even constructing their desires. The same concerns are reflected in postwar films, television shows, and other media, which routinely posit conspiracies of astonishing size and complexity. And as sociological studies have shown, many Americans now assume that such plots are not only possible, but operative and determining forces in their own lives.

Why, then, has conspiracy theory become such a fundamental form of American political discourse? And why is this way of thinking about political power common to both marginalized and relatively privileged groups? While paranoia and conspiracy theory are often seen as marginal forms—the implausible visions of a lunatic fringe—their ubiquity in contemporary American culture suggests that they are symptoms of a more pervasive anxiety about social control. Indeed, their popularity can only be explained by examining what they have in common with mainstream narratives and ideas. It is no accident that so many cultural expressions—from Vance Packard's *Hidden Persuaders* to postwar addiction discourse, and from David Riesman's *Lonely Crowd* to the Unabomber "Manifesto"—have lamented the "decline" of individual self-control and the increasing "autonomy" of social structures, especially government and corporate bureaucracies, control technologies, and mass media. Despite the diverse contexts in which these anxieties appear, they take a remarkably consistent form, which I call *agency panic*. Agency panic is intense anxiety about an apparent loss of autonomy, the conviction that one's actions are being controlled by someone else or that one has been "constructed" by powerful, external agents. *Empire of Conspiracy* traces this fear through postwar American culture, concentrating on its often melodramatic expression in fiction and film and revealing its importance to nonfiction genres, including cybernetics and systems theory, popular sociology, medical discourse, business and self-help literature, political writing, and cultural and social theory. The importance of agency panic, this book argues, lies in its troubled defense of an old but increasingly beleaguered concept of personhood—the idea that the individual is a rational, motivated agent with a protected interior core of beliefs, desires, and memories.

As I have worked on this project, I have discovered a form of agency panic to which scholars seem particularly susceptible. It is most often experienced at the library, in the dark spaces of the stacks or the quiet maze of the periodicals room. One is especially vulnerable to it while gazing at an on-line catalogue, an article index, or a list of new books. It is precipitated by the discovery of a text that appears, on first glance, uncannily similar to one's own work. The feeling that follows such a discovery may vary in intensity, but it is rarely good. It may be a sense of lost opportunity, a disappointment at having failed to be the first to bring a thesis to the public eye, but at times it amounts to nothing less than paranoia—a suspicion that one's ideas have somehow been accessed, duplicated, preempted, perhaps even stolen (but *how?*).

Such discoveries, and the feelings they provoke, usually fade away on reflection. But like the more dramatic instances at the center of this study, they arise in the first place because of tenacious, romantic assumptions about the autonomy and uniqueness of individuals (especially writers), assumptions reinforced by the atomistic lifestyle of the scholar. What such discoveries remind us is that our ideas are never *wholly* our own. They are influenced by the larger communicative systems in which we exist and to which we contribute. If such reminders come in the form of panic, no matter how momentary, they do so because it is sometimes difficult for us to discard the idea that we are unique and autonomous authorial agents. At least it has sometimes been difficult for me. Yet, the library, especially the contemporary, globally networked library, has repeatedly made me aware of the debt I owe to other thinkers, not only those cited in the pages to follow, but those whose insights I now take for granted.

There are also many institutions and individuals who helped me directly on this project. I would not have been able to devote myself to it without generous grants from the Andrew W. Mellon Foundation, Cornell University, and Miami University. I am also grateful to the following organizations for allowing me to present portions of it to an audience: the Midwest MLA, the Western Humanities Conference, the University of Washington Americanist Colloquium, the University of Louisville's twentieth-century literature conference, the Claremont Graduate School's conference on addiction and culture, *Rethinking Marxism's* conference on contemporary Marxism at the University of Massachusetts, and the Miami University English Department. Portions of this book have appeared elsewhere in slightly different form. Much of Chapter 2 appeared as "Bodies Incorporated: Scenes of Agency Panic in *Gravity's Rainbow*" in *Contemporary Literature* 35.4 (1994): 709–38. A version of Chapter 3 appeared as " 'Stalked by Love': 'Female Paranoia' and the Stalker Novel" in *differences* 8.2 (1996): 68–100. I am grateful to The University of Wisconsin Press and Indiana University Press, respectively, for permission to reprint this material.

It is a pleasure to acknowledge the immense debt I owe to Molly Hite, whose generosity, incisive criticism, and continuing support have been vital to this project. I owe great thanks as well to Mark Seltzer, whose brilliant approach to American cultural phenomena first helped me to conceptualize this project, and who provided much guidance along the way. My editors, Bernhard Kendler and Candace Akins, and the readers for Cornell University Press, Joseph Tabbi and Kathryn Hume, have been helpful and attentive. Many other colleagues and teachers have offered invaluable responses to this book. I am especially grateful to Barry Chabot, Mary Jean Corbett, Fran Dolan, Paul Downes, Malcolm Griffith, Susan Morgan, Naomi Morgenstern, Joel Porte, and Scott Shershow for their friendship and advice over the past several years. Finally, there are those personal debts too large to describe here. These are to my parents, Ellen and Dan Melley, and to Katie Johnson, who has been both a willing listener and my most faithful reader. This book, and a great many other things, would not have been possible without their love and support.

TIMOTHY MELLEY

Empire of Conspiracy

Introduction

The Culture of Paranoia

The Depth Boys

In 1957, Vance Packard described a postwar phenomenon he found deeply troubling. "Large-scale efforts," he claimed, are "being made, often with impressive success, to channel our unthinking habits, our purchasing decisions, and our thought processes by the use of insights gleaned from psychiatry and the social sciences" (3). According to Packard, a vast array of "subterranean operations," designed to manipulate the behavior of individuals, had been established by public relations firms, advertisers, "social engineers," and political operatives (8). "Typically," he wrote, "these efforts take place beneath our level of awareness; so that the appeals which move us are often, in a sense, 'hidden.' The result is that many of us are being influenced and manipulated, far more than we realize, in the patterns of our everyday lives" (3).

The notion that a network of agents might be operating "beneath the surface of American life" (9–10) was certainly not original. Nervousness about the supposedly extraordinary powers and dangerous motives of large organizations has long been a feature of U.S. political culture. In its classic form, which Richard Hofstadter termed "the paranoid style in American politics," this way of thinking insists that important events are controlled by "a vast and sinister conspiracy, a gigantic and yet subtle machinery of influence set in motion to undermine and destroy a way of life" (29). Of course, Hofstadter himself associated the paranoid style not with the sort of cultural criticism practiced by Packard, but with traditionally "political" texts—that is, documents having to do rather directly with the control of government bodies.

For a more conventional example of the paranoid style from the same period as *The Hidden Persuaders* we might consider J. Edgar Hoover's *Masters of Deceit* (1958), a popular account of communist infiltration. "The communist," Hoover warns, "is in the market places of America: in organizations, on street corners, even at your front door. He is trying to influence and control your thoughts" (191). Like Senator Joseph McCarthy and other practitioners of "paranoid," cold war politics, Hoover regards communism as a veiled "plot" (81), a revolutionary "conspiracy" (53) with extraordinary powers.[1] It is "virtually invisible to the non-communist eye, unhampered by time, distance, and legality" (81). Significantly, these extraordinary powers seem to lie less in the conspirators themselves than in their massive and half-hidden "thought-control net" (93). Despite the rhetoric of conspiracy, in other words, the real threat is not so much a specific agent or group as *a system of communications*, an organized array of ideas, discourses, and techniques.

In all of these respects, Hoover's account is remarkably similar to Packard's, which also posits a large and powerful program designed to manipulate unwitting Americans. Yet, there is a striking political difference between the two texts, and this difference makes their structural resemblance all the more odd: Packard's book exposes a dangerous facet of corporate *capitalism*, while Hoover's hopes to foil *communist* activity. The question, then, is why these accounts of national crisis look so similar when they seem to be at ideological cross-purposes.[2] One possible answer, a familiar one, is that they are part of a "paranoid" tradition transcending particular ideologies and historical conditions. But the notion of a transhistorical, paranoid style does not by itself explain why such politically different projects might find a strategic advantage in the notion of conspiracy. Nor does it account for the specific historical conditions that may have shaped these postwar accounts. Even Hofstadter, who traces political paranoia back to colonial America, notes that the nature of paranoid politics is different after World War II, focused on domestic rather than foreign threats and especially concerned about "the effects of the mass media" (24).[3]

These are significant changes, plainly visible in the texts at hand and striking in their consequences. In the first place, they crack open the notion of the paranoid style, making room for texts such as Packard's, which is not a traditional "political" document but which nonetheless detects a "gigantic yet subtle machinery of influence" at work in American mass culture. More important, changes in postwar "paranoid politics" indicate a shift in popular conceptions of political power. After all, to suggest that *conspiracies* are perpetrated through the mass media is to rethink the very nature of conspiracy, which would no longer depend wholly upon private messages, but rather upon mass communications, messages to which anyone might be privy. This new model of "conspiracy" no longer simply suggests that dangerous agents are *secretly* plotting against us from some remote location. On the contrary, it implies, rather dramatically, that whole populations are being *openly* manipulated without their knowledge. For mass control to be exercised in this manner, persons must be significantly less autonomous than popular American notions of individualism would suggest. The postwar model of conspiracy, in other words, is dependent upon a notion of diminished human agency. And it is *this* concept that makes *The Hidden Persuaders* and *Masters of Deceit* so much alike, despite their distinct ideological underpinnings. Like so many other postwar narratives, both are deeply invested in a traditional concept of individual autonomy and uniqueness, and both reveal this investment through expressions of nervousness about its viability.

One index of this shared anxiety is that Hoover and Packard each posit a secret effort whose real goal is the mass reengineering of persons. Hoover, for instance, insists that the Communist Party is "a vast workshop where the member is polished and shined, his impurities melted out" (159). The rhetoric of such passages connects communist indoctrination to deindividuation, simultaneously implying that capitalism guarantees human freedom and uniqueness. What is most frightening about communist training, in Hoover's view, is that it seeks to remove *all* "undigested lumps of independence" (163). The "communist thought-control machine" (188) is designed to refashion "renegades" and "deviationists" (185) through a program of "ruthless uniformity" (172). The hypocrisy of this view is rather stunning, because Hoover devotes his book (and devoted his career) to rooting out deviants in order to conserve the ruthless uniformity of *American* politics.[4]

My intention here, however, is not to critique the familiar illogic of cold war anticommunism. It is rather to show how that illogic governs the impulse toward conspiracy theory. Hoover's unwillingness to consider anything like *capitalist* "thought control"—that is, his failure to portray both communism and capitalism as ideologies—is central to his conspiratorial view of communist training. Because he refuses to see capitalist training as training, he views communist training as a *secret* and *total* means of social control. How else can we account for the fact that, when Hoover reveals the deep secret of communist thought control, it turns out to be nothing more sinister than education? The Communist Party, Hoover explains, is "an educational institution...One of the first things a new member does is to go to a school" (160). Of course, for Hoover, this is no ordinary school; through its diabolical curriculum, the originally autonomous individual "is made into *communist man*" (159). What allows Hoover to present this little tale of education in the form of a horror story is his assumption that education in a capitalist society, by contrast, is not ideologically shaped and does not construct individuals by its own mechanisms of "thought control." The ironic corollary to this view is not simply that it borrows (and hugely simplifies) an account of ideology from Marxism, but that it undercuts its own premises. If Americans are defined by their extra-ordinary individual autonomy, then why do they need powerful government protections from communism? The answer can only be that autonomy is precisely what they *lack*, because they are easily turned into "brainwashed" communist dupes. It turns out that for all their putative individuality, Hoover's Americans are deeply susceptible to ideological controls.

The same problem of agency haunts *The Hidden Persuaders*, which asserts that scientists have discovered secret new ways to manipulate human desire. According to Packard, these motivational researchers—"known in the trade as 'the depth boys'"(8)—exploit a model of personhood derived from psychoanalysis, employing special "triggers of action" and "conditioned reflexes" (24) to control components "deep" inside persons. They use packaging and display techniques to induce a "hypnoidal trance" in shoppers, causing them to "[pluck] things off shelves at random" and buy more than they can afford (107); they use "subthreshold effects" (subliminal messages) that might someday make "political indoctrination... possible without the subject being conscious of any influence being brought to bear on him" (43); and, in the words of one public relations expert, they are involved in "the most important social engineering role of them all—the gradual reorganization of human society, piece by piece and structure by structure" (217).[5] While Packard suggests that most of these depth experts "want to control us just a little bit" (240), he speculates that their work may lead to practices like "biocontrol" in which "a surgeon would equip each child with a socket mounted under the scalp" so that "subjects would never be permitted to think as individuals" (239–40).

For Packard, this lurid fantasy—in which "electronics could take over the control of unruly humans" (239)—reveals the real threat of motivational research: it is a technology for the radical reconstruction of persons (see Chapter 5). Even motivational researchers themselves, in Packard's view, are "custom-built men," barely separable from the "sample humans" on whom they perform manipulation experiments: each trade school "socially engineers" them to be more compatible with corporate needs (5–6). Such assumptions generate a problem of control much like the one implicit in Hoover's argument. If even the agents of persuasion have been constructed, then who governs the system of depth manipulation? Indeed, if we carry Packard's view to its logical extreme, the very idea of manipulation, in the sense of a *willful* attempt to control others, becomes obsolete, because attempts at manipulation are themselves only products of previous manipulation. In Packard's world, the system of depth manipulation is self-regulating. Control has been transferred from human agents to larger agencies, institutions, or corporate structures.

This way of understanding social control is certainly not new. Concepts of structural agency have long been a staple feature not only of economic and social theories, but also of aesthetic approaches such as literary naturalism, the late-nineteenth-century movement coupled to the development of sociology, machine culture, and deterministic theories of human behavior. In more sophisticated social theories, such as Louis Althusser's, they are often linked to the problem of ideology. We might even say that Packard and Hoover have begun to formulate crude theories of ideology—crude not because they are wholly mistaken (advertisers *do* try to manipulate us and communists *do* train new recruits), but because they view social control as a mysterious and magical process, activated instantaneously and capable of utterly disabling rational self-control. The concepts of thought control and depth manipulation provide theories of social conditioning not by accounting for the complex effects of numerous institutions, discourses, rules, and agents, but rather by reducing those effects into a simple mechanism—a "trigger of action" that almost instantantly converts people into automatons. In other words, Packard and Hoover both attempt to describe a *structural* form of causality while simultaneously retaining the idea of a malevolent, centralized, and *intentional* program of mass control.

It is this odd conjunction of the structural and the intentional that unites the narratives examined in *Empire of Conspiracy*. My interest lies less in the widely accepted idea that social and economic systems affect individual action than in a particularly nervous expression of this idea, an expression that gravitates toward representations of paranoia, conspiracy, and agency-in-crisis. In the postwar rhetoric of diminished individual agency, the power of social structures frequently comes as a shock. Texts from the last half of the twentieth century are replete with the frightening "discovery" that human behavior can be regulated by social messages and communications. This discovery in turn feeds the tendency to attribute motives to large social and economic organizations, bureaucracies, information-processing systems, communication networks, discourses, and social institutions. Such systems frequently seem to be autonomous agents in their own right, and worse, agents interested in the subordination of *all* humans. In a "technological society," Jacques Ellul remarked in 1954, "there can be no human autonomy in the face of technical autonomy. The individual must be fashioned by techniques...in order to wipe out the blots his personal determination introduces into the perfect design of the organization" (138). This sort of remark, which develops out of the sociological tradition of Oswald Spengler, Lewis Mumford, and Siegfried Giedion, is visible all across the postwar American landscape—particularly in the strain of popular sociology pioneered by David Riesman (*The Lonely Crowd* [1950]) and William Whyte (*The Organization Man* [1956]), who articulated for a mass audience the idea that individuals had fundamentally changed under the controlling influence of mass media, corporations, and other social organizations (see Chapter 1). Crucially, writers in this tradition rarely see technological rationalization producing different benefits and problems for different groups of people. Rather, they posit an opposition between individuals and techno-social structures so monolithic and abstract that it obscures the need for a class politics. To take merely one example, Charles Reich's *Greening of America* (1970), a recycled version of *The Lonely Crowd*, asserts that Americans "live under the domination of the Corporate State," a "single vast corporation" "autonomous" enough to have generated "a universal sense of powerlessness"—a sense that extends "even to the inhabitants of executive offices" (129, 89, 101, 10). What is striking about such bold pronouncements is not just their frequency, or even their fear of new technologies, but their sense that social control should be so ubiquitous, so effective, so *total*.

For these writers, and a great many others from this period, the idea of social control comes as a profound revelation and conjures up an empire of conspiracy, a vision of the world in which individuals are forever manipulated by secret agents, hidden persuaders, and malevolent organizations. One of its most important cultural functions, I shall suggest, is to sustain a form of individualism that seems increasingly challenged by postwar economic and social structures. Conspiracy theory, paranoia, and anxiety about human agency, in other words, are all part of the paradox in which a supposedly individualist culture conserves its individualism by continually imagining it to be in imminent peril.[6]

Agency Panic

Although I have begun with a few emblematic instances, this book is concerned with a broad cultural phenomenon, a pervasive set of anxieties about the way technologies, social organizations, and communication systems may have reduced human autonomy and uniqueness. This phenomenon is visible in a wide range of texts, many of which have strikingly different basic concerns and political implications. My intention in this introduction, therefore, is to outline the general contours of a popular way of thinking, but to do so less by generalization than by detailed discussion of different discourses and texts. Along the way, I will be focusing on one particularly nervous form of expression, a way of imagining social control that is extreme yet increasingly popular. This form of expression is often dismissed as paranoia or conspiracy theory—although as I will make clear, neither of these terms, with their sense of marginal and insane interpretive activity, adequately describes the broad-based phenomenon I have in mind.

"This is the age of conspiracy," says a character in Don DeLillo's *Running Dog* (1978), "the age of connections, links, secret relationships" (111). By all accounts, this view has become increasingly common in the postwar period. For several decades, cultural critics have observed that "a kind of paranoia has settled over many communities" (Toffler, *Third Wave* 347) and that many social groups seem to depend upon conspiracy theory for their survival. More recently, major news magazines have described the United States as a nation in the grip of "conspiracy mania" and have pronounced the arrival of a "new paranoid style in the American arts"—although such a style has clearly been flourishing for decades. "The rhythm of conspiracy," notes another, "once background noise, is now a dominant theme of everyday life."[7] Whether the postwar era is really an "age of conspiracy" seems uncertain at best; the important fact is that many people believe it is such an age. Americans now account for all sorts of events—political conflicts, police investigations, juridical proceedings, corporate maneuvers, government actions, and a wide range of other phenomena—through conspiracy theory. Conspiratorial explanations have become a central feature of American political discourse, a way of understanding power that appeals to both marginalized groups and the power elite.

Perhaps not surprisingly, conspiracy theory has also been a fundamental organizing principal in American film, television, and fiction since World War II.[8] Numerous postwar narratives concern characters who are nervous about the ways large, and often vague, organizations might be controlling their lives, influencing their actions, or even constructing their desires. Film and television, from cold war alien flicks to the highly popular *X-Files*, have so frequently depicted corporate, political, and otherworldly conspiracies that Richard Donner's 1997 film, *Conspiracy Theory*, seems at once historically emblematic and utterly redundant. Writers such as Kathy Acker, Margaret Atwood, William S. Burroughs, Don DeLillo, Philip K. Dick, Joan Didion, Ralph Ellison, William Gibson, Joseph Heller, Diane Johnson, Ken Kesey, Joseph McElroy, Norman Mailer, Thomas Pynchon, Ishmael Reed, Leslie Marmon Silko, Kurt Vonnegut, and Sol Yurick have all produced narratives in which large governmental, corporate, or social systems appear uncannily to control individual behavior and in which characters seem paranoid, either to themselves or to other characters in the novel. As Tony Tanner remarked in 1971, "The possible nightmare of being totally controlled by unseen agencies and powers is never far away in contemporary American fiction" (16).[9] Of course, this nightmare was never absent in earlier American moments and may indeed be traced to colonial traditions. But the postwar years have witnessed a dramatic intensification of interest in such a view of the world, and an increasing popular acceptance of its central premises.

Why this is so—not only in fiction and film, but in other cultural arenas as well—is a central concern of this book. Part of the answer is relatively straightforward. As others have noted, the idea of conspiracy offers an odd sort of comfort in an uncertain age: it makes sense of the inexplicable, accounting for complex events in a clear, if frightening, way. To put it another way, by offering a highly adaptable vision of causality, conspiracy theory acts as a "master narrative," a grand scheme capable of explaining numerous complex events (see Chapter 4). Most conspiracy theories are virtually impossible to confirm—yet this built-in impediment to certainty is precisely why they have flourished in an age supposedly marked by the disappearance of grand explanatory schemes and master narratives.[10] Because they are so difficult to confirm, they require a form of quasi-religious conviction, a sense that the conspiracy in question is an entity with almost supernatural powers. In fact, the term "conspiracy" rarely signifies a small, secret plot any more. Instead, it frequently refers to the workings of a large *organization, technology, or system*—a powerful and obscure entity so dispersed that it is the antithesis of the traditional conspiracy. "Conspiracy," in other words, has come to signify a broad array of social controls. And it is this enlarged sense of the term—the sense that allows J. Edgar Hoover to call communism "a conspiracy"—that interests me here.

8 Empire of Conspiracy

The increasing appeal of conspiracy theory is directly linked to this newly expanded definition, which accords the conspiracy broad explanatory power and enormous political utility. In its new form, "conspiracy" can be used to label political enemies who are doing nothing more devious or sinister than their accusers. In the midst of the Korean War, for instance, President Truman could declare that "the Communists in the Kremlin are engaged in a monstrous conspiracy to stamp out freedom all over the world" (568) without also observing that, by such a definition, he was also involved in a "conspiracy" to promote capitalism. At virtually the same moment, the Supreme Court could dramatically toughen its three-decade-old "clear and present danger" test on the grounds that a conspiracy to teach dangerous ideas must not be permitted, even though the "conspiracy" in question was an informal gathering of socialist educators who had neither taken nor advocated any action whatsoever against the state. In its ruling, the Court rejected "the contention that a conspiracy to advocate, as distinguished from the advocacy itself, cannot be constitutionally restrained, because it comprises only the preparation. *It is the existence of the conspiracy which creates the danger*" (*Dennis v. United States* 564, emphasis added).[11] In short, the panic-stricken rhetoric of conspiracy has often been sufficient to mobilize support for serious state action, even the significant abridgment of individual freedoms.

But the state has not had a monopoly on the rhetoric of conspiracy. In the United States, that rhetoric has been widely deployed by both disempowered and comparatively privileged groups to imagine the controlling power of private enterprise, of regulatory discourses and systems, of the state, or of some complex and bewildering combination of these entities. As Fredric Jameson has observed, postwar narratives deploying conspiracy theory and "high-tech paranoia" have provided important representations of global capitalist networks. Conspiracy theory, Jameson remarks, is "a degraded attempt—through the figuration of advanced technology—to think the impossible totality of the contemporary world system" (38), to map networks of power too vast to be adequately represented. In this account, conspiracy theory's oversimplifications stem partly from the sublime objects it attempts to make visible.[12] Instead of being merely a comforting form of misrepresentation, conspiracy theory is a reductive (or "degraded"), but still useful, form of political representation. Jameson's view thus allows room for a defense of some conspiracy theories. Yet, it leaves open a number of questions about the conspiracy form itself. Why represent a massive economic system as a conspiracy? Why conserve a sense of *intentionality* when explaining the manipulation of individuals by huge social and economic networks, labyrinthine webs of power?

These questions are crucial to a full understanding of the culture of paranoia and conspiracy. I will have a good deal more to say about them in the chapters to follow, but for now I want to outline several general observations about conspiracy-based narratives. First, in many texts I examine, conspiracies are understood to be hermetically sealed, marvelously efficient, and virtually undetectable. Second, as Jameson's comments imply, conspiracies typically serve to conceptualize the relation between individuals and larger social bodies. Third, and consequently, the conspiracy is often understood as a structure that curtails individuality, or that is antithetical to individualism itself. As the narrator of Don DeLillo's *Running Dog* puts it, "All conspiracies begin with individual self-repression" (183). According to this view, the members of a conspiracy "repress" their own desires and aims for a set of communal goals, a small social compact.

This assumption has a vital, though often-ignored, corollary: if conspiracy begins with self-repression, then conspiracy *theory*—the apprehension of conspiracy by those *not* involved in it—begins with individual self-protection, with an attempt to defend the integrity of the self against the social order. To understand one's relation to the social order through conspiracy theory, in other words, is to see oneself in opposition to "society." It is to endorse an all-or-nothing conception of agency, a view in which agency is a property, parceled out *either* to individuals like oneself *or* to "the system"—a vague structure often construed to be massive, powerful, and malevolent. This way of thinking is rooted in long-standing Western conceptions of selfhood—particularly those that emphasize the corrupting power of social relations on human uniqueness. As Ralph Waldo Emerson warned some 150 years ago in the classic American account of self *versus* society, "Society everywhere is in conspiracy against the manhood of every one of its members" ("Self-Reliance" 261). This familiar sense of individual struggle against a collectivity is essential to contemporary conspiracy theory. One of its problematic effects is to hide the specific political features of the struggle it attempts to represent. Its monolithic conception of "society" (or "system," or "organization") obviates the need to conceptualize particular interests within that collectivity, interests that might be based on class, gender, race, or other factors. Hence the similarities between politically opposed writers like Packard and Hoover, and the apparent contradictions of figures like the Unabomber, whose professed "ambition" was not only "to kill a scientist, big businessman, government official or the like" but also "to kill a Communist" (Kaczynski, qtd. in Johnston A16).[13] These facts offer a crucial lesson: by making diverse social and technological systems enemies of "the self," the conspiratorial views function less as a defense of some *clear* political position than as a defense of individualism, abstractly conceived.

It is not surprising that extremely self-defensive postures of this sort are often understood as "paranoid." Clinically paranoid individuals, after all, frequently express a general fear and distrust of their environment. Yet, the highly popular conception of self I have just outlined cannot simply be read as a sign of pathology. Indeed, conspiracy narratives would not be on the rise if that self-concept were not broadly popular. Only the continuing appeal of liberalism, and its vision of an autonomous self beleaguered by society, can explain why the controlling "agencies and powers" in postwar narratives are so often "unseen" or elusive, why they so rarely consist of specific conspirators, why they vary from text to text, and why they often look nothing like conspiracies in the traditional sense of the word. The broad appeal of liberal individualism also explains why, for at least the past several decades, conspiracy narratives have displayed such extraordinary political flexibility—why, for instance, they are as appealing to African Americans who wish to explain racial discrimination as they are to white racist groups who believe the United States is under the control of "Zionist Occupied Government" (ZOG) or some other coalition of foreigners and minorities.[14] It is significant that conspiracy theory has been attractive to both the left and the right and that it has registered concern about all kinds of social organizations, large and small. Its widespread appearance on the cultural landscape cannot simply be explained as a response to some *particular* political issue, historical event, or social organization. This does not mean, of course, that its application to social and political events does not have particular sources or political implications. As I have already suggested, conspiracy discourse has considerable political effects, the most important of which stem from its usefulness to both the disempowered *and* the powerful—the latter of whom sometimes further their own interests through a sense of their "manipulation" and "victimization" by some pernicious form of social control (see Chapter 1).

My point, however, is that the recent surge of conspiracy narratives stems not from a specific historical development—such as Watergate, the Kennedy assassination, or even the Cold War—but from the larger sense that, to quote one cultural critic, "our specialness—our humanness—has been taking it on the chin a lot lately."[15] It stems, that is, from a sense of *diminished human agency*, a feeling that individuals cannot effect meaningful social action and, in extreme cases, may not be able to control their own behavior. "At this moment in history," wrote R. D. Laing in 1967, "we are all caught in the hell of frenetic passivity" (51). For Charles Reich, "The American crisis…seems clearly to be related to an inability to act" (10). And for Donna Haraway, "Our machines are disturbingly lively, and we ourselves frightening inert"—a view, she admits, that once would have seemed "paranoid" though "now we are not so sure" (152). Sentiments like these are related to a widely circulated postwar narrative, a story about how the "postindustrial" economy has made Americans more generic and less autonomous than their rugged forebears and about how social structures— especially government and corporate bureaucracies, control technologies, and "the media"—have become autonomous agents in their own right.

Despite their appearance in diverse postwar narratives, these anxieties take a remarkably consistent form, which I will refer to as *agency panic*.[16] By agency panic, I mean intense anxiety about an apparent loss of autonomy or self-control—the conviction that one's actions are being controlled by someone else, that one has been "constructed" by powerful external agents. This anxiety is expressed most dramatically in fiction and film, though its underlying view of the world is central to many nonfiction texts as well. In most cases, agency panic has two features. The first is a nervousness or uncertainty about the causes of individual action. This fear sometimes manifests itself in a belief that the world is full of "programmed" or "brainwashed" subjects, addicts, automatons, or "mass-produced" persons, as is the case in Heller's *Catch-22*, Reed's *Mumbo Jumbo*, Kesey's *One Flew Over the Cuckoo's Nest*, virtually all of Burroughs's work, much science fiction, and many of the nonfiction texts I have already mentioned. Just as often, the anxiety consists of a character's fear that he or she has been personally manipulated by powerful external controls. Many postwar narratives depict characters who feel they are acting out parts in a script written by someone else or who believe that their most individuating traits have been somehow produced from without. Margaret Atwood's characters, for example, are forever enacting classically feminine behavior, even though they know it is harmful and undesirable. Some of Thomas Pynchon's characters suspect that their sexual responses, among other things, have been determined by a massive espionage program. DeLillo's Lee Harvey Oswald feels that his participation in Kennedy's murder has been planned by powerful forces beyond his control. And, in the junked-up world of William S. Burroughs, sadistic government and corporate technologies continually regulate all kinds of human behavior.

In addition to these primary anxieties about individual autonomy, agency panic usually involves a secondary sense that controlling organizations are themselves agents—rational, motivated entities with the will and the means to carry out complex plans. These organizations are sometimes concrete agencies, like DeLillo's CIA or Heller's corporatized Army, but they are just as often more diffuse structures—Pynchon's "Them," Burroughs's "junk virus," Atwood's "men," Reed's "Atonist" culture industry, cyberpunk's autonomous corporations, or even the general "world system" invoked by Jameson and much postwar political rhetoric. In moments of agency panic, individuals tend to attribute to these systems the qualities of motive, agency, and individuality they suspect have been depleted from themselves or others around them. Thus, agency panic not only dramatizes doubt about the efficacy of individual human action, it also induces a *postmodern transference* in which social regulation seems to be the intentional product of a single consciousness or monolithic "will."

Because the convictions I have been describing usually arise without much tangible evidence, they often seem to be the product of paranoia. Yet, they are difficult to dismiss as paranoid in the clinical sense of pathologically deluded. As Leo Bersani points out, the self-described "paranoids" of Thomas Pynchon's fiction are "probably justified, and therefore—at least in the traditional sense of the word—really not paranoid at all" (101). Theorists of schizophrenia working against traditional psychological models, from R. D. Laing and Gregory Bateson to Gilles Deleuze and Félix Guattari, have shown that pathologizing judgments of such abnormal modes of experience may stem from overidentification with normalizing clinical assumptions. In fact, Laing goes so far as to suggest that schizophrenia can be "a conspiracy" perpetrated *against the schizophrenic* by family and health care workers, who wish to reduce the patient's "full existential and legal status as human agent" (*Politics* 84).

Nonetheless, there is now a wealth of scholarship, following Hofstadter, that continues to view "political" paranoia as an easily identified and pathologized ailment, something that can be readily diagnosed by appeal to a universal authority.[17] What many such accounts refuse to recognize is that conspiracy theory arises out of radical doubt about how knowledge is produced and about the authority of those who produce it. Ironically, then, by uncritically labeling certain claims "paranoid" and dangerous to society (in general), such theories miss the most important meaning of conspiracy theory: that it develops from the refusal to accept someone else's definition of a universal social good or an officially sanctioned truth. This is not to say that we must open our arms to all manner of conspiracy theories. It is merely to assert that diagnoses of political paranoia are themselves political statements reflecting particular interests. Until we discover some magically unmediated access to reality, conspiracy theory cannot simply be pathologized in one sweeping gesture. Indeed, while many of the suspicions I examine throughout this book seem far-fetched, insane, or even dangerous, many others seem to be logical responses to technological and social change, to the radical insights of poststructuralism and systems theory, and even to the breathless sociologies of "future shock," "global village" and "postindustrial society" (Toffler; McLuhan; Bell).

For these reasons, I want to make it clear that my intention here is not to weigh in on the validity of particular conspiracy theories. I will not be offering historical analysis that might persuade readers to accept or reject the theories discussed in these pages. Nor do I mean to suggest that authors mentioned here are panicked or, even worse, deluded—although they are clearly in the business of *representing* panic about human agency, and some do at times seem to share the emotions so visible in their characters, often for good reason. Rather, my goal is to assess the cultural significance of the anxieties I have been describing.

I believe that those anxieties indicate a crisis in recent conceptions of personhood and human agency. The importance of agency panic lies in the way it attempts to conserve a long-standing model of personhood—a view of the individual as a rational, motivated agent with a protected interior core of beliefs, desires, and memories. This concept of the liberal individual, which C. B. Macpherson has termed "possessive individualism," derives from the liberal political philosophy of Hobbes and Locke, and has long been celebrated in American political culture, particularly in the guise of "rugged individualism" and atomistic "self-reliance."[18] That these forms of individualism have masculine associations helps to explain why so many of the texts I examine understand social communications as a feminizing force and why narratives of dwindling human autonomy are so often connected, in our culture, to masculinist outbursts of "regeneration through violence" (from John Birch tactics to the work of the Unabomber and contemporary "patriot" groups).[19]

Indeed, the culture of paranoia and conspiracy may be understood as a result of liberal individualism's continuing popularity despite its inability to account for social regulation. Agency panic dramatizes precisely this paradox. It begins in a discovery of social controls that cannot be reconciled with the liberal view of individuals as wholly autonomous and rational entities. For one who refuses to relinquish the assumptions of liberal individualism, such newly revealed forms of regulation frequently seem so unacceptable or unbelievable that they can only be met with anxiety, melodrama, or panic. Agency panic thus reveals the way social communications affect individual identity and agency, but it also *disavows* this revelation. It begins with a radical insight, yet it is a fundamentally conservative re-sponse—"conservative" in the sense that it conserves a traditional model of the self in spite of the obvious challenges that postwar technologies of communication and social organization pose to that model. Its widespread appearance on the postwar landscape indicates a broad cultural refusal to modify a concept of self that is no longer wholly accurate or useful, but that still underpins a long-standing national fantasy of subjectivity.

This concept of self stands in sharp contrast to poststructural and post-modern theoretical reconceptions of subjectivity, which have exploded the assumptions of liberal individualism, arguing that identity is constructed from without, repeatedly reshaped through performance, and (in extreme accounts) best understood as a schizophrenic and anchorless array of sepa-rate components.[20] "Instead of mourning the loss of the self," Gabriele Schwab remarks, poststructural theory "celebrates its end" (5). In the wake of such theories, many cultural critics have emphasized the relation be-tween postmodern narrative and these newly "fragmented" or "decentered" concepts of subjectivity—frequently associating modernism with paranoia and postmodernism with schizophrenia, respectively.[21] But when under-stood as stark oppositions, such associations are misleading. The texts I ex-amine here, many of which are routinely considered postmodern, invest heavily in themes of paranoia and rarely seem to *celebrate* the fragmenta-tion of the self. Rather, they depict the difficulty their characters have relin-quishing liberal humanist assumptions about themselves. Agency panic, therefore, may be understood as a nervous acknowledgment, and rejection, of postmodern subjectivity. Its appearance in writing commonly consid-ered postmodern is an index of liberalism's continuing appeal in the face of serious theoretical challenges. As one of Kathy Acker's characters puts it: "My total being could have somersaulted in and into that panic which is nihilism. But an act of will kept the fiction of 'me' going" (*Empire* 147).

Despite the significant problems with some panic-stricken defenses of liberal individualism—which include the encouragement of individual, rather than collective, forms of resistance to social control—I want to stress that agency panic is not simply a misguided or irrational response. In fact, I will show that it bears an important likeness to sociological thinking, often illuminating the obscure sources of social regulation. Yet, paradoxically, it produces quasi-sociological insights by attributing intentionality to the level of the social order. Those possessed by it find hidden communiqués inside generic social messages; they view mass social controls as forms of individual persecution; and they see social and economic patterns as the re-sult of *willful* malevolence. In other words, they unearth forms of human intentionality where a strictly sociological analysis would find only institutions, mores, economic structures, and discourses. Their attempt to trace social effects to an intending subject depends upon a form of misrecognition—yet one that is difficult to avoid and often fruitful. Thus, for reasons that will become clear, it is neither possible nor desirable to say that the forms of suspicion examined here are fundamentally misguided or mistaken. Their pervasiveness testifies to the difficulty of assessing their validity and is symptomatic of serious cultural concern about access to information and the production of knowledge. Even more important, some of the narratives examined here provide compelling critiques of the social and economic structures that cause this problem. As Noam Chomsky has pointed out, "institutional analysis" is often dismissed as mere "conspiracy theory" by those who believe our institutions (economic, communicational, judicial, and so on) are supremely fair. My refusal to make sweeping assessments of conspiracy theory in general, then, (despite the apparent lunacy of a good many conspiracy theories) depends partly on the intelligence and political power of many such narratives. But it also stems from a set of theoretical considerations, to which I now turn.

Crises of Interpretation

Because they attempt to unearth hidden forms of control and communication, theories of conspiracy and mass manipulation depend heavily on the interpretation of half-hidden clues, tell-tale signs, and secret messages. Both Packard and Hoover, for instance, rely on their sense that they have uncloaked concealed influences in apparently ordinary communications. In many of the fictional texts I examine, the business of reading messages is more vexed. In many of Margaret Atwood's novels, for instance, a woman feels she is being stalked by a man (possibly her lover), yet she is unable to determine who he is or whether he even exists. Thomas Pynchon's characters frequently believe they have stumbled on a massive plot, but are unable to confirm its existence. Don DeLillo's *Libra* (1988) foregrounds the difficulty of historical interpretation through the figure of Nicholas Branch, a CIA historian who is unable to write his account of the Kennedy assassination despite more than a decade of research. In each of these cases, a difficulty confirming the causes of complex social events leads to grave uncertainty about human agency and social regulation.

Given the frequency of this pattern, it is no accident that paranoia is a major theme in many of these texts. After all, paranoia is an interpretive disorder that revolves around questions of control and manipulation. It is often defined as a condition in which one has delusions of grandeur or an unfounded feeling of persecution, or both. Understood less judgmentally, it is a condition in which one's interpretations seem unfounded or abnormal *to an interpretive community*. I present both of these descriptions because they highlight a problem inherent in the definition of paranoia, and thus an issue I will confront throughout this study: despite the seemingly obvious marks of extreme (or pathological) cases of paranoia, it is remarkably difficult to separate paranoid interpretation from "normal" interpretive practices. Freud himself repeatedly noted that paranoid interpretations are akin to the very philosophical and psychoanalytic schemes necessary to define and diagnose the disorder.[22] "The delusions of patients," he writes, "appear to me to be the equivalents of the constructions which we build up in the course of analytic treatment" ("Constructions" 268). Because of this similarity, cases of paranoia take the form of *interpretive contests* between analyst and patient, each of whom claims to have unearthed the hidden truth about the patient's (apparent) persecution (see Chapter 3). Consider, for instance, Freud's remarks on the purported homoerotic foundation of paranoia:

> Paranoia is precisely a disorder in which a sexual aetiology is by *no means obvious*; far from this, the strikingly *prominent* features in the causation of paranoia, especially among males, are social humiliations and slights. But *if we go into the matter only a little more deeply*, we shall be able to see that the *really* operative factor... ("Psycho-Analytic Notes" 60, emphases added)

I could have cited many other passages from Freud's work, because going "more deeply" into the "obvious" would serve as a crude definition of psychoanalysis in general, but what is significant in this passage is how much Freud's description of paranoia has in common with paranoia itself. First, both psychoanalysis and paranoia depend upon interpretations that move beyond "prominent" or "obvious" factors. Second and consequently, both appeal to the category of the real—to the "really operative factor," foundation, or causal agent for certain events. (As the popular slogan insists, "It's not paranoia if they're *really* out to get you.")

It is this second move that has made the fictional representation of conspiracy and paranoia increasingly popular in a period marked by skepticism about unmediated access to reality. Because diagnoses of paranoia depend upon a strong concept of reality—a conviction that the patient's claims do not correspond to events transpiring in a measurable reality—the postmodern tendency to put "the real" in quotation marks has undermined the pathologization of paranoia. As a result, if what is real seems more and more to be a construct, and if the procedures for pathologizing insane interpretations seem increasingly indistinguishable from the procedures of the insane, then paranoia (or "paranoia") becomes an obvious vehicle for writers to use in illustrating the politics of interpretation, normalization, and knowledge production (this despite theories that continue to associate paranoia with modernism and not postmodernism).[23] This problem has underwritten virtually the entire corpus of Philip K. Dick's science fiction, which obsessively depicts characters attempting to assess their own sanity in situations of radical ontological uncertainty. It has also encouraged many postwar writers to represent paranoia as a positive state of mind, an intelligent and fruitful form of suspicion, rather than a psychosis. Pynchon's characters, for instance, often believe that "operational paranoia" and "creative paranoia" (*Gravity's Rainbow* 25, 638) can serve as effective forms of resistance to social or political control. In the other texts I examine, potentially paranoid theories are commonplace and often justifiable. Heller's "paranoid" bombardier Yossarian stays alive in part because he believes "everyone" is trying to kill him, a view that seems increasingly sound as *Catch-22* unfolds. The same strategy pays off for many of Margaret Atwood's characters, who come to learn that their fears of being watched or stalked are a reasonable response to heterosexual relationships. The postwar literature of conspiracy and paranoia, in other words, is driven by a sense that knowledge and power are inextricably linked and that to be "paranoid" may only be to reject the normalizing ideology of the powerful.

Yet given the political stakes of conspiracy theories, and the violence associated with some forms of political "paranoia," it may seem especially important to be able to say for certain who is paranoid and who is not. One might thus object to my association of psychoanalysis and paranoia because it seems to undermine the grounds for making such decisions. After all, do not severe cases of paranoia—such as Dr. Daniel Paul Schreber's famous "nervous illness," the subject of Freud's major study of paranoia—go well beyond a mere tendency to draw meanings from what is not clearly "prominent" or "obvious" to others? Schreber's apparent *conviction* that certain evils are being perpetrated against him, it might be argued, is quite different from more recent instances of "operational paranoia," which are marked by a self-critical *suspicion* of the world. We might then distinguish between cases where an individual develops a highly rigid and socially unacceptable interpretive scheme (Schreber's complex system of "nerves" and "rays," for instance) and cases where an individual merely feels uncertainty about the agency of apparently meaningful events (as is the case in most of the texts I examine here). This distinction would be of use in isolating cases of the sort that arise frequently in postwar narrative: cases where individuals not only *suspect* an array of invisible determinants to be at work but also *suspect their own suspicions.* The secondary suspicion seems to indicate the process of a rational, self-effacing, skeptical mind—precisely the opposite of irrational or delusional self-inflation.

This distinction, however, is not as easy to make as it first might seem, because a self-effacing uncertainty is not always absent from more serious or "pathological" cases of paranoia. Louis Sass has convincingly argued that extreme cases of paranoid schizophrenia often result from hypercognitivity and excessive self-reflection. Furthermore, interpretive certainty cannot by itself be a sign of insanity, because even Schreber, who was highly committed to a rigid and unorthodox interpretive scheme, is no more certain of his views than Freud is of his own. In fact, Sass's extraordinary analysis of Schreber's *Memoirs of My Nervous Illness* (1903) demonstrates that the apparently rigid claims of a pathological paranoiac may be, in part, the products of overly rigid interpretation on the part of the analyst (or reader of the *Memoirs*). A more self-effacing reader might begin to wonder, as Sass does, if Schreber's apparently insane claims are not actually the work of a brilliant and complex mind:

> One may be tempted to think that the delusions and near-hallucinations it describes are little more than the almost random products of a state of pure irrationality, perhaps of some kind of near-dementia, or of a delirium in which virtually any random fancy passing before the mind can be extracted and treated as real. Yet . . . one cannot help but wonder whether it is possible to discover a coherent system lying behind it all. (244)

Here, the interpretive drive of the analyst—the desire to find some kind of "coherent system lying behind" what initially seems to be "random fancy"—is structurally analogous to the interpretive drive of the paranoiac, whose disorder is characterized by the tendency to locate coherent motives in what others believe to be "random" or "chance" events. As Sass remarks earlier in his study, "paranoid thinking can be viewed as, in some sense, an almost obvious, logical development—in a world . . . where all events feel interpretable, so that nothing can seem accidental and everything therefore appears to be somehow consciously intended" (61).

If the sense that there are no accidents—that everything is connected, intended, and meaningful—is a hallmark of paranoia, then the difference between a paranoid theory and a brilliant theory may only be a matter of how much explanatory power the theory has for a given interpretive community. And if this is so, then the work of sorting out paranoid claims from justifiable claims—the work of diagnosing, pathologizing, and normalizing—will require a vision at least as penetrating as the one to be judged. Indeed, Sass's desire to match Schreber's own perspicuity seems to be part of what compels him to look for a "coherent system" in Schreber's account, where other analysts have found only "pure irrationality" and "random fancy" (244). Sass even goes on to suggest that Schreber's paranoid system bears a powerful resemblance to sophisticated social theories, such as Foucault's account of panoptic surveillance. Given such resemblances, we might say that the interpretive differences between Freud's account of Schreber and Schreber's account of himself amount to something like a contest between psychoanalysis and sociology—a disciplinary dispute about whether the "really operative factors" in a series of events are best located through study of individuals or analysis of social institutions. Even in the spectacularly delusional case of Schreber, then, serious and intelligent readers disagree about whether Schreber's vision is a profound perception of the social realm or a pure projection of internal material outward. To put the matter in the terms Kathy Acker uses in *Empire of the Senseless* (1988), "Dr Schreber was paranoid, schizophrenic, hallucinated, deluded, disassociated, autistic, and ambivalent. In these qualities he resembled the current Unites States President, Ronald Reagan" (45).

This sort of challenge to traditional conceptions of paranoia is a central preoccupation of many of the texts I examine hereafter. One of the reasons stories of paranoia and conspiracy have become so popular recently is that they stage a contest over the reality, or social basis, of a potentially paranoid individual's perceptions. Contests of this sort have become primary occupations of recent social and cultural theory because they reveal that "knowledge and power are simply two sides of the same question: who decides what knowledge is, and who knows what needs to be decided?" (Lyotard 8–9). Questions like these pose serious problems for anyone attempting a study of paranoia, because projection is a phenomenon afflicting not only those who articulate theories of persecution or conspiracy but those who would interpret such theories as well. Schreber's diagnosis, for instance, has everything to do with the degree to which Freud and Sass have projected their own theoretical assumptions onto the "raw material" of Schreber's account. This sort of interpretive quandary is inseparable from the deployment of pathologizing terms like paranoia, and is intensified by the study of literary texts that self-consciously embrace paranoia as an intellectual stance. Before I account for my own way of handling this issue, therefore, I want to explain more fully what is at stake in the analysis of narratives that attempt sociological description through what might be termed a "paranoid" method. And I want to do so by moving from the easily pathologized case of Schreber to a pair of theories drawn from the work of two prominent scholars, philosopher Leo Strauss and linguist Ferdinand de Saussure.

At the height of the cold war, Strauss advanced an unusual but influential theory of reading. In "Persecution and the Art of Writing" (1952), he suggested that in countries where writers are compelled to espouse government views, they might engage in the literary equivalent of leaving secret messages in their work. Such messages would be discernible only to those elite readers capable of penetrating the obvious. "Persecution," says Strauss,

> gives rise to a peculiar technique of writing, and therewith to a peculiar type of literature, in which the truth about all crucial things is presented exclusively between the lines. That literature is addressed, not to all readers, but to trustworthy and intelligent readers only. It has all the advantages of private communication... (25)

This literary theory not only contains the element of persecution central to paranoia, it also suggests that semiprivate communications are buried in public documents, and it relies on a technique of interpretation in which apparent accidents or "blunders as would shame an intelligent high school boy" are to be read as "intentional" (Strauss 30). Strauss's quasi-gnostic method, then, is barely separable from the paranoid view in which "nothing can seem accidental and everything therefore appears to be somehow consciously intended" (Sass 61). The obvious problem with it is the difficulty of confirming whether patterns in a text are intentional—or, more pointedly, whether they are even patterns. In DeLillo's *Libra*, to take merely one example, Lee Oswald's Straussian attempts to "read between the lines" of a communist newspaper never provide him with a clear sense of mission because he cannot locate the "message buried in the text" (372). Even if Oswald were a good reader (and he is not), this sort of confusion would be inevitable because attempts to locate hidden messages hinge upon the paradoxical assumption that any message one can easily detect must not be the *truest* message of the text.

This assumption applies to the detection of all kinds of conspiracies, secret plots, and hidden influences—and it has two consequences. First, it so divorces signification from normative reading practices that interpretation may depend upon the (often self-declared) authority of a charismatic interpreter ("trustworthy and intelligent readers only"). Strauss's method is, for instance, structurally indistinguishable from the method employed by Charles Manson, who claimed that the Beatles were "speaking to him across the ocean" (Bugliosi 423) from "between the lines" of songs from their *White Album*—a case to which I will return momentarily. The other odd consequence of a secret hermeneutics is that it casts doubt on the value of "surface" communications, messages that would be obvious to most members of a discourse community. In Robert Coover's *Origin of the Brunists* (1966), for instance, a community becomes so convinced that the survivor of a mining accident has prophetic powers that they develop an apocalyptic religion based on "deep" readings of his most prosaic remarks. Similarly, it turns out that Ezra Pound's war broadcasts, whose overt fascism brought him into disgrace in England and America, were "mistrusted" by the Italian government because they were suspected to contain coded (i.e., *anti*-fascist) messages for Allied intelligence. Kurt Vonnegut's 1961 novel *Mother Night* addresses a situation like Pound's through the story of Howard Campbell, an American artist-turned-agent who transmits secret Allied codes in his highly popular pro-Nazi radio program. After the war, however, Campbell finds that no one knows about his secret work or believes he was really an Allied spy. Vonnegut's novel makes clear that whatever value the hidden messages may have had for American intelligence, their more obvious content did extraordinary harm by encouraging Germans to embrace Nazi principles.[24]

Despite its numerous problems and dangers, however, reading for buried messages cannot be dismissed as a practice of only the lunatic fringe, or the intelligence community, or even its aficionados in the postwar literary community, because it cannot be divorced from normal interpretive practices. It is for precisely this reason that literary criticism is so often understood to be a matter of unearthing "secret" meanings and intentions in texts. While few literary critics are likely to explain their work in this way, they would not be entirely wrong to do so because the work of interpretation always seems to produce *secret* meanings to those who do not know how the meanings in question are coded. This is what the lawyer Harry, in William Gaddis's *Frolic of His Own* (1994), has in mind when he says, "Every profession is a conspiracy against the public, every profession protects itself with a language of its own" (251).

With these remarks in mind, I want now to consider the second case: Ferdinand de Saussure's theory of anagrams, which held that Latin poets hid anagrams of proper names in their poems.[25] This theory, like Strauss's, depends upon a potentially paranoid interpretive method, a conviction that what may be merely the accidental result of combining 26 letters is in fact an intentional form of communication. Yet, as Jonathan Culler points out, the significance of Saussure's theory, which some have called "*la folie de Saussure*," is that it is "a special case of a more general phenomenon":

> Signs are not simply given to perception: to perceive the signifier at all is to confer on some patterns and not on others the status of meaningful expressions.... The idea that prior linguistic conventions enable listeners or readers to identify signifiers and know their meaning seems to be undermined from both sides by the processes anagrams expose: there is patterning that seems to work without prior conventions or listeners' recognition, and there is patterning that seems willfully created by readers, who must determine what to count as a signifier. (Culler 127–28)

To put these remarks into the terms of the present discussion, the existence of messages that work without our recognition (hidden persuaders) and the creation of meaning by readers (paranoia) are central to the operation of texts *in general*. Yet, the unstable relation between such elements of a sign system is precisely what generates the impasses I have been sketching here. The *apparent* presence of anagrams—or, more generally, of "hidden messages"—in cultural artifacts generates a problem analogous to the central problem of paranoia: are these apparent messages "motivated" (produced intentionally) or are they "accidents" (merely seen as intentional by a highly motivated, or paranoid, reader)?

It is critical to see that such interpretive dilemmas revolve around issues of agency—questions about *who* or *what* is producing the meaning in a set of signs.[26] One of the reasons I have focused this study on agency rather than paranoia is that I am less interested in adjudicating between different interpretations than in revealing what is at stake, both philosophically and politically, in the assumptions undergirding certain kinds of interpretations. What I hope to show is that "paranoid" interpretations are often complex and self-defeating attempts to preserve a familiar concept of subjectivity. They stem from a desire to think sociologically about agency while *simultaneously* retaining a concept of individual action that is at odds with sociological work. They sometimes amount, then, not only to a self-defensive posture in the face of external controls, but to a fraught and paradoxical defense of liberal individualism itself.

In order to get a larger sense of this thesis, it is instructive to examine Freud's early encounter with the problem we have just been considering, an encounter that occurred in his 1901 study of motive and accident and became pressing as he attempted to make the critical distinction between psychoanalytic and irrational forms of interpretation. When explaining potentially meaningful coincidences, Freud claims that "superstitious" persons behave "just like paranoics" (*Pyschopathology* 259), while he, on the other hand, explains coincidence rationally:

> The differences between myself and the superstitious person are two: first, he projects outwards a motivation which I look for within; secondly, he interprets chance as due to an event, while I trace it back to a thought. But what is hidden from him corresponds to what is unconscious for me, and the compulsion not to let chance count as chance but to interpret it is common to both of us. (257–58)

A strict definition of the boundary between self and world grounds Freud's distinction between rational and irrational interpretation. While "irrational" interpretations find motive in *external* determinants, psychoanalytic interpretation locates motive and agency *within* the individual. This distinction underwrites Freud's later understanding of "projection" as "the most striking characteristic of symptom-formation in paranoia" ("Psycho-Analytic Notes" 66). Because the "interior" of the individual is the privileged site where the *real* meaning and "motive" for apparently persecutory events reside, attempts to locate persecutory motives in the external world must be viewed with great suspicion.

This would seem to separate psychoanalytic and paranoid approaches rather nicely. Yet, it must be noted that the deepest "inside," the unconscious, is in some ways only another kind of "outside"—a region outside conscious control. Locating motive there, in other words, is not *radically* different from locating it in the suprapersonal agencies (or gods) of the superstitious or in the collective networks (or conspiracies) of the paranoid. Indeed, we might even say that psychoanalysis solves the problem of whether interpretation is overzealous, or paranoid, by relocating motive from the unitary consciousness of an *intending* subject to a shadowy agent (the unconscious) whose deliberations are veiled and not easily subject to interrogation. This "solution" bears a striking resemblance to conspiracy theory. After all, the unconscious, as Freud later theorized it, is not an affective state, but a mental agency or "system" ("Unconscious" 172). Freud's "discovery of unconscious processes," writes Paul Ricoeur, "invites us to form the idea of 'belonging to a system'" (119)—precisely the idea so terrifying to the conspiracy theorist. The "systems" in both cases, we might add, govern human actions, thoughts, and desires, and are frequently described in a rhetoric according them motive, unity, and efficacy.[27] Lest my comparison of these mental and social systems seem far-fetched, it is worth adding that the same analogy allowed Freud to develop social and historical theories on the basis of his mental model.

The real difference between irrational and rational interpretation, then, lies not so much in *whether* one believes in uncontrollable determinants or agents as in *where* one locates those determinants—and, thus, in how one conceptualizes the agency of persons. For Freud, human action is governed by a complex of mental systems. Freudian theory, to borrow Ricoeur's words, results in a "wounded Cogito...a Cogito that posits itself but *does not possess* itself" (439, emphasis added). This conception of the self reverses the basic presumption of possessive individualism, which identifies self-possession and "freedom from dependence on the wills of others" as "the human essence" (Macpherson 3). Freud's model also dispenses with the voluntarist aspects of the liberal self—the idea that rational will is the primary determinant of human action—even as he rejects the paranoid compulsion to interpret "chance" external events as the work of willful actors. We can thus begin to see a relation between the so-called paranoid stance and liberal, or possessive, individualism. We can in fact hypothesize that paranoia is a defense of—perhaps even a component of—liberal individualism. If the paranoid, like the superstitious, are overzealous in their interpretations, they nonetheless retain the liberal notion that *intentions* are the supreme cause of events in the world. In the words of William S. Burroughs, postwar America's high priest of agency panic, "there is no such thing as a coincidence. ... Nothing happens in this universe... unless some entity *wills* it to happen" ("On Coincidence" 99, 101).

Whether such a view is "paranoid" in the sense of "wrong" is hard to say. More clear is its implicit view of the self as an atomistic, rational agent beleaguered by other (often immense) rational agents—a view that the writing of Burroughs, among others, articulates with great frequency (see Chapter 5). Rather than accepting a view of self-control as divided and *less than absolute*, the so-called paranoid stance retains an all-or-nothing concept of agency. And unlike Freud, the paranoiac finds the idea of being dispersed into an ineffable system of control (even if it is only his or her own unconscious) wholly intolerable. Paranoia is therefore not just an interpretive stance, but part of a discourse about agency. Within that discourse, it often produces compelling insights about social control, yet it also tends to promote forms of hyperindividualism—extraordinary desires to keep free of social controls by seeing the self as only its *truest* self when standing in stark opposition to a hostile social order.

Bodily Symptoms, Cultural Pathologies

"Since the assassination of John F. Kennedy," Norman Mailer has remarked, "we have been marooned in one of two equally intolerable spiritual states, apathy or paranoia" ("Footfalls" 129). No one has mapped these "spiritual states" as obsessively as Thomas Pynchon, whose self-proclaimed paranoids (the obsessive Herbert Stencil of *V.*, for instance) are often set into relief against apathetic figures (like *V.*'s "human yo-yo," Benny Profane). Such alternatives are also essential to popular conspiracy fictions, where a potentially paranoid individual often attempts to convince more apathetic characters that a dangerous plot is afoot. The repeated connection of these rival postures in postwar literature seems to indicate a serious cultural problem: on the one hand, a deep suspicion about the causes of important social events, and on the other, a feeling that no matter how aggressively pursued, those causes will never be fathomed. It also represents a form of "paranoia" that is self-critical, tempered with skepticism about its own theories.

I have been suggesting that if we view this sort of "paranoia"—the sense, in Pynchon's often-cited words, that *"everything is connected"* (*Gravity's Rainbow* 703)—as more than an interpretive pathology, then we can begin to understand its emergence in the postwar period as part of a cultural conversation about human autonomy and individuality. To do so would be to move past critical accounts that have used the category of paranoia largely to label fictional characters or their assertions and that have tended to overlook the historical significance of paranoia as a postwar theme, particularly its relation to postmodernism.[28] Such a view would also recognize the literature of paranoia as only *part* of a larger discourse on social control, many expressions of which could not be labeled paranoid, even if the term were construed broadly. I want now to show how this strategy might be applied to specific postwar narratives. My first example is Joan Didion's stunning essay on late-1960s California, "The White Album," a narrative that concisely registers many of the issues I will be examining in greater detail in the chapters to follow.

"The White Album" is about a period of deep uncertainty and nervousness in Didion's life, a period during which she becomes increasingly unable to understand her relationship to the chaotic world around her. The immediate cause of this unease is a series of coincidences between crises in her own life and larger social upheavals—the most inexplicable and disturbing of which is the murder campaign conducted by Charles Manson and his "family." As these events unfold, Didion begins to wonder if they are somehow connected and, thus, if she is being influenced by some invisible social logic. Her suspicions culminate in a panic attack that brings her to a Los Angeles hospital. "The White Album" thus provides an interesting instance of agency panic, but it is also an essay *about* agency panic because its central goal is to provide an account of why Didion suffered her attack and whether or not her anxiety was somehow justified.

Initially, Didion characterizes her nervousness and dread as part of the widespread "paranoia of the time" (12), despite her belief that the feeling is justified. This is a paradoxical gesture, yet one that surfaces repeatedly in the postwar period. To view one's own feelings as both justified *and* paranoid is to admit a belief in hostile forces surrounding one, while also acknowledging that the ontological basis of such suspicions cannot be confirmed. What Didion describes in "The White Album," then, is something like paranoia, but a bit too self-effacing to fit neatly into the category. It is rather a *crisis of interpretation*—a frustrating inability to account for pernicious developments that seem too patterned to be accidental. Ultimately, this crisis becomes so intractable that Vietnam-era Los Angeles seems to Didion a place where "all connections were equally meaningful, and equally senseless" (44).

The most important result of this interpretive stalemate is that it disables Didion's understanding of human action and agency. "I am talking here about a time," she writes, "when I began to doubt the premises of all the stories I had ever told myself" (11). Usually, she suggests, "We interpret what we see." By this she means that we attempt to fathom the *motives* behind individual acts (seeing a "naked woman on [a] ledge," for instance, "we tell ourselves that it makes some difference whether the naked woman is about to commit a mortal sin or is about to register a political protest" [11]); and we impose "a narrative line upon" such acts ("we look for the sermon in the suicide, for the social or moral lesson in the murder of five" [11]). But during the period of "The White Album," Didion discovers she is "no longer interested in whether the woman on the ledge outside the window...jumped or did not jump, or in why. I was interested only in the picture of her in my mind" (44). Here, Didion's lack of interest in motive and cause seems to be a version of postmodern skepticism about the sources and authority of explanatory narratives. Her dismissal of interpretation and her increased concern with image—the substitution of surfaces for depths—seems to epitomize the radical view that postmodernism privileges "aesthetics" over "ethics" and "images" over "narratives" (Harvey 328), a purported development Jean Baudrillard has called "the triumph of effect over cause...the triumph of the surface and pure objectality over the profundity of desire" (*America* 6).

Yet a refusal to determine real causes and motives cannot fully account for Didion's feelings because she does not wholly turn away from the categories of motive, cause, and desire. She only turns away from their traditional association with the rational human subject. That is, while she loses interest in *individual* intentions or motives, she simultaneously begins to sense that events are "motivated" in a more *systemic* way. As she gets to know Linda Kasabian, the star witness in the Manson trial, she learns that "Linda did not believe that chance was without pattern. Linda operated on what I later recognized as dice theory, and so, during the years I am talking about, did I" (18). This sense, that seemingly unrelated incidents are actually governed by a deeper logic, is a hallmark of paranoid conceptions of the world. Yet, the contradictory rhetoric in which Didion expresses this idea—her paradoxical view that "chance" events are "patterned," that *randomness* could be the product of *organization*—indicates not so much a paranoid conviction as a serious difficulty conceptualizing issues of agency. Didion is moving toward a view of causality that would account for regularities in individual acts while also explaining why such acts seem to be determined by unrelated individual actors. That is, she is trying to explain apparently intentional outcomes without resort to intentions—a major sociological challenge and a task that the postwar literature of social control has been unable to achieve. It is significant, therefore, that in formulating this view Didion turns to examples about suicide, because the attempt to explain suicide without recourse to individual motive was the inaugural act of sociology. Didion's reenactment of this act comes in an attempt to see *individual* actions as a product of *social* determinants or influences. As Durkheim put it in *Suicide* (1897), "Intent is too intimate a thing to be more than approximately interpreted by another. It even escapes self-observation" (43). In short, Didion's lack of interest in individual intentions represents an attempt to think in systemic terms—to work along the lines of sociology rather than psychology.

This would seem to be an appropriate way to interrogate anonymous social outcomes, but unfortunately, social outcomes are not the only crises punctuating the long, hot Los Angeles summer. Didion herself begins to suffer a series of psychological and physical problems, and these personal crises bring her up against the interpretive dilemma I described earlier. She cannot adopt a systemic model because it cannot rule out the possibility that she is projecting her own problems onto the social realm—that she is, in other words, paranoid. This possibility seems especially strong when "an attack of vertigo and nausea" (15) brings her to a psychiatric clinic in Santa Monica. After a battery of psychological tests, her doctors tell her that she has an "increasing inability...to mediate the world of reality"; that her "basic affective controls" and "basic reality contact [are] obviously and seriously impaired at times"; and that she feels "all human effort is foredoomed to failure" because she "lives in a world of people moved by strange, conflicted, poorly comprehended, and, above all, devious motivations" (14–15). Didion's feelings here contain a paradox repeated throughout the essay: others seem to be "devious," yet their motives are "conflicted" and incomprehensible. In other words, their actions suggest both sinister purpose and bumbling randomness—and thus seem to generate in Didion versions of those pervasive postwar "spiritual states," apathy and paranoia (Mailer 129).[29]

In Didion's case, however, these states are not opposed but unified. Her doctors suggest that both states are produced by the same problem—the difficulty of locating connections between apparently discrete social events. Both states, moreover, suggest that the individual is a victim, that power is elsewhere. Didion's interpretive problem is thus induced by anxiety about diminished individual agency. This anxiety conditions her attempts to understand the cause of her own symptoms. Are they *products* of the social order—her body a sort of leading economic and social indicator? Or is she merely *projecting* them, understanding the social world through the distorting filter of her own serious personal problems? While her doctors suggest that she is paranoid, she suggests that her psyche is an index of social conditions. "An attack of vertigo and nausea," she remarks, "does not now seem to me an inappropriate response to the summer of 1968" (15). Indeed, shortly after her illness, she is named *Los Angeles Times* "Woman of the Year"—a correspondence reinforcing the sense that her agency panic is a reasonable response to the bizarre and violent events of the time. She understands her subsequent development of multiple sclerosis in a similar fashion. The symptoms of this disease, a doctor tells her,

> might or might not appear, might or might not involve my eyes. They might or might not involve my arms or legs, they might or might not be disabling...It could not be predicted. The condition had a name...but the name meant nothing and the neurologist did not like to use it. The name was multiple sclerosis, but the name had no meaning....The startling fact was this: my body was offering a precise physiological equivalent to what had been going on in my mind....In other words it was another story without a narrative. (46–47)

Less tautologically put (since a story is a narrative), the onset of Didion's condition is a development that resists narration, because it has obscure determinants and an uncertain outcome, much like the events occurring around her in Los Angeles. What makes this story hard to narrate is the difficulty of specifying causes. Her condition is thus a *bodily* incarnation of the feeling of lost agency that earlier drove her to the outpatient mental clinic.

Didion's story thus establishes a pattern that echoes through many of the other cases of agency panic I will examine. What begins as an attempt to understand the relation between individual acts and social patterns leads to a dramatic and troubling sense that individuals are no longer as autonomous or unique as they once seemed. This latter sense is visible not only in Didion's feeling that her own life is out of control, but in her view of others. It is central, for instance, to her description of Huey Newton talking like a machine as he defends the work of the Black Panthers, "his voice gaining volume as the memory disks clicked" (32). It is also vital to the most enigmatic and powerful moment of the essay—Didion's description of the following encounter with a motel manager:

> During the course of checking out I was asked this question by the manager, who was a Mormon: *If you can't believe you're going to heaven in your own body and on a first-name basis with all the members of your family, then what's the point of dying?* At that time I believed that my basic affective controls were no longer intact, but now I present this to you as a more cogent question than it might at first appear, a kind of koan of the period. (46)

The crucial feature of the manager's statement is its expression of anxiety about the impermanence of individual identity. The "koan," or paradox, of the statement lies in its presentation of the inevitable (death) as something that needs motivation or intent (a "point"). The expression thus compensates for an apparent erosion of individuality by returning individual intention (the essence of liberal individualism) to that which is not usually intended—death—recovering, in a sense, the suicidal intention depleted from the sociological subject. If this gesture seems to Didion emblematic of the period, it is so because it concisely expresses what creates her "paranoia" in the first place: the sense that individual motive is important, but that, in its recognizable forms (jealousy, greed, anger), it cannot account for any of the violent acts she describes; such actions seem better, if still not fully, accounted for by veiled connections between individuals and social messages—the sort of connections, for instance, between the Beatles' *White Album* (which contained the song "Helter Skelter") and the Manson murders, connections unmentioned by Didion and invisible to most everyone but Manson himself.[30]

We can see, then, that agency panic works as a set of negotiations between sociological and psychological perspectives of human action. It flirts with both of these views—attempting on the one hand to gain a sociological purchase, but on the other hand conserving the view of individual action and identity with which sociology must dispense if it is to do its business. Such negotiations may be seen in a wide array of cultural settings, but the pattern is often quite similar. Consider, for instance, this anxious prediction from literary critic Sven Birkerts: "One day soon we will conduct our public and private lives within networks so dense, among so many channels of instantaneous information, that it will make almost no sense to speak of the differentiated self" (20). A character in DeLillo's *Running Dog* understands the technological threat in slightly different, but equally familiar, terms:

> When technology reaches a certain level, people begin to feel like criminals....
> Someone is after you, the computers maybe, the machine-police. You can't escape investigation. The facts about you and your whole existence have been collected or are being collected....Devices make us pliant. If *they* issue a print-out saying we're guilty, then we're guilty. (93)

What is striking about such accounts is the way their vision of the social order, and specifically of a dense communicative network, generates a rhetoric of lost individuality and autonomy. It is as if the perspective required by sociological description so diminishes individuals that they seem incapable of social influence. The result is often anxiety or dread.

For the same reason, attempts to unveil social influences are frequently viewed as paranoid—as Didion's are by her psychiatrist. Because of the sheer vastness of social systems, describing them means delineating a web of influences that is not clearly visible—means, in other words, employing something like a paranoid logic. It is possible to extend this comparison to much more extreme cases. Even the striking form of paranoia that Victor Tausk called the "influencing machine delusion"—a paranoid psychosis in which one's persecutor allegedly controls one with a complex machine— bears a family resemblance to sociological theories in which individuals are controlled by a social "machine." If Tausk's influencing machine is "a suggestion apparatus" (544), a mechanism that makes the patient a mechanical extension of itself, then it is not unlike Ellul's technological society, which "pursues its own course," attains "autonomy," "has for its object the elimination of all human variability and elasticity," and ensures that "the human being becomes a kind of machine" (Ellul 135, 383).

We might substitute for Ellul's any number of other accounts. Charles Reich's view is that "under the domination of the Corporate State...man is deprived of his own being, and he becomes instead a mere role, occupation, or function. The self within him is killed, and he walks through the remainder of his days mindless and lifeless, the inmate and instrument of a machine world" (129). The idea that social controls are part of a centralized control apparatus, in short, is visible not only in the annals of the insane, but in a wide range of cultural sites. What distinguishes "influencing machine" theories from more mainstream accounts is not the idea that technology controls persons, or even that technology has a will of its own. It is that influencing machine patients view the machine as a device directed at them in particular.

Influencing Machines

The comparisons I have been making suggest that the postwar culture of "paranoia" is driven by both a desire for sociological analysis and a sense of individual autonomy in decline. Another important facet of this culture is that it frequently represents social controls as *feminizing* forces, domesticating powers that violate the borders of the autonomous self, penetrating, inhabiting and controlling it from within. It is no accident that Schreber's classic struggle "against sexual transformation...is, at the same time, a struggle against the undermining of his *manly will* principally by the insinuation into his body of 'female nerves'" (Shapiro 149). Nor is it an accident that examples of technological control are frequently supported by more traditional stories of enervated "manly will," like that of the young pilot who must "abandon his profession" because his wife's hysterical joy upon his return each day makes him too "accident conscious" (Ellul 138). What the pilot gives up, of course, is an equally constraining adaptation to "technical functions" (Ellul 139)—an adaptation that is already feminizing because, as Donna Haraway puts it, "Work is being redefined as both literally female and feminized, whether performed by men or women" (Haraway, "Cyborg" 166).

Gendered tales of socialization have a long and well-documented history in American letters, the most canonical documents of which often tell the story of men "lighting out for the territory" in order to escape the cloying pressures of a female social order.[31] In the postwar period, this tradition becomes coupled to a narrative of violated identity and agency-in-crisis—a story about the implantation of social controls into previously self-enclosed, integral, atomistic subjects. Such stories privilege the male body and heterosexual norms in conceptualizing human agency and subjectivity. While the earlier tradition imagines the mechanism of control to be a constraining environment, the postwar narrative imagines it as a bodily violation, an *introjection* of the social order into the self. This latter notion continues to influence accounts of "empty" or "depthless" postmodern subjectivity, especially those that view the contemporary social order as an insidious system capable of regulating human desire or even (in extreme cases) protest against the system itself. For Baudrillard, who advances the most "dramatic and 'paranoiac-critical' expression of this dilemma" (Jameson 203), the postmodern subject is an "effect" of power precisely because "he" is *open* to the strategies of the system.

> No more hysteria, no more projective paranoia, properly speaking, but this state of terror proper to the schizophrenic: too great a proximity of everything, the unclean promiscuity of everything which touches, invests, and penetrates without resistance, with no halo of private protection, not even his own body... The schizo is bereft of every scene, open to everything in spite of himself, living in the greatest confusion. ("Ecstasy" 132–33)

What Baudrillard finds so frightening about the total system, in other words, is not only its control of the social realm, but its penetration and "emptying out" of the individual. And what underwrites his panic-stricken story of a new postmodern subjectivity is nostalgia for both a "lost" male autonomy and the historical moment in which it supposedly flourished.[32] In short, like so many postwar texts, Baudrillard's version of agency panic romanticizes the old self-enclosed and "inner-directed" masculine subject by way of its apparent devastation.

Despite the masculinist implications of this tradition, it is essential to see that a similarly gendered conception of social control has also been mobilized for progressive, feminist purposes. This should hardly be surprising. One reason the masculinist tradition encodes social control as feminization is that feminization is a pervasive and tangible form of disempowerment. To depict feminization as a dangerous hollowing out and occupation of the *female* subject, therefore, is to advance a critique with powerful feminist possibilities. Writers such as Acker, Atwood, and Diane Johnson mount just such a critique, using scenes of agency panic to illuminate the violent effects of patriarchal social scripts. Much like Schreber, their characters discover that they have been programmed to display self-destructive, feminine behavior by the insinuation into them of something like "female nerves." If this discovery leads them to panic about the invasion of their bodies by forms of external regulation, it also gives them a feminist perspective on their own control and allows them a vision of resistance to that control (see Chapter 3 and Epilogue).

The gender implications of agency panic, then, depend greatly on who is articulating it. What is constant about it, however, is its tendency to romanticize the inviolate, liberal subject. This tendency becomes clearer when we compare it to other viable feminist options. Donna Haraway, for instance, has suggested "another route to having less at stake in masculine autonomy," one that does not privilege "the return to wholeness" or imagine "the drama of life to be individuation, separation, the birth of the self, the tragedy of autonomy" ("Cyborg" 177). Her path rejects "the founding myth of original wholeness" (176) and proposes a view of the self as "multiple, without clear boundary, frayed" (177). The characters of Atwood, Johnson, and Didion, however, have difficulty accepting this view of themselves as "partial" and "fluid" (Haraway 180). They are deeply concerned about becoming pregnant—a state of divided selfhood diametrically opposed to liberal, male autonomy. Atwood's characters frequently feel "suffocated" and "choked" by this notion of unbounded selfhood, and they associate images of maternity with visions of being stalked, violated, and controlled. Similarly, Johnson's protagonist in *The Shadow Knows* begins to experience feelings of persecution—feelings her friends believe may be paranoid—just after she has aborted a pregnancy. And after being pressured into having an abortion, the actress Maria Wyeth in Didion's *Play It As It Lays* (1970) has recurrent dreams that "a shadowy Syndicate" is drawing her into a mysterious "operation" to be conducted in a Beverly Hills home—a dream that always ends with "hacked pieces of human flesh" in the kitchen sink (96–97) and reinforces her sense that she has no "knack for controlling her own destiny" (20–21). In short, the pernicious regulation of female bodies underwrites a desire, in these narratives, for just the sort of mythic subjectivity Haraway attempts to discredit. Despite their radically different political implications, these texts bear a structural and theoretical similarity to many of the male-authored texts I consider here.

To give a better sense of both this similarity and its political variability, I want to offer an example from the other side of the equation—Ken Kesey's *One Flew Over the Cuckoo's Nest* (1962). Kesey's narrator, Chief Broom Bromden, is perhaps the most well-known "influencing machine" patient in postwar American fiction. His opening remark, "they're out there" (3), sets him up as a classic paranoiac, and he is in fact the inmate of a mental hospital. The hospital, he believes, is equipped with machinery designed to control and reshape its occupants. Its attendants are able to turn on a blinding fog machine; the head nurse "is able to set the wall clock at whatever speed she wants" (73); and patients are sometimes transported to "a big machine room down in the bowels of a dam where people get cut up by robot workers" (87). To Bromden, the hospital is a machine, "like the inside of a tremendous dam. Huge brass tubes disappear upward in the dark. Wires run to transformers out of sight. Grease and cinders catch on everything, staining the couplings and motors and dynamos red and coal black" (83–84). This machine, in turn, is in the service of a social system Bromden calls "the Combine," his term for "the technological society."

Though presented as delusional, this view of the hospital is part of a compelling, if familiar, account of mass control. As Bromden explains,

> The ward is a factory for the Combine. It's for fixing up mistakes made in the neighborhoods and in the schools and in the churches, the hospital is. When a completed product goes back out into society, all fixed up good as new, ... something that came in all twisted different is now a functioning, adjusted component, a credit to the whole outfit and a marvel to behold. Watch him sliding across the land with a welded grin, fitting into some nice little neighborhood ... And the light is on in his basement window way past midnight every night as the Delayed Reaction Elements the technicians installed lend nimble skills to his fingers as he bends over the doped figure of his wife, his two little girls just four and six, the neighbor he goes bowling with Mondays; he adjusts them like he was adjusted. This is the way they spread it. (38)

This description presents psychological adjustment as an oddly material process involving the implantation of mysterious "elements" in the patient. Yet, in its basic claims, it is not substantially different from Ellul's view that "the purpose of psychological methods is to neutralize or eliminate aberrant individuals ... in order to 'immunize' the environment against any possible virus of disagreement" (410). Like Schreber's delusions, Bromden's bear a compelling resemblance to Foucault's analysis of insanity as a discursively produced form of subjectivity. As Foucault suggests, "The asylum reduces differences, represses vice, eliminates irregularities" (*Madness* 258).

Yet there is a striking difference between Kesey's asylum and the Enlightenment asylum described by Foucault. In the latter, Foucault writes, "the madman remains a minor, and for a long time reason will retain for him the aspect of the Father" (254). In Kesey's novel, the madman is also infantilized, but reason retains the aspect of the *mother*. Kesey's ward is run by Nurse Ratched, whom the narrator describes as "that smiling flour-faced old mother there with the too-red lipstick and the too-big boobs" (46). The other men on the ward frequently call "Mother Ratched" a "ball-cutter" and "bitch" (57–60), and she is not the only woman with whom they have problems. Many claim to be on the ward because of what women have done to them. The novel thus places a potentially powerful story of institutional normalization into a gender framework that equates social control with emasculation and female power. "In this hospital," one patient explains, "the doctor doesn't hold the power of hiring and firing. That power goes to the supervisor, and the supervisor is a woman, a dear old friend of Miss Ratched's; they were Army nurses together in the thirties. We are victims of a matriarchy here, my friend" (61). Once power and gender are set into this relation, the plot then develops around the efforts of its hero, Randle Patrick McMurphy, to liberate the men from oppressive female control through a long series of profoundly misogynistic acts. In this novel, social control "retains the aspect of the mother," but it does so only because *true* reason is a property of "the insane" and not of the oppressive institutions designed to normalize individuals in its name. Like other postwar novels of paranoia, this one reverses the traditional privileging of reason over madness, but it does so only by retaining the patriarchal gendering of those terms.

It is important to stress that the misogyny of Kesey's novel stems not from its sociological vision but from its commitment to a masculinist version of liberal individualism, a sense that to be "free" means to be separate from the domestic sphere and protected from a technologically invasive society that threatens "the manhood of every one of it members" (Emerson 261). While Kesey's tale is an extreme example, it is not uncommon to find less violent associations of social control with women. When the narrator of Ralph Ellison's *Invisible Man* (1952) is given shock treatments similar to those endured by Kesey's patients, he is asked his mother's name in order to confirm that his identity has been erased. His response, however, is to see the shocking device itself as his mother ("A machine my mother? ... Clearly, I was out of my head" [240]). "I had the feeling," he says afterward, "that I was in the grip of some alien personality lodged deep within me" (249). This surreal scene is designed to reveal the ideological role of Ellison's paint factory—a business that profits by whitewashing American institutions and that is "making" persons as much as it is making paint. But the relevant point here is that the scene conceptualizes ideological power as a female force that invades, empties, and reconstructs the male subject. The same logic is essential to Joseph Frankenheimer's *Manchurian Candidate* (1962), whose picture-perfect American mother is not only the wife of a top presidential candidate but also a communist spy using her own brainwashed son as an assassin.

Similarly gendered visions of the hapless, "programmed" subject appear in many postwar texts—as do associations of masculinity with freedom from social control. It is no accident that the Unabomber's project involved *both* a violent resistance to technological society *and* a zealous reenactment of the great masculinist tradition of getting "outside society" in the manner of Thoreau. Nor is it an accident that the legal defense team of Theodore Kaczynski, who was convicted of the Unabomber crimes, attempted to argue that he suffered from the influencing machine psychosis, despite the fact that his widely dismissed jeremiad, "Industrial Society and Its Future" (F,C. 1996), borrows many of its ideas from popular, mainstream attacks on techno-capitalism (see Chapters 4 and 5). Similarly, Timothy McVeigh, who was convicted in 1997 of bombing the Murrah Federal Building in Oklahoma City, reportedly complained that the U.S. Army had implanted a computer chip in his buttock for the purpose of controlling him.[33] These examples indicate what may be at stake in some cases of agency panic. When a sociological vision is combined with extreme anxiety about individual autonomy, the result may be a form of hyperindividualism that sees violent resistance as the only answer to the threat of technological and social control.

Postmodern Transference

If agency panic is an attempt to conserve the integrity of the liberal, rational self, then its widespread appearance in postwar culture must be understood partly as a response to discourses that have articulated new ideas about subjectivity. *Empire of Conspiracy* is concerned with a number of such discourses, both popular and academic. I have already referred to one influential strain of writing about technological development and its influence on individuals. This sociological discourse runs roughly from *The Lonely Crowd* and *The Organization Man* through recent accounts of addiction and is distinguished by its insistence that various "new forms of control" (Marcuse, *One-Dimensional* 1) have produced a breed of persons significantly less independent than those of an earlier era. While diverse in scope, texts in this tradition assume that a major historical, cultural, and economic change has occurred since World War II—a second (or third) industrial revolution leading to a "postindustrial society," an "information age," or some other brave new world that has moved beyond our capacity to understand or control it: it is "postcivilized," "postmaturity," "postideological," "posteconomic," "postliberal," "posttraditional," and, of course, "postmodern."[34] As James Beniger notes in his superb *Control Revolution* (1986), "a steadily mounting number of social scientists, popular writers, and critics have discovered that one or another revolutionary societal transformation is now in progress" (2).[35] These stories of transformation are inseparable from the anxious fictional responses at the center of this book, because their tendency for hasty periodization has contributed to a feeling that radically new social and economic forces now manipulate individuals in frightening ways. The result, many analysts have concluded, is that people are no longer what they used to be (see Chapter 1).

Because many such narratives valorize liberal subjectivity, it is crucial to contrast them with alternative postwar conceptions of human agency—especially those advanced by the information sciences and poststructural theory. The notion that individual actions or desires can be controlled by large systems is not unlike the theoretical proposition—now widely accepted in the humanities—that individuals are "constructed" by powerful systems of knowledge or discourse. For several decades, theorists from a wide range of disciplines have relentlessly challenged the assumptions of liberal humanism. Cybernetics, for instance, mounted an early and influential challenge to liberal conceptions of human agency, one that profoundly affected writers such as Vonnegut, Pynchon, DeLillo, Heller, and Burroughs.[36] Developed by Norbert Wiener in the years following World War II, cybernetics theorized the use of "messages as a means of controlling machinery and society," beginning with the premise that humans and machines are fundamentally alike (Wiener, *Human Use* 15). Later developments of the theory held that individual actions are determined not by *internal* properties of the subject, but by communicative relays extending beyond the self. Consider, for instance, the model of agency proposed by anthropologist and early cybernetics enthusiast Gregory Bateson: "The total self-corrective unit which processes information, or, as I say, 'thinks' and 'acts' and 'decides,' is a *system* whose boundaries do not at all coincide with the boundaries either of the body or of what is popularly called the 'self' or 'consciousness'"("Cybernetics" 319). In Bateson's "cybernetic epistemology," the important controlling unit—what used to be called the person—extends outward along endless communicative connections between the individual body and other material entities.

This view is surprisingly like Schreber's notion that the "human soul is contained in the nerves of the body" (45), which are "the determined recipients of influences from outside themselves" (Sass 249). Yet, the difference between Bateson's view and Schreber's—and, by extension, between cybernetic theory and paranoia—is the level of comfort each has with this radical conception of subjectivity. For Schreber, the idea of a dispersed and penetrable self provokes an intense desire to *protect* the self from external influences—a desire, that is, to transform it back into the inviolable, atomistic self of liberalism. For Bateson, on the other hand, communicative influences are *unavoidable* and not necessarily harmful. Bateson feels this way because he rejects the assumptions of liberal individualism in favor of a view that conceives of the "self" as part of a larger system of social relations. Indeed, he connects the basic assumptions of liberal individualism (which he calls both "purposive thinking" and "the epistemology of 'self-control'") with the central symptom of paranoia: "a phenomenon which seems to be almost universal when man commits the error of purposive thinking... is called by the psychologists 'projection.' The man... does not see himself as part of the system... and he either blames the rest of the system or he blames himself" ("Conscious Purpose" 436). Psychic projection seems improperly individualist to Bateson because, like many systems theorists, he views "the system" as a beneficent entity that includes all of us. "Call the systemic forces 'God' if you will," he says ("Conscious Purpose" 434). That, of course, is precisely what Schreber does. But in Schreber's account, "God" is a fierce tormentor and violator of Schreber's autonomy, a controlling totality bent on his destruction. The difference between each view, in other words, concerns not only the nature of persons but also the nature, or "personality," of the larger system.

More recent systems theory has strenuously resisted this reifying tendency. As Cary Wolfe explains, there are substantial differences between "first-order systems theory" of the sort practiced by Bateson and the "second-order systems theory" of writers such as Humberto Maturana, Francisco Varela, and Niklas Luhmann. While the former approach posits a "total system" that subsumes innumerable smaller systems (ranging from cells to biological organ systems to human beings to families to large environmental or social networks), second-order systems theory does not. It views systems as "operationally closed" to their larger environments—that is, closed on the level of the relationships that define the system, but open to material and informational exchanges with the environment.[37] This more complicated idea of the self-reproducing (or autopoietic) system understands the social order not as one big system, but as multiple, interlocking, and heterogeneous systems. And because it is able "to bypass entirely the logical geography of inner and outer" (Varela et al. 172) in thinking about control, it allows for "high degrees of systemic autonomy *and* [it explains] how systems change and 'adapt' to their environments" (Wolfe 66). This more sophisticated approach to agency still requires us to jettison traditional assumptions about human action. As

Katherine Hayles points out, "Like many postwar systems, including Foucault's epistemes and Lacan's psycholinguistics, autopoiesis is profoundly subversive of individual agency" ("Making" 93).

Given this subversiveness, it should come as no surprise that much postmodern theory has been met by intense defenses of humanism—defenses that frequently resemble agency panic. These rejoinders often exaggerate or misconstrue the implications of postmodern theory, yet they respond directly to postmodernism's new language of agency, a rhetoric that attributes rationality and motive to structures larger than individual persons while simultaneously representing individuals as constructions and "subjects" of those agencies. This rhetorical shift, or *postmodern transference*, is in fact precisely what systems theory proposes. As Jürgen Habermas puts it, systems theory "replaces the self-relating subject with a self-relating system" (353). The humanist fear of such a replacement, I have been suggesting, is one of the things that can give rise to agency panic.

From the point of view of poststructural theory, of course, self-relating systems have "always already" compromised the autonomy of the subject. Yet, from a humanist perspective, poststructuralism effects a total and imaginary transfer of agency from subjects to systems, which it treats as more human than human beings. This does not seem to me an accurate criticism, yet poststructuralists have not exactly discouraged it. If poststructuralism has attempted to "free [itself] of" what Paul de Man calls "all false questions of intent" (18), it has not entirely discarded the humanist rhetoric of intention and motive. As Jacques Derrida reminds his readers, "deconstruction takes place, it is an event that does not await the deliberation, consciousness or organization of a subject" (Derrida, "Letter" 274). Such statements have inspired Derrida's followers to account for the complexity of signification by according agency, at least nominally, to what Barbara Johnson calls "warring forces of signification *within the text itself*" (xiv) and what Jonathan Culler calls "forces in language" (130), "the forces of attraction that link signifiers in the most productive ways" (132). In Jacques Lacan's version of this rhetoric, "the subject, too, if he can appear to be the slave of language is all the more so of a discourse... in which his place is already inscribed at birth, if only by virtue of his proper name" ("Agency of the Letter" 148). And, in his landmark attempt to devise a new mode of historical analysis, Michel Foucault shifts attention away from "a cogito... the speaking subject" and toward the "strategies" in discourse—the rules, themes and organizing patterns that give the discourse a measure of coherence and an *appearance* of purpose (*Archaeology* 122). This method becomes more pronounced in Foucault's later accounts of "power," which designates the "over-all effect" (*History* 93) of numerous social relations through reference to strategies and aims (see Chapter 2).

In all of these cases, then, we have an emphasis on the way discursive and social systems influence human activity and identity, and yet this emphasis is made through a rhetorical maneuver in which agency is "transferred" from the autonomous individual to a discursive or social system. While all of the writers I have just cited would stress the *purely nominal* or rhetorical nature of this transfer, their critics have often understood it more literally. As Charles Newman remarks, "We have become acutely aware of language not as a mediating tool, but as an independent agency in its own right, a force which is not an adjunct of perception, but a competitor" (15). If the first half of this claim restates the lesson of anagrams (that language is not a transparent medium for the intentions of individual agents), the second draws an extreme conclusion from that lesson: *the medium itself is an agent.* This vision of quasi-human discursive agency is often understood by its detractors to imply an *annihilation* of human agency. According to John Patrick Diggins, for instance, poststructuralist theory "sees power activating itself with no human agent consciously involved. All that can be perceived are endless contexts of domination that develop on their own, and the authority of truth is powerless to resist such developments, since there is no rational subject to render it" (373).[38]

Impassioned defenses of liberalism, such as this one, conceive of agency in an all-or-nothing fashion. They assume that the poststructural emphasis on discursive construction amounts to a complete transfer of agency from persons to social formations. Critics of poststructuralism, notes Judith Butler, often view social construction as the work of "a *godlike agency,*" even though it need be understood neither "as a unilateral process initiated by a prior...willful subject" nor as an "evacuation or displacement of human agency" (*Bodies* 6, 9). What is mistaken about such readings is not their view that poststructuralism stresses the influence of social structures, but rather their conclusion that a theory of social influence implies a *drastic* reduction of human agency. If such readings misunderstand power as a godlike agency, in other words, then they are like the misunderstanding by which Schreber believed the agency of his own torment to be *God Himself.* Both involve attempts to conceptualize a complex array of social influences—and both amount to a misunderstanding insofar as those influences are reduced to a monolithic, unified, external agent.

The dramatic form of agency panic may therefore be seen as a response to theories that have reimagined the subject in relation to discursive and social systems. What is most interesting about this response is its tendency to exaggerate and reify the rhetoric of agency in poststructural and systems theory, to compress an array of determinants into a single entity. Its tendency toward postmodern transference results in a terrifying and sublime object, an entity that seems to possess in giant form precisely those qualities so horribly depleted from the individual. Despite its terror, such a vision can offer considerable psychic rewards. As William Whyte observed in his account of the 1950s "organization man": "Only by using the language of individualism to describe the collective can he stave off the thought that he himself is in a collective as pervading as any ever dreamed of" (5). By transferring the attributes of persons to the level of the collective, in other words, one can maintain a fantasy of separateness and autonomy in the face of evidence that one has been incorporated into something larger. While such fantasies have shaped many "paranoid" texts, their basic elements are not restricted to the insane or even to the "shamans of the paranoid novel" (Lentricchia 205). Rather, they are part of a widespread phenomenon tied both to social and technological changes, and to new theories about the relation of persons to the social order.

The Representation of Social Control

The chapters to follow are not intended to provide a historical map of postwar social writing or the outline of a general "cultural logic." They are case studies, each of which centers on an aspect of the trend I have set out in this Introduction. The opening chapter, "Bureaucracy and Its Discontents," examines pervasive postwar anxieties about the tendency of bureaucracies and social systems to deindividuate and control persons. By tracing such efforts to rethink the status of persons through early postwar popular sociologies (including Whyte's *Organization Man,* Marcuse's *One-Dimensional Man,* Wiener's *Human Use of Human Beings,* Reich's *Greening of America,* Ellul's *Technological Society,* and Riesman's *Lonely Crowd*), I show that agency panic was a pervasive way of confronting the apparent challenges of postindustrial society. One remarkable feature of these texts is their suggestion that large social systems or social bodies are the "enemies" of a dying American individualism—a suggestion central to the fiction of Joseph Heller, which is the subject of the second half of the chapter. My interest throughout is in how a certain form of "paranoia" about the motives of large bureaucracies functions as an antidote to the deindividuating tendencies of postindustrial mass culture.

Chapter 2, "Bodies Incorporated," begins by assessing the bizarre premise of Thomas Pynchon's 1973 novel *Gravity's Rainbow:* that German

V-2 rockets are striking London precisely where an unwitting American lieutenant has recently had sexual intercourse. This uncanny correspondence generates an intense interpretive dilemma about the causes of individual action, a dilemma that is thematically identical to theoretical debates between psychoanalytic (Freud and Lacan) and deconstructive (Derrida) accounts of the way social relations might "determine" the subject. The scenes of agency panic in which the novel's characters attempt to resolve such dilemmas are characterized by radical uncertainty about the status of persons. The novel continually attributes the qualities of human beings— motive, consciousness, agency—to all kinds of systems, including technologies, cells, cartels, and economies. Drawing on Norbert Wiener's analogies between the human body and the self-guided rockets of World War II, as well as Michel Foucault's account of the way sexuality has been used to reinvent the subject, I argue that Pynchon offers a new understanding of the relation between male bodies and systems of communication. I also show that the ubiquitous panic of the novel's male characters dramatizes their difficulty accepting this radical view.

In "Stalked by Love" (Chapter 3), I take up women's narratives of male persecution. My chief examples are texts in which a woman's belief that she is being stalked induces subsequent feelings of panic about her self-control: they include Freud's brief study of "female paranoia" and the remarkable stalker novels of Margaret Atwood (*Bodily Harm; The Edible Woman; Lady Oracle; Surfacing*) and Diane Johnson (*The Shadow Knows*). By locating these stories in the context of contemporary legal and popular discourse on stalking, I show that their apparently "paranoid" claims provide compelling analyses of sexual violence against women. Moreover, the figure of the *anonymous* stalker in these narratives solves a pressing theoretical problem: how to represent the immense system of institutions, discourses, and practices that contribute to such violence. The shadowy stalker, I argue, stands in for these systems while simultaneously resisting the popular desire to trace sexual violence to individual psychopaths.

A fourth chapter, "Secret Agents," continues this investigation by taking up the unsettled and unsettling problems of agency central to one of the most enduring American epistemological dilemmas of the postwar era: the assassination of John F. Kennedy. Kennedy's murder epitomizes the condition of knowledge and history in postmodernity because it turns on an unbridgeable gap between historical events and historical narrative. My analysis of this case centers on the cultural significance of the rival "lone gunman" and conspiracy accounts that so routinely structure national discourse about the murder. By way of official documents, news sources, and fictional representations—including Oliver Stone's *JFK* and Don DeLillo's *Libra*—I argue that these rival theories operate in tandem, conserving a model of subjectivity threatened by some of the evidence in the case itself. I also connect DeLillo's "men in small rooms," the secretive and anxious characters populating his fiction, to an American tradition of masculinist resistance to social conditioning—a tradition that has surfaced most recently in the Unabomber "manifesto."

Chapter 5, "The Logic of Addiction," addresses postwar addiction paradigms, which have become a major repository for representations of agency-in-crisis. My primary goal here is to suggest that addiction has become an increasingly pervasive malady because it dramatizes problems and contradictions in American conceptions of agency. Addiction culture, in other words, is intimately related to other prominent postwar discourses on autonomy and individuality. Most of my examples come from the writings of William S. Burroughs, whose "terminal" subjects are addicted not only to drugs but also to commodities, images, words, human contact, power, and even control itself. I show that the lurid scenes of mass control in these novels are not simply the product of Burroughs's intoxicated imagination, but are derived from much more popular cold war texts, including *The Hidden Persuaders*. I also argue that while Burroughs creates the forms of "schizophrenic" or "decentered" subjectivity frequently allied with post-modern writing, he does so in the mode of panic and thus his anxiety represents longing for a traditional view of the individual agent as the privileged site of rational self-control.

The epilogue, "Corporate Futures," takes up the fiction of William Gibson and Kathy Acker (*Neuromancer* and *Empire of the Senseless*) alongside Ridley Scott's film, *Bladerunner*. While cyberpunk often explodes the very category of the human, it also imagines corporate structures to be immense individuals in their own right, monolithic agents with uniform motives and the means to carry them out. By linking this claim to earlier assertions, I conclude with the suggestion that, despite claims to the contrary, postmodern narratives have been remarkably reluctant to abandon the coherent, liberal subject.

Together, these studies suggest that the rise of conspiracy and paranoia as major themes in late-twentieth-century American culture is connected to changing social and technological conditions and to new conceptions of human subjectivity. The numerous narratives that grapple with these challenges are often conflicted in their attempts to represent social control while defending a fantasy of individual autonomy and distinctness. With their intimations of conspiracy, their interpretive uncertainties, and their curious expressions of paranoia, these texts register serious cultural concerns about the power and autonomy of persons. Their cultural function, *Empire of Conspiracy* demonstrates, is not only to articulate such fears but also to reassert the vitality of a more familiar and comforting model of self in response.

1 Bureaucracy and Its Discontents

The analogy between the process of civilization and the path of individual development may be extended in an important respect. It can be asserted that the
community, too, evolves a super-ego under whose influence cultural development proceeds.

—Sigmund Freud, *Civilization and Its Discontents* (1930)

Indeed, in the most highly developed areas of contemporary society, the trans-
plantation of social into individual needs is so effective that the difference between them seems to be purely theoretical.

—Herbert Marcuse, *One-Dimensional Man* (1964)

The New Line of Americans

In the years immediately following World War II, a handful of popular
sociological studies suggested that a fundamental change was occurring in
American society. This transformation, so the story went, was a response
both to the rise of the information sciences, systems theory and cybernetics, and more fundamentally to an economy in which the production and
distribution of information was taking unprecedented priority over the
production and distribution of material goods. As David Riesman put it in
the popular edition of his 1950 classic, *The Lonely Crowd*, a "revolution" was
in progress, "a whole range of social developments associated with a shift
from an age of production to an age of consumption" (Riesman, rev. ed. 6).
Scores of subsequent studies described these developments as the rise of a
new "post-industrial society," a "global village," an "information age," a

"second industrial revolution," and, in cultural criticism, a "condition of postmodernity."[1]

Among the more prominent anxieties animating early accounts of this condition was that new social arrangements had produced—or mass-produced—a new, and somewhat frightening type of American: a "lonely crowd" of "posthistoric men," "one-dimensional men," and "organization men."[2] For many observers, individuals had grown alarmingly generic and pliant as they became enmeshed in ever-larger bureaucratic and corporate structures. This pervasive concern about individual agency in turn gave rise to a second, more pressing worry about the "agency" of postindustrial systems. Because bureaucracies seemed to efface essential human attributes and distribute them across a system comprised of many human beings, they were often described as if they possessed human attributes. As a result, they were increasingly viewed as autonomous "social bodies" dangerously out of human control, even the control of those individuals nominally at their "head."

Such worries were not wholly new. Several decades earlier, Max Weber had described the tendency of rational, bureaucratic structures to grow somewhat uncontrollably. But Weber maintained that "the mechanism" of bureaucracy could be put into motion "only from the very top" and that bureaucracy was "a power instrument of the first order *for one who controls the bureaucratic apparatus*" (987–88, emphasis added). In the postwar sociologies I have been describing, Weber's claims seem outmoded. The postindustrial worry about bureaucracy is not that it may be misused "from the top" but that those at the top of a bureaucracy do not *really* run it. In the words of Bob Slocum, Joseph Heller's consummate "organization man," "Nobody is sure anymore who really runs the company (not even the people who are credited with running it), but the company does run" (*Something Happened* 13).[3]

In this chapter, I trace a widespread, anxious narrative response to this vision of "postindustrial" society. The type of narrative in which I am interested attempts to rally support for a supposedly threatened form of American individualism. Its primary cultural function is to defend the idea that individuals are inviolable, autonomous repositories of internal differences, ideas, and motivations—and to defend it specifically against the consequences of postindustrial economic developments, especially the incorporation of cybernetic ideas into the modeling and operation of large bureaucratic systems. The texts I consider in this chapter attempt to conserve this form of individualism by urging individuals to treat large systems as "enemies," resisting their demands for corporate identity and collective behavior. The cultural work of these narratives, in other words, is not only to describe how postindustrial culture might diminish individual agency but also to offer an "antidote" to that problem. The antidote, interestingly enough, takes the form of a "paranoid" suspicion of social connections— and a commitment to the idea that persons are atomistic units threatened by various forms of social communication and collective identity.

In tracing the rise of this "reasonable paranoia," I must leave the regions of lurid conspiracy theory for more familiar territory. My aim is to locate the early foundations of a popular postwar story about human agency, one that would usher the potentially marginal forms of conspiracy theory and paranoia toward the center of American life and would eventually provide a "legitimate," mainstream basis for more dramatic expressions of agency panic. My central literary examples in this endeavor come from the fiction of Joseph Heller, whose novel of rationalization-gone-mad, *Catch-22*, is perhaps the best-known fictional embodiment of the cultural tendency I have been outlining. Before I turn to *Catch-22*, however, I want to examine in detail several of the nonfictional narratives I mentioned above.

Social Characters

One of the most influential such narratives came from sociologist David Riesman. Shortly after World War II, Riesman made an observation about individual autonomy that would become the basis of many other works, both fictional and nonfictional. "One kind of social character, which dominated America in the nineteenth century," he declared, "is gradually being replaced by a social character of quite a different sort" (rev. ed. 3).[4] The new, or "other-directed," sort of character seemed to "find itself most at home in America" and was like other recently diagnosed products of "highly industrialized, and bureaucratic America: [Erich] Fromm's 'marketer,' [C. Wright] Mills's 'fixer,' Arnold Green's 'middle-class male child'" (orig. ed. 20). Like these figures, Riesman's new Americans seemed far less admirable than the rugged, "inner-directed" individuals they seemed to be replacing. The difference between the two types, Riesman was quick to point out, lay not in *whether* they were socially conditioned but in *how frequently* and *from whom* they received guidance: "direction in *both* cases," he noted, "comes from outside and is simply internalized at an early point in the life cycle of the inner-directed" (172). Yet the results of this difference were dramatic. Inner-directed children grew up to be unique and self-governing adults. Like the hard-working, driven individuals of Weber's "Protestant ethic," they possessed a "rigid though highly individualized character" (15) allowing them to "gain a feeling of control over their own lives" (18). Other-directed persons, by contrast, were easily influenced and controlled by social pressures. They were highly flexible and uncertain of themselves, continually adjusting their desires in response to "signals from others," especially "the school and the peer-group" and "the mass media: movies, radio, comics, and popular culture media generally" (22). As a result, they seemed to be shallow "glad-handers" and manipulators, extremely needy of approval and guidance from others.[5]

The appearance of the "other-directed" type indicated a fundamental change in American society, and one that did not bode well for the nation. The bad news was not merely that America had become populated by shallow and insecure individuals. The situation was much graver, for while inner-directed persons had a rich internal life—the mark of personhood in the dominant tradition of liberal individualism—other-directed types were generic inside. Their most "individual" aspects, even their "inner experiences," were regulated by external communications, which penetrated and inhabited them. This conclusion, as we shall see, raised the specter of a serious social dilemma. If one's contemporaries were the source of one's goals and desires, and if *they too* were other-directed, then who or what determined *their* goals and desires? If the answer was the "anonymous voices of the mass media" (23), then who or what controlled those influences? Even the nonconformist, Riesman noted, had to be aware that "his efforts at autonomy are taken as cues by the 'others'" and might merely "degenerate into other-directed play-acting" (304). The theory of other-direction posited nothing short of a national crisis of agency—not only a severe decline in individual autonomy, but a new imperative to trace human behaviors to their diverse *social* origins.

Riesman was not alone in offering his dramatic and captivating thesis. Its basic tenets would be advanced in a staggering array of texts. In 1954, Jacques Ellul described a process called "involuntary psychological collectivization" and asserted that its "inevitable consequence is the creation of the mass man" (406–7). He added, "We can get a general impression of this new type by studying America, where human beings tend clearly to become identified with the ideal of advertising" (407). Two years later, William Whyte would trace the same problem to U.S. corporate culture. The result, he claimed, was not "'Mass Man'—a person the author has never met" (10)—but rather "the organization man," a social character whose desires and ideas seemed indistinguishable from corporate propaganda. For Whyte, this new corporate tool signaled "a major shift in American ideology" (4), a movement away from Weber's "Protestant ethic" toward a new "social ethic." This was a dangerous development, in Whyte's view, because it made "morally legitimate the pressures of society against the individual" (7) and suggested that "society's needs and the needs of the individual are one and the same" (7). Organization men were ideologically conditioned subjects—"not only other-directed, to borrow David Riesman's concept," but convinced that "it is right to be that way" (396).

It is important to emphasize that the central element of such accounts— a story of individual agency in crisis—was deployed not only by those who longed for a return to the Protestant ethic of market capitalism but by those favoring socialism as well. In his *One-Dimensional Man* (1964), the Marxist critic Herbert Marcuse argued that postindustrial Americans had been so "introjected" with "social controls" that "even individual protest [was] affected at its roots" (9).[6] Like Whyte's organization men, Marcuse's conditioned subjects were unable to recognize their own conditioning. And like Riesman's other-directed persons, they lacked an *internal* "gyroscope" or guidance system. In Marcuse's version of the story, however, the internal aspects of the individual were no longer simply "adjusted" by social and economic pressures. Rather, the political economy *wholly* evacuated and occupied their private space, rendering them "one-dimensional." For Marcuse, the problem was so severe that the term "introjection" no longer described the way individuals internalized social controls:

Introjection implies the existence of an inner dimension distinguished from and even antagonistic to the external exigencies—an individual consciousness and an individual unconscious *apart from* public opinion and behavior. The idea of "inner freedom" here has its reality: it designates the private space in which man may become and remain "himself."

Today this private space has been invaded and whittled down by technological reality. Mass production and mass distribution claim the *entire* individual, and industrial psychology has long since ceased to be confined to the factory.... The result is, not adjustment but *mimesis*: an immediate identification of the individual with *his* society and, through it, with the society as a whole. (10)

One-dimensional man, in other words, suffered from a *terminal* case of other-direction.

"Other-directed" subjects have become increasingly commonplace in postmodern representation and theory. The cultural landscape is now populated not only with the artifactual replicants, terminators, and "meat-puppets" of science fiction but also with theoretical subjects such as Jean Baudrillard's "schizo," a figure so open to mass communication that his politics can be nothing more than "a hyperconformist simulation of the very mechanisms of the system" ("Masses" 219). Similarly pliant subjects wander through the fiction of Ralph Ellison, William S. Burroughs, Ishmael Reed, Kathy Acker, and Thomas Pynchon, whose Mucho Maas, for instance, increasingly becomes "less himself and more generic... a walking assembly of man" (*Crying* 140).[7]

But we can perhaps get the most vivid sense of what life might be like for the "other-directed" by studying Bob Slocum, the protagonist of Heller's 1974 novel *Something Happened*. Slocum's most stable characteristic is his tendency to take on the characteristics of those around him. "I always have the disquieting sensation that I am copying somebody," he confesses (73). When he spends the day with a man who limps, he comes home with a limp. Around a loud and assertive talker, he becomes loud and assertive. "It's a weakness," he admits, "a failure of character or morals, this subtle, sneaky, almost enslaving instinct to be like just about anyone I happen to find myself with" (72). Slocum is not just an impersonator, but a compulsive impersonator. His tendency toward other-direction "operates unconsciously... with a determination of its own" (72). As he puts it, "I do not realize I have slipped into someone else's personality until I am already there" (72). It quickly becomes apparent, in other words, that Slocum lacks what Riesman calls an "internal gyroscope." His most individual qualities turn out to be simulacra. "Even my handwriting is not my own!" he confesses (77). This is a significant admission because handwriting has long been not only the legal index of consent, agency, and will but also the conventional sign of individuality. The "science" of handwriting analysis is built on the assumption that one's writing offers a snapshot of one's psychological makeup. The fact, then, that Slocum has painstakingly internalized the writing of a coworker reveals that his most individuating traits have come from the outside.[8] His problem is not that he wears a gray flannel suit to work but that he wears gray flannel *on the inside*, so to speak.

Like Whyte, Heller suggests that Slocum's "inner surrender" (Whyte 10) makes him invaluable to his organization. Yet it also generates problems for Slocum himself. For one thing, he suffers from a permanent identity crisis. "I don't know who or what I really am," he confesses (74). Second, because the sources of his identity seem to lie outside himself, he feels unable to control his own actions. He worries perpetually about his ability to act autonomously, feels "enslaved" by his imitative tendencies, and fears that he might "break free and go permanently out of control" (73). Finally, as in most narratives of agency-in-crisis, Slocum suspects that his actions are being determined by some entity he cannot name or see, and he tries to find the causal forces that shaped him, the "something" that "decided to sort [him] into precisely this slot" (210). That the ensuing search turns up little is not surprising, because when one imagines persons as Heller does Slocum, the sources of their "own true nature" (73) are dispersed across an array of social connections and communicative networks.

What, then, are the basic elements of the story of agency-in-decline that became widely accepted in the early postwar years? The first concerns the nature of the newly-spawned individuals themselves, who are not only insufficiently individual but also lacking in agency, ideologically controlled, and too closely identified with advanced industrial society. Second, the controlling "system" in such accounts has an extraordinary uniformity and coherence, despite its obscure workings. It is not a complex array of competing interests, powers, and classes, but a monolithic totality whose mandates and goals seem utterly noncontradictory. Constructed this way, it seems to be dramatically opposed to the puny individual, as in the familiar but reductive formula "individual *versus* society." Finally, the impact of this system on the individual is conceptualized through a rhetoric of interiority and exteriority, an imagined penetration, invasion, and occupation of the individual's formerly private and protected interior, a process designed "to rob him of the intellectual armor he so badly needs" (Whyte 13). As I show later, the intimacy between this rhetoric and the values associated with masculinity helps to explain why the story often ends with a series of prescriptions to restore the "lost" masculine vitality of yesteryear.

What are we to make of the lineaments of this story? The answer has much to do with the way it relates to Enlightenment conceptions of the individual. After all, it depicts a stunning erosion of liberal individualism's fundamental assumptions, the most important of which include the following: that persons are atomistic and autonomous; that they contain a protected "internal" core of unique memories, desires, and ideas guaranteeing their individuality; and that "every man is naturally the sole proprietor of his own person and capacities—the absolute proprietor in the sense that he owes nothing to society for them" (Macpherson 231). This final proposition—that one's internal qualities are one's *property*—assumes that persons are self-made and acquire their own attributes through the labor of self-creation. It is against the backdrop of these assumptions about personhood that the concept of "other-direction" acquires its force, because the other-directed person is a dramatic inversion of the liberal individual. Indeed, the other-directed might be defined as those individuals who are "made" and "possessed" by others and who thus have little ownership of their own capacities.

It is crucial to recognize that, in defining this new subject, texts such as *The Lonely Crowd* and *The Organization Man* do not overturn the assumptions of liberal subjectivity. Rather, by suggesting that persons *should be* internally directed proprietors of an "inner dimension" and by viewing "society" or "the system" as a natural antagonist of the self, this genre reasserts the value of liberal individualism by announcing its decline. Once this paradoxical strategy is clear, so is its central implication. This genre does not simply describe a shift in the nature of individuals; it suggests that individuality itself is in danger of becoming *extinct.*

How, then, can we account for the widespread popularity of such a dramatic thesis? One possibility is that there really has been a wholesale change in the nature of persons in the United States and environs since World War II. Such a shift is not out of the question, but there are many reasons to be suspicious of such a story. First, it is uncomfortably similar to a stock generational tale about how young people "these days" seem motiveless, poorly behaved, too easily influenced by mass culture, and more obedient to their peers than their parents (who are always the ones telling the story). More important, the story of a drastic *historical* shift in the nature of persons is itself riddled with contradictions that become evident when the story moves beyond the purely theoretical realm and into the historical. As Riesman attempts to give examples of the inner- and other-directed, for instance, it becomes apparent to him that inner-directed people also conformed noticeably to the standards of their peers. He then finds himself trying to distinguish this conformity from the conformity of the other-directed:

> The inner-directed person, though he often sought and sometimes achieved a relative independence of public opinion and of what the neighbors thought of him, was in most cases very much concerned with his good repute and, at least in America, with "keeping up with the Joneses." These conformities, however, were primarily external, typified in such details as clothes, curtains, and bank credit. For, indeed, the conformities were to a standard, evidence of which was provided by the "best people" in one's milieu. In contrast with this pattern, the other-directed person, though he has his eye very much on the Joneses, aims to keep up with them not so much in external details as in the quality of his inner experience.... That is,... his desire... for guidance in what experiences to seek and in how to interpret them. (24-25)

Here, in order to explain away troubling signs of other-direction among the inner-directed, Riesman qualifies his definitions. The inner-directed, he now notes, *also* respond to external influences—from the Joneses and, by extension, from the acquisitive logic of liberal market capitalism. This is a significant modification, one that threatens to erode the distinction between the two character types. In order to prevent that result, Riesman recovers his original distinction by insisting that the other-directed conform not only in superficial ways but also in terms of their "inner experience." But this proposition requires us to believe, rather absurdly, that consumer *desires*—the desires of inner-directed consumers to keep up with the Joneses—are not "inner experiences." In fact, Riesman's backtracking here is a smoke screen for the real difference implicit in these examples, which is not a difference in "internality" but a difference in class. At bottom, inner-directed people imitate the "standard" set by the "best people," while other-directed people imitate only what is standard in the sense of "common."

Class distinctions divide the inner- and other-directed throughout *The Lonely Crowd*. One of Riesman's key contentions is that the "other-directed person's tremendous outpouring of energy is channeled into the ever expanding frontier of consumption, as the inner-directed person's energy was channeled relentlessly into production" (79). When Riesman presses himself a bit, however, he is forced to admit that inner-directed people were also conspicuous consumers (79). As a result, he finds himself once again redefining the types through class difference. The inner-directed person, he argues, "pursued clear acquisition and consumption goals with a fierce individualism. To be sure, his goals were socially determined, but less by a contemporary union of consumers than by inherited patterns of desire" (79–80). There is something odd about applying the term "fierce individualism" to the pursuit of consumption goals that are "socially determined." Even more problematic is the suggestion that these goals are *socially* determined by "*inherited* patterns of desire." The only way to understand such contradictions is to read the term "inherited" as a figure for *inheritance*, for the sort of acquisitions goals that can be realized only by the upper classes. Only this meaning can explain why other-directed shoppers seek out items purchased by their peers (i.e., mass-produced items) while the acquisition goals of the inner-directed consumer are "investments" such as "fine houses, fine horses, fine women, fine objets d'art" (80). The inclusion of "fine women," moreover, clearly marks this latter consumer as male—a "fiercer" and more autonomous forefather of the feminized, postwar mass-consumer. As Ann Douglas has argued, the rise of mass culture has been equated with "the feminization of American culture," and here Riesman makes a point of noting that, during the period of other-direction, "women are the accepted consumption leaders in our society" (81). Such assertions are a cultural shorthand for the mass-consumer's conditioned behavior and "implanted" tastes. What Riesman seems to miss is that the consumption practices of various classes might be conditioned not by a massive shift in human autonomy but simply by class itself. The "fluctuating" and generic tastes of the other-directed are better explained as the result of a rapidly expanding middle class and the relative affordability of mass-produced items. If the other-directed shopper *appears* to have "most of his individuality trained out of him by his membership in the consumers' union" (80), in other words, perhaps it is not because he is any different from his inner-directed forebears, but because he does not have enough capital to buy a "fine house" or an "objet d'art." And if "he" does not wish to acquire "a fine woman," perhaps it is because *she* already is one.

The rise of a more visible and privileged middle-class consumer and the increasing entrance of lower-class laborers into service-oriented and white-collar positions no doubt helps to account for the purported rise of an other-directed type. It also explains why such persons would constitute a "lonely crowd," a group that possesses individual attributes (like loneliness) *only as a group* or "social body." Yet the point I wish to emphasize is that such narratives were born and popularized not merely in response to changes in the socioeconomic structure but also out of a cultural desire to defend the values of liberal individualism—values vital to the interests of the propertied classes. Only by indulging in a fantasy about the individualism and autonomy of past generations could the "new" Americans seem so sadly lacking.

Paranoid Prescriptions

Once we understand that such narratives come into being through a nostalgia for the "lost" individualism of past generations, then we can understand the *antidotes* they offer for restoring individual autonomy. These prescriptions take somewhat different forms, depending upon who is offering them, but they all have one thing in common. They insist that collectives, organizations, and groups, despite their deceptively pleasant appearance, must be recognized as the true enemies of the individual. While the autonomous figures of the nineteenth century "had no doubt as to who their enemies were," notes Riesman (rev. ed. 257), postwar individuals "are incapable of defining the 'enemy'" (orig. ed. 302). The new systems of domination "are not the *visible* and *palpable* barriers of family and authority that typically restricted people in the past" but rather a set of "shadowy entanglements" whose "demands appear so reasonable" that they go virtually unnoticed (301–02, emphasis added). Marcuse's view of the new enemies ("a system of anonymous powers" [*One-Dimensional* 46]) is similar. These powers form a "society without opposition," because they "institute new, more effective, and more pleasant forms of social control and social cohesion" (Marcuse ix, xv). In William Whyte's view, "there is—or should be—a conflict between the individual and the organization" (13), a fact people have forgotten because "it is not easy to fight benevolence" (397). What we have forgotten, Whyte says, is that we "must *fight* The Organization" (404), and *The Organization Man* contains detailed instructions on how to do so.[9]

On its face this sort of resistance seems admirable, particularly given the ongoing rationalization of the corporate workforce, the ruthless expansion of capital into unregulated labor markets, and the unrelenting corporate drive to stimulate new consumer demand. Yet resisting "the system" in these cases (Marcuse's excepted) does not mean engaging in a collective struggle to modify capitalist practices.[10] Nor does it imply combating a *particular* class of individuals within the society or the organization—for instance, stockholders, or management, or even the upper classes more generally. Rather, the directive to *fight* is a declaration of war on a unified and reified "system." This directive has the effect of encouraging resistance to social commitments *in general*. While such resistance might be liberating for some, it also amounts to a defense of the liberal values undergirding free market capitalism—atomism, privacy, competitiveness, and *strict* opposition to the social order.

This problem becomes most clear in *The Organization Man*, where the story of declining individualism is driven by a masculinist fantasy of resistance in which the only actors are "the individual" and "the organization." The primary problem with modern society, in Whyte's view, is its tendency to promote cooperation and "belongingness" (the opposite of alienation). In place of that domesticating organizational kindness, Whyte recommends a return to the "hard-boiled ... Protestant Ethic" (15), a "gladiators' school" mentality in which "combat was the ideal—combat with the dealer, combat with the 'chiseling competitors,' and combat with each other" (117). The "committee way," he insists, "simply can't be equated with the 'rugged' individualism that is supposed to be the business of business" (18). In short, the prescription for ailing individual agency in America is nothing so much as a healthy dose of masculinity. What is so telling about this sort of struggle is the ease with which it becomes a struggle against social commitments of any kind. "Fella," Whyte fondly recalls a master salesman advising him, "you will never sell anybody anything until you learn one simple thing. The man on the other side of the counter is the *enemy*" (117).

The strategy by which "the system" is treated as an enemy of the self promotes a hyperindividualist defense that sees enemies *everywhere*—or rather, does *not* see them because they are *hidden* in organizations that seem, on the surface, benevolent and reasonable. Such a view is structurally analogous to paranoia—a way of thinking, I suggested earlier, that may be viewed as both an extraordinary form of individualism and a way of conceptualizing ideological conditioning. In other words, it seems reasonable to translate Whyte's prescriptions into the more recent terms of business professor Andrew Grove, who declares, "when it comes to business, I believe in the value of paranoia" (3). By introducing the term *paranoia* in my analysis here, I do not mean to dismiss Whyte's brand of individualism. There is much to agree with in all of these accounts, particularly their acute sense of the pressures placed on individuals by postwar economic conditions.

Yet these powerful observations are purchased at the price of some telling reductions. To understand the organization as enemy, one must first make two tacit assumptions. First, one must conceive of the organization not as a system of complex relationships and structures, but as a unified *totality*. Second, one must imagine it as an active, living agency, against whose *will* to subdue and incorporate one must struggle. In order to save the imperiled liberal agent from incorporation into a larger controlling body, in other words, that social body must itself be imagined *as a liberal individual,* as an agent with a coherence and identity of its own, a sort of superindividual. To make the point in terms of recent writing on organizational behavior, it is a short step from the view that *Only the Paranoid Survive* (Grove) to a full-blown vision of *The Paranoid Corporation*—a collectivity that, like a paranoid person, "sincerely believes that its bizarre behavior is normal and necessary" [Cohen and Cohen 53–54]. This sort of reification, or postmodern transference, is a direct result of the initial presumption that human agency is in short supply. To demonstrate this point, I must turn to the moment at which these texts link their reimagination of persons to a new vision of corporate and social structures.

The Shadow of the Firm

"If one had to set a date for the change" from inner-direction to other-direction, remarks Riesman, "one might say that the old epoch ended with the death of Henry Ford" (139). This historical marker is interesting for several reasons. First, it quite literally (no doubt too literally) indicates the end of "Fordist" production, which has been viewed as a vital index of both the shift from monopoly capitalism to "late" or global capitalism and the rise of a postmodern economic condition. David Harvey, for instance, has drawn on the terminology of "regulationist school" economics to characterize postmodernity as the result of a shift from "Fordist accumulation" to "flexible accumulation." Given such descriptions it is not insignificant that Riesman's "other-directed" type develops because inner-directed types are "no longer sufficiently *flexible*" (19, emphasis added) or that the "inner-directed" character prefers the occupations of a dying Fordist regime, "the banker, the tradesman, the small entrepreneur," to the favored occupations of "the 'new' middle class—the bureaucrat, the salaried employee in business, etc." (21). In fact, the other-directed type develops in response to a host of socioeconomic changes that have since been linked to postmodernity and late capitalism: a "centralized and bureaucratized society and a world shrunken and agitated by the contact—accelerated by industrialization—of races, nations, and cultures" (18); a movement from "production and extraction" to a "tertiary" service economy (21); and an increase in the way "relations with the outer world...are mediated by the flow of mass communication" (21–22).[11]

But there is another reason why Riesman selects the death of Ford as a historical marker. It symbolizes a transformation in the agency and control of corporate bodies, the end of an era in which corporations could (supposedly) be "run" from the top down by a single, powerful individual like Ford.[12] It is vital to see that the apparent death of such institutions relates directly to Riesman's initial presumption that individual autonomy is on the wane. If individuals are no longer unique and autonomous, then organizations must also be fundamentally different, because their "heads" can no longer provide the charismatic leadership that marked the era of monopoly capitalism. As Riesman explains, there once was a time when, "if [one] founded a firm, this was his lengthened shadow. Today the man is the shadow of the firm" (146). *The Lonely Crowd* and *The Organization Man* are obsessed with this eclipsing of the heroic CEO. They are in some ways elegies for the loss of individual genius—for the replacement of charismatic bosses like Ford and "inner-directed" inventor-heroes like Edison (who would "try and try again, sustained by his internal judgment of his worth" [Riesman 129]) with a new and depressingly uniform "generation of bureaucrats" (Whyte 63).

What I wish to emphasize, however, is how this elegiac narrative invites an imaginative transfer of agency to the corporation as a totality. We can witness such a transfer by examining one of Whyte's deepest concerns—the difficulty in tracing corporate products to *individual* human origins. The typical postwar organization, Whyte laments, wants a worker "who does not think up ideas himself but mediates other people's ideas" (135). The difference between this new sort of "middleman" and the maverick thinkers of the past epitomizes the shift from "making" to "processing" that supposedly characterizes postindustrial society. "If the corporation concentrates on getting people who will process other people's ideas," Whyte worries, "where will it get the other people—that is, the people with ideas?" (136). For Whyte, making and processing are radically opposed. Making is done by individuals, while processing is done by a system into which individuals have been incorporated. This opposition ensures that true creation can never be the result of a *social* process and, in so doing, protects the romantic notion of the individual agent as *sole* source of genius and creativity. But it is precisely this latter notion that seems most unsettled by the practices of postwar organizations:

> The whole tendency of modern organization life is to muffle the importance of individual leadership. In studying an organization, one of the most difficult things is to trace a program or innovation back to its origins, and this is just as true of organization successes as it is of failures. Who started what and when? This kind of question is the kind that makes organization people uncomfortable. (53)

Of course, it is Whyte who is made uncomfortable by these questions. After all, an organization that turns work into processing not only undermines what we might call the "great man theory" of the corporation—the view that an organization is merely the "tool" of its autonomous leader—but seems to confirm the dramatic historical shift that Riesman locates in "the death of Ford," and that, to borrow the terms of literary theory, we might locate in the "death of the author" or even in the postmodern "precession of simulacra," those representations whose own referential origins seem deeply in question.[13]

But there are deeper reasons for Whyte's concern. If creativity has been transferred from the individual agent to the system, then so must other signs of agency, such as decision making, leadership, and control more generally. This possibility—that control is not centralized in *human* individuals—is deeply unsettling to Whyte. To begin with, it seems to indicate an increasing uniformity among all the workers of the company. It has become difficult, he complains, to tell the difference between "the staff" and "the line" (3). "It is no longer clear," Riesman agrees, "which way *is* up even if one wants to rise" (Riesman 48). In such suggestions we can once again detect an anxious desire to maintain class boundaries. Riesman regrets that we no longer know who "ranks" whom in society (48) and bemoans the fact that a manager "is compelled to personalize his relations with" his staff, whereas before he "never 'saw' his secretary...as an individual" (311–12). The reinvigoration of individualism would presumably "solve" such problems by allowing individuals to establish their proper social rankings through hard-driven competition.

But it is the ominous and self-aggrandizing figure of the corporate system itself to which all of these other symptoms of corporate change point. If the workers *and* the leaders of corporations have been homogenized, "Who, then," asks Whyte, "is to be in charge?" (29). One wonders, writes Riesman, "who really runs things" in a modern organization and "how things get done at all" (rev. ed. 220). "Nobody is sure anymore who really runs the company," says Heller's Slocum, and Marcuse notes that "the organizers and administrators themselves become increasingly dependent on the machinery which they organize and administer" (*One-Dimensional* 33). In such accounts, the rising power of the organization itself is registered through a story about the enervation and decline of the autonomous CEO. In modern organizations, says Whyte,

> *Creative leadership is a staff function.* Organizations need new ideas from time to time. But the leader is not the man for this; he hires staff people to think up the ideas....His job is not to look ahead himself but to check the excesses of the kind of people who do look ahead. He does not unbalance himself by enthusiasm for a particular plan by getting involved with the basic engine. He is the governor. (136)

This final metaphor is widely visible in postwar writing. Charles Reich's *Greening of America* (1970), for instance, suggests that in a modern corporation, "No one at all is in the executive suite. What looks like a man is only a representation of a man who does what the organization requires. He (or it) does not run the machine; he *tends* it" (107). Such a bureaucratic engine is notably different from Weber's "iron cage," which is "put into motion or arrested...only from the very top" (988). Postwar CEOs, by contrast, may still have the power to arrest the organization, but they do not because they have allowed decision making to become a collective function instead of an individual act.

In texts like *The Organization Man* we thus witness the rebirth of the corporation as a self-regulating entity outside the control of any one human. This way of imagining corporate power is by now a familiar subject of films and novels. It is not difficult to see that, by imaginatively homogenizing all of the human components of a system, this vision simultaneously disables a class-based analysis of labor relations and creates sympathy for the corporate chieftains who are now subject to the very system they nominally head. Indeed, this is one reason why the "total system" model of the corporation has had a certain appeal for corporate managers and executives themselves. A CEO in Richard Powers's *Gain* (1998), for instance, finds himself amused, "drawing the salary he does, how little say a CEO has about anything." He is simply the "corporation's point man, the passive agent of a collective bidding" (349).

Such visions of the corporation, like their postwar predecessors, are deeply rooted in cybernetics. In fact, when Whyte and Riesman describe the corporation as an "engine" and its executive head as a "governor" (rather than a "leader"), they specifically invoke the discourse of cybernetics. According to Norbert Wiener, the term "cybernetics" was "derived from the Greek word *kubernētēs*, or 'steersman,' the same Greek word from which we eventually derive our word 'governor'" (*Human Use* 15).[14] It should thus come as no surprise that Whyte blames the rise of organization culture on the introduction of "cybernetic principles" into the workplace (26), because cybernetics challenged the idea that one could understand the governance of complex systems by looking at individual actions. Indeed, cybernetics reconceptualized the relations between information-processing machines and "the special sort of machine known as a human being" by suggesting that human action is the product of messages between parts of the individual and other, external sources (Wiener, *Human Use* 79).

The cybernetic approach to problems of control, in other words, is diametrically opposed to an approach that would distinguish individual acts from social influences or, by extension, "inner-direction" from "other-direction." As cybernetics enthusiast Gregory Bateson remarks, " 'inside' and 'outside' are not appropriate metaphors for inclusion and exclusion when we are speaking of the self" (*Mind and Nature* 145–46). For Bateson, the mistaken tendency to explain human action through reference to "a factitious inner tendency, principle, instinct, or whatnot" can easily cause a "descent…to paranoia" (147). And this, as we have seen, is what happens throughout the postwar narrative of diminished agency. While "panic" is perhaps too strong a term for the texts I have been discussing, they nonetheless contain the basic elements of agency panic. They begin with an insight about the way persons are regulated by large systems. Yet because they cling to a traditional conception of agency, they recoil from this insight, understanding social influence not as a structural feature of social relations but as the result of a radical historical transformation in the very nature of human beings.

We can understand the values behind this response, I have been suggesting, by comparing it to "cybernetic" approaches to the same problem. From the viewpoint of cybernetics, the idea that persons are regulated by larger systems is not a terrifying discovery but a basic assumption necessary for understanding human behavior.[15] For the writers I have been discussing here, however, the vision of a self-regulating system that reduces its human components, even its titular "head," to mere relays or "switches" in a larger "processor" of information, implies the existence of a "society which is self-expanding and self-perpetuating in its own preestablished direction—driven by the growing needs which it generates and, at the same time, contains" (Marcuse, *One-Dimensional* 34). From this latter perspective, which views agency as a property of integral subjects, the system appears to be a self-governing superindividual with its own intentions or goals. Thus, the idea of adopting a cybernetic view seems suicidal because a cybernetic viewpoint, with its *acceptance* of systemic controls and its *weakened* sense of individuality, seems to be precisely what the system "wants" us to adopt. The proper way to respond, therefore, is with a form of individualism so intense that it is barely distinguishable from paranoia. One must identify the organization as a totality, unmask its false benevolence, reject its cybernetic ideology, and treat it as an enemy:

> In the 1984 of Big Brother one would at least know who the enemy was—a bunch of bad men who wanted power because they liked power. But in the other kind of 1984 one would be disarmed for not knowing who the enemy was, and when the day of reckoning came...they would be a mild-looking group of therapists who, like the Grand Inquisitor, would be doing what they did to help you. (Whyte 31)

As this dystopian parable makes clear, the enemy no longer consists of "bad men," but is rather a seemingly beneficent system that wishes to "adjust" its human components in order to perfect its own being. The only thing left to do, Whyte suggests, is to recognize this incorporating logic as evil and to resist it, thus conserving the threatened model of competitive individualism.

Anti-Socialism

Perhaps no post–World War II fiction more compellingly resists the culture of "organization men" than Joseph Heller's *Catch-22* (1961). Centered on an Air Force bombardier named Yossarian, *Catch-22* is the story of Captain Yossarian's extraordinary and often comical attempts at self-preservation while serving on a small Mediterranean island in World War

II. But this is an unusual war story because the forces from whom Yossarian is trying to protect himself are not just his foes in the Axis armies. They also include the officers in his own Group Headquarters, whose concern with public relations victories over military victories and whose "happy facility for getting different people to agree" (119) mark them as organization men par excellence. Yossarian's primary problem is his commanding officer, Colonel Cathcart, who, like the other leaders at Group, is deeply concerned with matters like getting "a tighter bomb pattern" on missions, because *his* commanding officer, General Peckem, "feels it makes a much nicer aerial photograph" (190). Cathcart tries to get himself into the *Saturday Evening Post* by concocting a condolence letter campaign and then volunteering his men for dangerous missions in order to "get some casualties" (277). Most problematic for Yossarian is that Cathcart tries to increase his own stature at Group by raising the number of missions his men must complete just before any of them is scheduled to be sent home.

Like Riesman and Whyte, Yossarian understands his "enemies" in this image-obsessed corporate environment as the larger organizations that demand "corporate" forms of behavior from their members, including himself. These organizations include not only the military bureaucracy with its complex system of catch-22s—self-contradicting rules that frustrate one's ability to follow them—and his squadron's famous transnational supply "syndicate" in which "everyone has a share," and which eventually becomes an emblem of the emerging global economy. They also include the nation itself, whose ultimate catch-22 is a demand that its male citizens sacrifice their lives in order to preserve its identity. "All over the world," says the narrator, "boys on every side of the bomb line were laying down their lives for what they had been told was their country, and no one seemed to mind, least of all the boys who were laying down their young lives" (16).

Yossarian minds. "They're trying to kill me," he tells his fellow officer Clevinger. "Every one of them" (16–17). "No one's trying to kill you," Clevinger explains. "They're shooting at *everyone*... They're trying to kill everyone" (16). But Yossarian insists, and his proof is that "strangers he didn't know shot at him with cannons every time he flew up into the air to drop bombs on them" (17). What Yossarian forcefully resists in making such assertions is Clevinger's reasonable insistence that the cannonfire is directed not at Yossarian personally but at the Allied forces generally. By Clevinger's way of thinking, the real antagonists here are "social bodies"—not their individual members. Any casualty suffered by an individual is thus an accident of sorts, a result of his membership in the larger American "corps." In other words, the threat against Yossarian himself is not *motivated*, but rather depends upon a sort of collective identification that is so familiar it almost goes unnoticed. It is this concept of collective identity, and thus collective risk, that Yossarian cannot accept. His refusal to associate himself with the national project or with the collective body under attack leaves him with only one way of comprehending an attack on his unit: it is an attack on him personally. Furthermore, because Yossarian refuses to identify himself with national aims, he views the actions of his own leaders as threats equally hostile and deliberate as those presented by the German forces. Virtually everyone, it seems, is out to get him. To many of Yossarian's colleagues, and to many readers, this response seems paranoid.[16]

In his classic account of the "paranoid style," Richard Hofstadter writes,

> Any historian of warfare knows that it is in good part a comedy of errors and a museum of incompetence; but if for every error and every act of incompetence one can substitute an act of treason, we can see how many points of fascinating interpretation are open to the paranoid imagination: treason in high places can be found at almost every turning... (24–25)

This would seem to be a fitting description of Yossarian's attitude toward the massive incompetence of his own unit. Not only is he intolerant of explanations that focus on "error" and other "non-motivated" causes, but he views the massive incompetence of his own leaders as intentional malice. In Clevinger's view, Yossarian has "an unreasonable belief that everybody around him [is] crazy," an "unfounded suspicion that people [hate] him and [are] conspiring to kill him," "a Jehovah complex," and "antisocial aggressions" (19–20)—all classic symptoms of paranoia.[17] Yet Heller makes it clear that Yossarian's paranoia is a *reasonable* response to both war and organizational culture. Indeed, one of the central missions of *Catch-22* is to challenge institutional definitions of sanity and insanity by illustrating the ways in which military service requires an "insane" form of self-denial.

The central concept of the catch-22, for instance, is designed to illustrate the collective insanity of the highly rationalized military bureaucracy. A catch-22 is any one of numerous mutually contradictory, but inescapable, bureaucratic precepts that create for their victims what Gregory Bateson called "the double bind" ("Toward"), and R. D. Laing, following Bateson, called "a position of checkmate" (*Politics* 79). These disorienting and destructive "iron cages" cannot be broken except by extraordinary self-negation that, in clinical cases, can lead to schizophrenia or "ontological insecurity" (Laing, *Divided* 40ff.). The most basic catch-22 in Heller's military is the rule that to be relieved of combat duty one must simply claim to be mentally ill; the "catch," however, is "Catch-22, which specified that a concern for one's own safety in the face of dangers that were real and immediate was the process of a rational mind" (46). Through this double logic, the military demands sanity while institutionalizing insanity. It creates a system in which one "would be crazy to fly more missions and sane if he didn't, but if he was sane he had to fly them. If he flew them he was crazy and didn't have to; but if he didn't want to he was sane and had to" (46). In the context of this topsy-turvy rhetoric, Yossarian's "paranoia" can hardly be called insane.[18] Indeed, if we accept the terms of the novel, he is utterly sane, because *Catch-22* defines insanity as a willingness to sacrifice oneself for a larger, "corporate" body—such as one's nation.

The question, then, is not whether Yossarian's stance is a form of pathology, but rather what is at stake in representing it as such. The answer, I believe, stems from Heller's association of insanity with corporate or collective forms of self-denial. Within the framework of that association, Yossarian's paranoia is a form of individualism that is especially uncompromising and, in a sense, antisocial. Yossarian's sense that collective acts of war are directed at him personally, for example, is antisocial in the sense that it involves a denial of the social nature of the acts in question. Yossarian does not deny that antiaircraft fire is meant for other individuals. He simply refuses to see the nation as the unit under attack. His thinking is fiercely (his colleagues might say *insanely*) individualistic. As he says to Clevinger later, "It doesn't make a damned bit of difference *who* wins the war to someone who's dead" (122). When Clevinger rebukes him for failing to support his comrades and giving "comfort to the enemy," Yossarian replies, "The enemy...is anybody who's going to get you killed, no matter *which* side he's on, and that includes Colonel Cathcart" (122). Yossarian thus employs precisely the sort of resistance to the organization suggested by cultural critics like Whyte. He recognizes the enemy through its deceptively benevolent mask and its seemingly rational, but actually insane, bureaucratic rules—and he fights it. The only difference between Yossarian's anti-corporatism and Whyte's is that Yossarian resists both the organization he works for and the larger "corporation" for which it stands, the United States. His "paranoia" is thus a form of resistance to the ideological demands of the *nation* and to social commitments in general.

The other person in the novel who assumes this unabashedly antisocial and antinationalist view is the 107-year-old Italian whose national allegiances change whenever Italy is reoccupied. "What is a country?" this man asks Nately, a pilot in Yossarian's squadron:

A country is a piece of land surrounded on all sides by boundaries, usually un-natural...There are now fifty or sixty countries fighting in this war. Surely so many countries can't *all* be worth dying for.... They are going to kill you if you don't watch out, and I can see now that you are not going to watch out. (242)

This account of the nation as an "imagined community" (Anderson) could function as a form of utopian collectivism. Yet here it is a reassertion of individualism. Its attack on the importance of national boundaries is a reaffirmation of the individual's boundaries, because these are what must be sacrificed to sustain the "unnatural" contours of the nation state—for instance, when male bodies are violently opened up in order to "protect" their country. While Nately and others view this response as deeply unpatriotic, they do not view it as paranoid. Nonetheless, it has the same function as Yossarian's "paranoia," which is a method of protecting an integral self against social pressures, including those of the nation.

Once we understand Yossarian's "paranoia" as a form of the resistance advocated by popular critics of mass culture, we can see why Yossarian suddenly abandons both the military and his country at the end of *Catch-22*. As he approaches this final decision, he comes under increasing pressure from the squadron's commanding officers, Colonels Korn and Cathcart, who have been attempting unsuccessfully to squelch his continual insubordination. Eventually, they decide to get rid of him by offering him a seemingly simple choice: either face court-martial or be sent home with a promotion, a medal, and a hero's welcome. The only condition of the latter option is that he publicly support and "like" them. Although the second choice will mean abandoning his campaign to reduce the number of missions for the rest of the squadron, Yossarian says, "what the hell!...let them stand up and do something about it the way I did" (418).

After some reflection, however, Yossarian changes his mind and decides to take a third course. Following in the footsteps of his colleague, Orr, he deserts and flees to Sweden. From one point of view, this ultimate decision seems to be an act of solidarity with the men of the unit. Yossarian sacrifices the thing he has been fighting for all along: a safe return home. In doing so, moreover, he refuses to help raise the number of missions for others. On its face, then, this decision would seem to display an altruism that flies in the face of the antisocial ethic I have been attributing to him. Yet it is essential to recognize that while Yossarian's solution is not self-aggrandizing it *is* self-preservative. Indeed, he explains his refusal to go home a hero in these striking terms: "I've been fighting all along to save my country," he says. "Now I'm going to fight a little to save myself. The country's not in danger any more, but I am" (435). This is an odd way to talk about going home safely to a hero's welcome. Yossarian's desire to "save" himself from this trip home only makes sense if the return to American civilian life is a major *threat* to Yossarian. And what makes it such a threat is that it would commit Yossarian to "the Organization" he has so stridently resisted thus far. To go back to the States with a promotion would be to abandon his individualist opposition to the "corps" and to become *incorporated* in a military-industrial system that seems to reduce its members to mindless automatons and mere public relations images. Instead, Yossarian flees not only the army but the nation. In doing so, it is important to note, he does not reduce the number of missions for his unit. He merely *abandons* his social commitments. It is in this sense that Yossarian is an antisocial character. And it is for this reason that the novel must end in a familiar flight to the displaced American frontier. Like Huckleberry Finn and other inner-directed heroes of the American past, Yossarian cannot find himself in the social realm, and so he lights out for the territory.

Bureaucratic Individuals

Part of Heller's critique of mass culture, then, involves a model of individual resistance to the corporate nightmare of the armed forces. This resistance, which is expressed by the inner-directed hero Yossarian, takes the form of a reasonable, self-protective "paranoia" about being killed during wartime. The other prong of Heller's critique is directed at the more unfortunate products of mass culture. In this part of his project, Heller depicts failures of resistance, forms of corporate behavior and identity that have violated the integrity of individuals.

No figure more concisely registers these deindividuating pressures than the novel's "soldier in white," a mysterious and disturbing figure who appears each time Yossarian is in the hospital. His mere presence generates conspiracy theories among the men on the ward. Part of what makes them nervous is the utter anonymity of this patient. He is Heller's version of the unknown soldier, a man without noticeable identification or identity, "constructed entirely of gauze, plaster and a thermometer" (165), which is balanced twice daily on the rim of the single, small hole over his mouth. But the most puzzling feature of the soldier in white's treatment concerns the two jars of clear fluid that seem to constitute his food and bodily waste:

> When the jar feeding the inside of his elbow was just about empty, the jar on the floor was just about full, and the two were simply uncoupled from their respective hoses and reversed quickly so that the liquid could be dripped right back

into him. Changing the jars was no trouble to anyone but the men who watched them changed every hour or so and were baffled by the procedure. (168)

The soldier in white's "treatment," then, consists in first receiving a generic external casing, and second, being reduced to a pure "processor," a machine that circulates material without altering it or producing something with it. The soldier in white is thus a miniature version of the postindustrial bureaucracy, which is designed more to manage and "process" things than to "make" them, and which ultimately seems to efface the most basic functions of humans. He is a perfect cybernetic organism, a model of homeostasis and self-regulation, a closed system.

What is disturbing about this figure is that the pure and purely circular processing of material through his body seems to make his body itself unnecessary. This, of course, is still the central anxiety about technological systems. As a colonel on the ward asks, "Why can't they hook the two jars up to each other and eliminate the middleman?" (168). The other men on the ward wonder, in somewhat different terms, if this is already the case. They suspect that the soldier in white may be "constructed entirely" out of plaster, with literally nothing inside. Eventually, their fears seem to be confirmed when the original soldier in white dies and is replaced by a plastered individual indistinguishable from the first. "It was, indeed, the same man," says the narrator. "He had lost a few inches and added some weight, but Yossarian... would recognize him anywhere. He wondered who he was" (358). The joke here—that Yossarian "recognizes" this patient without knowing who he is—grows out of Yossarian's willingness to associate identity with a purely exterior surface (the plastered body). What makes the joke operational—indeed, what drives the representational logic of the whole novel—is that Yossarian privileges those traits created *for* the soldier by the organization. The same emphasis on the plaster-thin *exterior* of the solider allows Dunbar to shout first "He's back" and then immediately declare "They've stolen him away!...He's hollow inside, like a chocolate soldier" (356, 358)—claims which begin to echo throughout the ward as one after another of the men goes into a state of panic. This mass expression of anxiety is telling. To say that the soldier in white is hollow inside is not only to express a certain paranoia about the material removal of the soldier by a malicious, bureaucratic "Them" but also to recognize that the soldier has been deindividuated (or "hollowed out") by his treatment. Because the "inside" is the site of individual difference and agency, a hollow individual can only be a symptom of a collective, anti-individualist logic.

The soldier in white thus represents the deindividuating effects of the military and of postindustrial society by extension. Although they rarely represent it so literally, many stories of military life focus on such effects. As Elaine Scarry notes in her study of war and the body,

> The boy in war is, to an extent found in almost no other form of work, inextricably bound up with the men and materials of his labor: he will learn to perceive himself as he will be perceived by others, as indistinguishable from the men of his unit, regiment, division, and above all national group. (83)

Heller renders this effort to make men "indistinguishable" from one another not in the familiar story of regimental drilling, training, and physical discipline but in a story about what Max Weber calls "rational discipline." Of all those powers "diminishing [the] importance of individual action," Weber writes, "the most irresistible force is *rational discipline*" (1148–49). Heller repeatedly dramatizes what he believes to be the consequences of this sort of discipline, one of which is the transfer of human decision-making capacities to an external and abstract set of rules and procedures. The result is an early version of the postmodern landscape so comically rendered in Don DeLillo's *White Noise* (1985), which satirizes our reliance on mass media for validation of our own experiences, even when media reports contradict "the evidence of our senses" (23).

Heller's novel is replete with such behavior. Consider, for instance, the case of Doc Daneeka. Although he never flies, Daneeka routinely has his name added to flight logs in order to gain flight credit. Eventually, however, one of the planes on which he is falsely registered crashes. As Sergeant Knight watches it go down, he laments to Yossarian that Daneeka is still on board. While they speak, however, Daneeka is standing right next to Knight, whom he corrects. A moment later, Knight repeats his sorrow and concern for Daneeka, who in turn insists, "I'm right here....I'm not in the plane" (333). Nonetheless, when no one emerges alive from the place wreck, the administrative staff sergeant strikes Daneeka's name from the squadron roster, asks the War Department to notify Daneeka's wife of his death, and tells Daneeka himself to "remain out of sight...until some decision [can] be reached relating to the disposition of his remains" (335). Even worse for Daneeka is that most of the squadron treats him as if he's dead. "The records show that you went up in McWatt's plane," one enlisted man tells Daneeka. "You didn't come down in a parachute, so you must have been killed in the crash." "Gee, I guess he really is dead," says another soldier, "I'm going to miss him" (335).

Excerpted this way, these remarks may seem to be good-natured kidding directed at Daneeka. But in the representational logic of *Catch-22* they are much more than that. The most basic strategy of the novel is to create characters who treat bureaucratic representations—official military reports and the like—as if they had absolute, ontological validity. Even Daneeka's wife tosses out her husband's "impassioned letter begging her to bring his plight to the attention of the War Department" because she receives one of Cathcart's "personal" condolence letters, which begins "Dear Mrs., Mr., Miss, or Mr. and Mrs. Daneeka..." (338). Similarly, when an officer named Mudd is killed before having "officially gotten into the squadron, he [can] never officially be gotten out" (106), and from that point on he acquires an odd ontological status as "the dead man in Yossarian's tent." He is assigned a bed that remains empty and can never be filled because no procedure exists for doing so. As in Daneeka's case, the problem is not simply that characters cannot escape the "iron cage" of bureaucracy; it is that they have no conception of such a cage and thus no desire to escape it. The satiric force of the novel reveals them to be ideologically conditioned subjects. They have internalized bureaucratic rules in their behavior and even their perceptions of the world.

The most striking example of this tendency is the brief episode in which a doctor asks Yossarian to impersonate a soldier who has just died moments before his entire family arrives from New York to visit him in the hospital. "But they came to see their son," Yossarian objects. "Maybe they won't even notice the difference," the doctor replies. "As far as we're concerned, one dying boy is just as good as any other, or just as bad" (181). If this seems at first to be only a military doctor's callous disregard for individual difference, it becomes something much more bizarre when the substitution of one individual for another does not bother the family at all. And it is not simply that they are deceived by a physical resemblance, for Yossarian identifies himself by name. When the mother continues to call him Giuseppe, her (other) son corrects her: "His name is Yossarian, Ma. Yossarian, don't you recognize me? I'm your brother John" (182). Oddly enough, then, the family seems content to ignore any traits that might distinguish Yossarian from Giuseppe, even in this most personal of circumstances, the deathbed scene. The drama that unfolds fully supports the doctor's original proposition that "one dying boy is just as good as any other."

Heller's fictional strategy here dramatizes people relinquishing certain internal, decision-making capacities to a larger system of communications and rules, a system that does its business, just as Weber described, "according to purely objective considerations"—that is, "according to *calculable rules* and 'without regard for persons'" (975). The result of this strategy is the creation of what we might call "bureaucratic individuals," persons imagined as if they had been stripped of traditional human features: not only individual difference (the soldier in white, the "Italian boy") or material presence (Mudd, Daneeka) but also the ability to make reasonable judgments and the ability to act autonomously within the rationalized procedures of the military system—to "fight the organization" as Whyte puts it (12). Much of the grim humor in Heller's novel stems from his characters' extraordinary lack of reasonable judgment and their simultaneous "worship" of The Organization's "beneficence" (Whyte 12–13)—their commitment to the idea that bureaucratic constructs, rules, and reports are the most ontologically secure things in the world. These characters believe whatever the military's "official" reports say—even when such reports contradict their own observations. They have "surrendered" to The Organization.

One of Heller's primary targets in *Catch-22* is the notion that representations, particularly bureaucratic communications, supersede the material reality of the war—a view that many of the organization men in the squadron hold dear. When the men in the unit want to avoid a dangerous bombing run to Bologna, for instance, they hope that the squadron "bomb line" (a cartographic representation of the areas already taken by Allied forces) will magically move past Bologna, making the run unnecessary. Clevinger describes this hope as "a complete reversion to primitive superstition. They're confusing cause and effect" (118). As he sees it, the bomb line is merely a representation that refers to a more vital, material reality. But the reliance of the organization on this representation threatens to undo Clevinger's common-sense realism, because when Yossarian moves the bomb line in the night, word quickly makes its way through the command and control structure that Bologna has been captured. The mission is canceled, and General Peckem awards himself a medal. Eventually, of course, the truth is discovered and the men must complete the mission.

What such scenes lampoon is the organization's tendency to confuse communications with the serious, material reality of war. *Catch-22* suggests that such confusions are symptoms of bureaucracy gone wild. It seems important to point out, therefore, that in the years since *Catch-22*'s appearance, similar propositions have become widely accepted tenets of cultural theory. One of the central claims of poststructuralism, for instance, is that we do not have unmediated access to the real, to an ontological level beyond "mere" communications. In Jacques Derrida's often-cited formulation, "there is nothing outside of the text" (*Grammatology* 158). The same emphasis on the determining power of communications has been central to cybernetics and systems theory. Heller's mockery of these propositions, therefore, allies him with the likes of Whyte and Riesman, and against most poststructuralists and systems theorists. Like Riesman, he recognizes that "relations with the outer world and with oneself are mediated by the flow of mass communication" (Riesman 37), but rather than viewing mediation as a permanent feature of social relations, he sees it (in the manner of Baudrillard) as a new and dangerous phenomenon, an opportunity for pure fabrication and simulation.[19] Unlike Baudrillard, however, Heller adopts a realist stance. He lampoons the idea that management techniques have become "more vital than content" and "relatively independent of the content of what is being managed" (Whyte 7). He does so primarily, I have been suggesting, by caricaturing the "empty" human products of postindustrialism. Yet Heller's most forceful and serious realist argument comes through the story of Snowden.

Snowden is a young tail-gunner who dies in Yossarian's arms during a bombing run. The grisly scene of Snowden's death recurs throughout the narrative and frequently interrupts other scenes. As Snowden lies in the back of the plane dying, Yossarian treats a gash in his leg, unaware that Snowden has a much more serious wound in his abdomen. Eventually, though, Yossarian cuts through Snowden's flak suit, and, to his horror, Snowden's insides pour out onto the floor of the airplane.

> Here was God's plenty, all right... liver, lungs, kidneys, ribs, stomach and bits of the stewed tomatoes Snowden had eaten that day for lunch. Yossarian... gazed down despondently at the grim secret Snowden had spilled all over the messy floor. It was easy to read the message in his entrails. Man was matter, that was Snowden's secret. Drop him out a window and he'll fall. Set fire to him and he'll burn. Bury him and he'll rot, like other kinds of garbage. The spirit gone, man is garbage. That was Snowden's secret. (429–30)

This final, full description of the Snowden incident, placed just before Yossarian rejects Korn and Cathcart's deal, functions as an epiphany— Yossarian's realization of something that has haunted him throughout the novel. It is meant partly to suggest that Yossarian decides to turn down the Colonels in order to preserve his own "spirit" and avoid becoming "garbage." But it also articulates a notion about persons that Heller has been at pains to portray as endangered. It suggests that persons are defined by the precious spirit they contain *inside* them like a secret. The opening of Snowden's body is synonymous with the destruction of his spirit because, in the model of subjectivity being defended here, the protected cavities of the body are essential sources of the self.

This dramatic celebration of the humanist self is inextricably linked to a sense that postindustrial bureaucracy cannot comprehend the basic reality of war, that it is too caught up in its representations, rules, and communications. In *Catch-22*'s humanist vision, the secret that pours out of Snowden cannot be reduced or misrepresented. It conveys no state ideology or platitude about the war. Its message has to do only with the nature of persons. Snowden's body is what Elaine Scarry calls a "body in pain" and as such it is meant to function as the "bedrock reality" upon which all kinds of falsifications are typically based and made to seem substantive.

> The declaration of war is the declaration that "reality" is now officially "up for grabs"...The lies, fictions, falsification, within war, though authored by particular kinds of speakers in any given instance (government officials, journalists, generals, soldiers, factory workers) themselves together collectively objectify and extend the formal fact of what war is, the suspension of the reality of constructs, the systematic retraction of all benign forms of substance from the artifacts of civilization, *and simultaneously*, the mining of the ultimate substance, the ultimate source of substantiation, the extraction of the physical basis of reality from its dark hiding place in the body out into the light of day, the making available of the precious ore of confirmation, the interior content of human bodies, lungs, arteries, blood, brains, the mother lode that will eventually be reconnected to the winning issue, to which it will lend its radical substance, its compelling, heartsickening reality, until benign forms of substantiation come into being. (Scarry 137)

For Scarry, as for Heller, the interior of the body is the ultimate ontological marker. It is the site of "heartsickening reality," because to see its secret truth, one must open up "the interior content of human beings." Ideologies and representations are inessential "ideas" that only become powerful once connected to the material reality of wounded bodies, which seem to substantiate those ideas.

Yet this is not the only possible account of the meaning of Snowden's death. A poststructural or cybernetic alternative to this reading might point out that only communications can mobilize bodies for war in the first place. According to this second view, wounded bodies are not the reality that "anchor" abstract ideas and representations. Rather, they are an index of the *material* power of representations, because representations are what induce persons to risk injury for an abstract idea (such as nationality) in the first place. Could it not be said, for instance, that Snowden dies in part because he has already been mobilized, first as a citizen and then more specifically as a soldier, by "abstract" ideas about the propriety of going to war "for his country"? Once this anti-realist position comes into view, it is clear that, like Scarry, Heller champions a humanist alternative to the improperly bureaucratic (and, as we shall see, cybernetic) logic of the organization. For Heller, Snowden is ultimately a victim of his commitment to "the system" and the nation. He is a heartsickening version of the soldier in white—literally "hollowed out" by his commitment to the collective logic of the military and the nation alike. The glimpse Yossarian receives into the secret of Snowden's being establishes his "body in pain" as the firm ontological footing against which the blunders of the novel's organization men seem obscene. To confuse representations of death with this death, the novel suggests, is a crime. What is significant about this view is the degree to which it is rooted in liberal individualist assumptions.

Syndicate-Nation

I have been describing the way Heller imagines the effects of postindustrial organizations on human agency and identity, but what about his representation of organizations themselves? The primary organization in *Catch-22* is Heller's highly corporatized military. Yet there is also Milo Minderbinder's transnational supply cartel, which is a model for the nascent global economy and its dangerous multinational corporations. Much of the comedy of *Catch-22* stems from the "improperly" cybernetic structure of these organizations. Like Whyte, Heller's characters continually find themselves unable "to trace a program or innovation back to its origins" in an individual agent (Whyte 53). When Yossarian, and later Major Major, forge the names "Washington Irving" and "John Milton" on documents, for instance, they provoke serious crises of identity and control. Several Criminal Investigation Department (CID) men are assigned to track the culprits, but cannot locate the origins of these signatures—not even, apparently, their literary origins—and eventually end up investigating each other. The same difficulty allows Yossarian's alteration of the bomb line to cause the mission to be aborted.

A major reason for such problems is that the people who *really* run things in Heller's Air Force are not at its head. Its most influential members are in fact the *lowest*-ranked enlisted man and officer in the novel: ex-PFC Wintergreen, a mail clerk at twenty-seventh Air Force Headquarters, and Lieutenant Milo Minderbinder, the mess hall officer. At the twenty-seventh, in other words, there seems to be little difference between "the staff" and "the line" (Whyte 3). "In the older ideology," laments Whyte, "it was the top leader who was venerated," But "in the new managerial ideology, it is not the leaders…that are idealized—if anything, they are scolded—but the lieutenants" (44). This is exactly the case in *Catch-22*'s military, whose ultimate "top leader," General Scheisskopf, is a shit-for-brains promoted up the ranks through a series of bureaucratic errors and superficially motivated decisions. At the same time, as Yossarian points out, the lowest-ranked man, Wintergreen, "is probably the most influential man in the whole theater of operations. He's not only a mail clerk, but he has access to a mimeograph machine" (296). By sorting and changing key communications that move through his post, Wintergreen exercises as much, or more, influence on Group decisions as Generals Dreedle and Peckem—whose orders he occasionally destroys or edits for being "too prolix" (26) and for offending his taste for bureaucratic efficiency.

Postwar representations of technological society have frequently satirized the breakdown of traditional social and organizational hierarchies. Comic masterpieces such as William Gaddis's *JR* (1975) and Don DeLillo's *White Noise* depict a technologically complex culture in which young children possess more technical skill and knowledge than their elders. One of the things that links their inverted hierarchies with Heller's is an emphasis on the increasing power of communicative technologies. Heller clearly relates the inverted command structure of his military to the difficulty of managing its communications. The bureaucracy's most comic feature— and its most terrifying potential—is how little control its leaders have over it. When General Peckem sends out a memorandum designed to restructure the bureaucracy so that he can subordinate General Dreedle's command to his own, he inadvertently transfers both commands to newly promoted General Scheisskopf. The appointment of Scheisskopf as new leader, therefore, is governed purely by bureaucratic rules and not by the intentions of any individual. In Scheisskopf's appointment, we have moved past the point at which bureaucracy is "a power instrument of the first order—for one who controls the bureaucratic apparatus" (Weber 987). Heller's bureaucracy enacts its own unwelcome effects, which include the promotion of an astonishingly "empty" and incompetent leader—a veritable *anti-Ford*—to its own apex. And what better figure than Scheisskopf— a man who has been promoted up from lieutenant at record speed only because of his singular competence at leading parades, the material embodiment of a purposeless, postindustrial circulation or "processing"? In *Catch-22*, we have come a good distance toward the imaginary reassignment of control that I call "postmodern transference." While Heller's bureaucracy is not utterly autonomous, it *is* dangerously out of control.

And while the situation is presented as a comedy of errors rather than a nightmare (the form it takes in many subsequent representations), its implications are unmistakably serious.

If anyone governs the military-industrial system in *Catch-22*, it is those individuals who control the distribution of goods and communications in the system—Wintergreen and Milo Minderbinder, whose *utterly rational* and bureaucratic values lead them to join forces in a mammoth trade cartel, M & M Enterprises. This corporation grows from Milo's squadron supply syndicate. The syndicate is essentially an international goods brokerage, a thoroughly postindustrial firm engaged purely in processing goods, moving them from country to country, often selling and repurchasing them many times to create the illusion that it provides them to the mess for less than what it paid.[20] Milo operates this cartel initially out of the squadron mess, but it soon becomes a multinational corporation, with political and material ties to a number of states—including those with whom the United States is at war. This early product of the military-*post*industrial complex thus begins to override both military and national interests—a subject that Thomas Pynchon would explore with fanatical precision in *Gravity's Rainbow* a decade later. Milo uses U.S. military equipment, at no cost, and no one ever questions him because, as he puts it, "they know that what's good for the syndicate is good for the country" (228). This proposition is a form of Whyte's social ethic, the ideology that paints the organization as a beneficent and paternalistic entity whose overall health and interests are identical to the interests of its employees.

Like Whyte, Heller suggests that this ideology is false. But unlike Whyte, who simply urges generalized resistance to the organization's logic, Heller shows specifically *who* benefits from that logic—and here it is the opportunistic capitalist, who profits from a manipulative public relations campaign and a concerted effort to hide the complex sham transactions that allow him to skim government funds into his own pocket. Although Milo repeatedly asserts that "everyone has a share" in his syndicate, Yossarian pressures him until he admits that "the syndicate benefits when I benefit" (228). The visible connections between Milo's interests and the syndicate's and the syndicate's and the nation's reveal how capital uses the ideology of classlessness and equality ("everyone has a share") to paint individual interest as national or collective welfare. According to Milo's logic, if everyone has a share in the syndicate and if what is good for the syndicate is good for the nation then the syndicate's goals are coextensive with the nation's. But when the Germans offer Milo a contract to bomb his own squadron, and he does so, it becomes clear how disparate the interests of these two collective bodies are. His supervisors are initially outraged at the attack on U.S. troops—until they find out what a profit he has made. "Frankly," Milo remarks, "I'd like to see the government get out of war altogether and leave the whole field to private industry" (254). This is precisely the implication of such an international cartel: it warns of the decline of national boundaries, economies, and identities. ("The Germans," says Milo, "are not our enemies" [251].) Once the economic stakes of war are revealed, and the nationalist rhetoric of the corporation is exposed as a sham, it makes perfect sense for a unit to bomb its own troops for profit.

This view is what Yossarian's antinationalist, hyperindividualist stance recognizes all along. If Whyte's corporate social ethic "converts what would seem in other times a bill of no rights into a restatement of individualism" (Whyte 6), then the social ethic of Heller's military-syndicate-nation converts "dying for one's country" into "patriotic heroism." Part of the aim of texts like Whyte's and Marcuse's, Reich's and Riesman's is to reconvert the organization's ideology back into the repressive, deindividuating set of propositions it really is, and part of Heller's goal in *Catch-22* is to build a critique of what we might call the *American nationalist ethic*—those propositions asserting that America is a classless society, that all Americans share common interests, and that, as Milo Minderbinder reiterates, "the business of government *is* business" (260).

Yet Heller moves a step beyond the abstract "individual versus society" logic that governs so many postwar sociologies. Those accounts rarely specify (at least consciously) what kind of class interests might be aligned with corporate interests—something that Heller does with ruthless precision. Riesman and Whyte locate resistance to the corporate ethic and the other-directed environment in a *competitive*, self-interested "Protestant ethic" that would at best only advance corporate interests through increased individual competition. Yossarian's final repudiation of the military bureaucracy is significantly more radical because it suggests that nationalism and capitalism themselves—and not merely a new managerial ethic—are his enemies. Yossarian's "paranoid" suspicions allow him to see the *nation* as a "Them" that can do whatever it wants: "Catch-22," he discovers, means "they have a right to do anything we can't stop them from doing" (398). And it is because of this discovery that Major Danby can honestly say to him, "destroying you…would be for the good of the country" (433). In the end, Yossarian's resistance is the realization of a profoundly antisocial vision, a response to power that is based on the premises of an individualist ethic that cannot conceptualize resistance to power in anything but all-or-nothing terms. Yet Yossarian does not simply reject the corporate ethic on its own competitive terms. Rather, he rejects both the competitive ethic of capitalism *and* the duties of citizenship—for in a world where multinational corporations are more than willing to violate national interests for a profit, the social ethic known as citizenship already seems outmoded.

2 Bodies Incorporated

Everything is a machine. Celestial machines, the stars or rainbows in the sky, alpine machines—all of them connected to those of his body.

—Gilles Deleuze and Félix Guattari, *Anti-Oedipus* (1972)

Here, too, one is reminded of the astonishment of boys when they become aware for the first time of erection. The fact, moreover, that the erection is shortly conceived as an exceptional and mysterious feat supports the assumption that erection is felt to be a thing independent of the ego, a part of the outer world not completely mastered.

—Victor Tausk, "The Influencing Machine" (1919)

Incoming Mail

A screaming comes across the sky. This is how *Gravity's Rainbow* opens— not with a *scream*, nor with a screaming *rocket*, but simply with *a screaming*, a bodily expression of panic so disembodied that it only hints at a cause beyond itself. This first line, in other words, presents a problem of agency that will characterize the plot of the novel: an unsettling bodily phenomenon manifests itself; its cause has been obscured from sight; and the difficulty of reading it has to do with the way a comforting separation between cause and phenomenon (or effect) has collapsed.[1] *Something* is coming across the sky, but what?

Materially speaking, it is a letter. It is, as British agent Pirate Prentice says to himself, "incoming mail" (6)—not just military slang for the Nazi V-2 rocket about to arrive in London, but, quite literally, incoming *mail*, for hidden in a capsule aboard that rocket is a letter, sent to Prentice by a double agent in Holland. The considerable "bodiliness" of this letter—

which I will take up momentarily—is rivaled only by the bodily correspondence that appears to mark its delivery: like every V-2 in *Gravity's
Rainbow*, this initial rocket arrives in London exactly where American
Lieutenant Tyrone Slothrop has had sex not long before. Not only,
then, does the rocket deliver mail, but it appears to have been delivered *as
if it were mail*. This latter form of correspondence—the bizarre but un-
mistakable geographical relation between Slothrop's sexual desire and the
subsequent landing of the rockets—seems to indicate a conspiracy of immense proportions. It is the novel's most significant agency problem, a
mystery that haunts the novel's characters and readers alike. In the pages to
follow, I suggest that this agency problem and others like it mark a new
way of thinking about the status of the body in relation to global communications and social systems, a radical reimagining of the relations
between persons, bodies, and discursive structures. I also show how this
extraordinary conception of personhood induces episodes of agency
panic—a response that not only registers anxieties about mass control,
but helps to sustain the idea of autonomous individuality against such
threats.

For now, I want to sketch the novel's approach to such issues by looking
at the brief scene in which Pirate Prentice anxiously reads his airborne
letter—or, rather, writes it, because what arrives via rocket is only a
blank scrap of paper. On that paper, a coded message has been written in
"kryptosam," an invisible chemical reagent that becomes visible skin pigment upon reaction with seminal fluid. The reading of this mail must
therefore be mediated by male sexual desire: Prentice has to ejaculate onto
the scrap of paper in order to decipher the message, and an erotic drawing
of a woman is enclosed to provide the "proper stimulus" for the reading.
But there is something uncanny about the efficiency of this drawing in
producing desire. It has come from someone who does not know Prentice
intimately, and yet it depicts a personal fantasy he has never mentioned,
an erotic idea closely allied with his sense of individuality. This odd
coincidence (coincidence?) produces a moment of panic. The drawing not
only features "a dead ringer" for one of Prentice's old flames, it also presents
a complex scene that

he daydreamed about often enough but never—
     No, of course he never told her. He never told anyone. Like every young man
growing up in England, he was conditioned to get a hardon in the presence of
certain fetishes, and then conditioned to feel shame about his new reflexes.
Could there be, somewhere, a dossier, could They (They?) somehow have man-

aged to monitor everything he saw and read since puberty...how *else* would They know? (71–72)[2]

At the center of this melodrama of agents and reagents is a serious question about agency, about what it means to be in control of one's own actions and desires. Prentice's panic stems from the uncanny sense that he is not only out of control—he "barely gets his cock out of his trousers before he's spurting all over the place" (72)—but that he is under the control of someone or something else.

I say "uncanny" because, as in Freud's treatment of the uncanny, something which "ought to have remained secret and hidden...has come to light" and it "forces upon us the idea of something fateful and inescapable when otherwise we should have spoken only of 'chance'" ("Uncanny" 225, 237). That familiar "something," in this case, is a fantasy forming a significant part of Prentice's identity as an individual. Although it is *heimlich*—both "familiar" and "concealed, kept from sight" ("Uncanny" 222–223)—it nonetheless arrives at, or is returned to, its place via airmail. Not long afterward, Prentice is described as an automaton (the quintessential embodiment of the uncanny and its theory), his "robot hands" (72) searching for vouchers and forms.[3] Over the course of the scene, agency appears to have been shuttled, through the channels of desire, from the person of the agent to a personified and potentially fantasized agency with vast powers of surveillance and control: "Them."

But perhaps this is to understand agency, as much recent cultural criticism has done, too much as a "property" of the subject—a sort of *pure* autonomy and volition—and to forget an older sense of the agent as "middleman," or "factor." In fact, the passage I have been discussing registers some of the tension present in the terms "agent" and "agency" themselves—terms that have historically signified both autonomous action (so-called free agency) and instrumentality (action on behalf of another).[4] What is unusually uncanny about Prentice's apparent loss of autonomy (or "agency" in the dominant current sense) is the way his body becomes a "factor" (or "agent" in the older sense) assisting in the return of the (un)familiar to its place: he must reconstruct the message literally using his penis as a pen or prosthesis, so that he can, in turn, read a message written in the bodily medium of skin pigment. This mode of communication has serious consequences for a model of persons as autonomous individuals. If Prentice's body can be used as a factor (or *facteur*, postman) in the transmission of information around the globe, then, at the very least, his autonomy is not as great as he thought. But the situation may indicate something far more dramatic. It may mean that part of his person—that which defines and controls him—has been dispersed into a network extending far beyond his individual, material body.

This latter possibility suggests a conception of persons similar to the one anthropologist Gregory Bateson developed from early systems theory. In Bateson's cybernetic epistemology, the "system" responsible for individual actions "is not the physical individual but a wide network of pathways of messages. Some of these pathways *happen* to be located outside the physical individual, others inside; but the characteristics of the *system* are in no way dependent upon any boundary lines which we may superpose upon the communicational map" ("Minimal Requirements" 251). If such systems are not circumscribed by individual, physical bodies then the most "characteristic" elements of persons (their "character," if it could still be called that) would be open to, even shared by, others.[5]

This is precisely the dilemma generated by Prentice's airmail. And Pynchon appears to offer two competing explanations for it. The first is that a dangerous, monolithic "Them" may mysteriously gain access to an individual's private fantasies for regulatory purposes. Like most conspiracy theories, this one appeals to the intentionality and immensity of large corporate and social systems. The second explanation is quite different. It suggests that male heterosexual desire is mass-produced by something like Pavlovian conditioning: male desire is first given an object when young men are "conditioned to get a hardon" in the presence of generic representations of the female body, and then it is driven into secret when they are "conditioned to feel shame." In such a regime, male desire is generic but seems nonetheless to be highly individual because each individual is conditioned in private. In other words, Prentice's "individual" fantasy may be knowable precisely because it is not individual at all. This second explanation is less melodramatic than the first, but it still paints an unhappy picture of the postwar individual, one consistent with popular accounts of psychological manipulation. It is worth noting that like so many of Pynchon's characters, Vance Packard's "depth manipulators" were said to have steeped themselves in texts such as "Reich's *Character Analysis,* Reik's *Masochism in Modern Man,* and Pavlov's *Lectures on Conditioned Reflexes*" so that they "might invade the privacy of our minds" (Packard 36, 266).

More than anything else, the rival explanations of Prentice's experience in this scene indicate a hesitation about whether to "locate" agency in individuals or social systems. Together they delineate the basic features of agency panic. As I have already suggested, that response typically involves both a recognition of the way subjects may be controlled by social formations (including discourses, narratives, and institutions) and a rejection of that knowledge. In the scene at hand, the second explanation, based on cultural conditioning, is a *systemic* description of the way entire *populations* of individuals may be both created and controlled by the dissemination of certain cultural forms—an account that begins to erode notions of individual action and motive. The first explanation, on the other hand—Prentice's attribution of control to a mysterious "Them"—centers on an *individual* experience. Paradoxically, this explanation conserves the very concepts of individuality and autonomous subjectivity apparently under threat, but it does so by assigning the most threatened qualities of that subjectivity—intention and coherent action—to a social or systemic level.

There is, of course, a third possible explanation for the uncanny events in this scene. They could be accidents or coincidences, and Prentice's fears about them could be mere paranoia.[6] To stabilize the uncertain status of agency in the passage would mean choosing between these alternatives, taking a position—but that is just what the passage seems designed to prevent. The narrator slides surreptitiously between Prentice's "private" thoughts and a position of detached, but still limited, omniscience. A similar ambivalence is written into the structure of the scene. A nearly unreadable correspondence between Prentice's person and a global network comes to light through the production of nearly unreadable epistolary correspondence. In reading the latter, Prentice appears to be receiving information from the outside and, simultaneously, to be producing it with his person; he does not have a stable position as either reader or writer. By analogy, any attempt to read the former correspondence—to decide whether the whole uncanny set of events is motivated or accidental—might result in the same thing: the transformation of this veiled correspondence into a more visible message, but a message whose "production" has been mediated by the desire of its reader.

Given all of this, it is significant that this little scene of agency panic is provoked by "the arrival of a letter at its destination." The delivery of mail was central to Pynchon's second novel, *The Crying of Lot 49*, in which a subterranean postal system—glimpsed through unsettling "chance" events and uncanny patterns—appeared to be sorting and distributing information to the members of an immense secret society.[7] But the trope of arriving letters has also been important to literary theory—particularly to a debate over the agency of letters in Poe's "Purloined Letter." Initially an exchange between Jacques Lacan and Jacques Derrida, that debate focused on Poe's story because the story seemed to emblematize crucial problems of agency in signification. Like Prentice's letter, the purloined letter is what Lacan calls a nonfunctional signifier because Poe's "tale leaves us in virtually total ignorance of the sender, no less than of the contents, of the letter" ("Seminar" 41). Yet, Lacan notes, the movement of the letter "determines the subjects in their acts, in their destiny..." ("Seminar" 43)—again, in much the same way that Prentice and Slothrop appear to be defined and controlled by the arrival of incoming mail. I say "appear" because *Gravity's Rainbow* only puts into *question* whether persons are controlled or "constructed" by discursive or social systems. The uncanny sense of control conveyed by all of the novel's very male "mail" (rockets and letters alike) may be only the result of a paranoid reading of accidents. And this is precisely the objection Derrida raises to Lacan's reading of Poe. Lacan's assertion that "a letter always arrives at its destination" ("Seminar" 53)—that certain patterns of meaning and behavior are inevitable—cannot, in Derrida's view, account for the possibility of accidental, lost, or residual meaning. Derrida goes on to accuse Lacan of "finding" the truth of psychoanalysis (the "law of the signifier and of castration as the contract of truth" [*Post Card* 441–42]) wherever he looks, by ignoring the disseminating power of language.[8] Again, *Gravity's Rainbow* appears uncannily to literalize the terms of this debate: Slothrop narrowly and accidentally misses being *castrated*, only to be *disseminated* bodily across a continent.

But I draw attention to these parallels less for thematic reasons than to show that issues of bodily control and threatened individual autonomy in *Gravity's Rainbow* have an intimate connection to interpretive questions debated in recent cultural theory.[9] In the instances I just sketched, the central interpretive question seems to be whether meaningful events are directed by a supremely competent mailman—a symbolic order or a "Them"—or whether they are merely made meaningful by a discourse (psychology) or a psychosis (paranoia) that finds *everything* significant. This problem—the absence of a "Real Text" (*Gravity's Rainbow* 520) or metanarrative that would stabilize signification and control the endless play of language—has been a central insight of poststructuralism. And perhaps not surprisingly, poststructuralist solutions to these problems have given rise to melodramas of lost agency similar in structure to the one I outlined earlier. In these theoretical dramas, poststructural accounts of signifying *systems* come into conflict with accounts critical of the apparent transfer of agency from *individual* authors and readers to texts or textuality in general. As M. H. Abrams recently said in a defense of humanist criticism, poststructuralist practice results in a "theory world, in which people are not agents but agencies, not users of language but used by language, not effectors but themselves only effects" (13). But to say that a discourse has its own "secret workings" (Abrams 7)—that it appears, in short, to be a "Them"—

is only another way of formulating the problem of agency dramatized bodily in *Gravity's Rainbow*. And this is not simply because "there is nothing outside of the text" (Derrida, *Grammatology* 158) but because, in *Gravity's Rainbow*, the body is already a medium of communication.

The Body We Can Measure

The notion that the autonomic processes of a human body could be associated with the movement of missiles is not something first imagined in *Gravity's Rainbow*. In 1948, Norbert Wiener, the founder of cybernetics, claimed that the self-propelled rockets of World War II were modeled on the human body and that the body was indispensable in accounting for them:

> They contain sense-organs, effectors, and the equivalent of a nervous system to integrate the transfer of information from the one to the other. They lend themselves very well to description in physiological terms. It is scarcely a miracle that they can be subsumed under one theory with the mechanisms of physiology. (*Cybernetics* 43)

That this sort of thinking has become commonplace in recent techno-culture is largely a result of its striking, early influence on a range of popular conceptions of personhood. Pop psychologists like Maxwell Maltz, to take just one example, used Wiener's work to develop a self-help cure for uncontrolled behavior. In his highly popular *Psycho-Cybernetics: A New Way to Get More Living Out of Life* (1960), Maltz tells his readers that "Every living thing has a built-in guidance system or goal-striving device" (14). This "servo-mechanism," he says,

> operates automatically to achieve a certain goal, very much as a self-aiming torpedo or missile seeks out its target and steers its way to it. Your built-in servo-mechanism functions both as a "guidance system" to automatically steer you in the right direction to achieve certain goals...and also as an "electronic brain" which can function automatically to solve problems. (16–17)

In short, we can regain control over our lives by recognizing the smart bomb inside of us. Paradoxically, however, we *do not have access* to this mechanism. Rather, our "goal-striving device"—what used to be called simply "human desire," the essence of liberal selfhood—is for Maltz an internal machine that operates "automatically" and strives for predetermined goals. The question then becomes, if a servo-mechanism guides each of us, who guides this servo-mechanism—an even smaller mechanism within the servo-mechanism itself?

This quandary—the *mise-en-abyme* of centralized control—has long troubled philosophers of mind.[10] Here, we might understand it as an artifact of Maltz's crude formulation, but it also stems from a symptomatic difficulty in the cybernetic theorization of the subject—one that we have already begun to explore in Pynchon's novel. Because cybernetics posits an essential similarity between humans and servo-controlled machines, as well as other kinds of self-regulating systems, it generates challenges to the notion that self-control is a property only of embodied, human subjects. And it does so by identifying self-control (or "autopoiesis," to use the language of systems theory) as a quality of machines, collective entities, and social systems. Bateson's early "cybernetic epistemology," for instance, unsettles the idea of a "tight fit" between persons and their bodies. Hence, by rejecting the idea that the boundaries of the material body are the boundaries of the person, cybernetic thinking offers, simultaneously, the exhilarating prosthetic extension of the person into other systems and the frightening effacement of the liberal subject. This is part of what media theorist Friedrich Kittler has in mind when he declares, "The self-guided weapons of World War II eliminated the two modern concepts of causality and subjectivity and introduced the present as the age of technical systems" (332).

These changes offer us a way of understanding some of the oddest features of Pynchon's novel, so it is worth exploring them for a moment longer in the writings of Wiener himself. Wiener formulates the distinction between the person and the material body through the concepts of matter and information or "process": "the physical identity of an individual," he writes, "does not consist in the matter of which it is made" but "in a certain continuity of process" (*Human Use* 101). This radical view leads Wiener to an unexpected theoretical dilemma. And the route by which he arrives at that dilemma is interesting because it involves a story about both the delivery of letters and the delivery of persons *as if they were letters.* Wiener embarks on this route when, after articulating his view of individuality, he allows himself a strange diversion—a meditation on Rudyard Kipling's "remarkable little story" (96) of bureaucratic repression and mass control, "With the Night Mail." The result is a fantasy as bizarre as anything in Pynchon's novel. "If," he says,

> we consider the two types of communication: namely, material transport, and transport of information alone, it is at present possible for a person to go from

one place to another only by the former, and not as a message. However, even now the transportation of messages serves to forward an extension of man's senses and his capabilities of action from one end of the world to another. We have already suggested…that the distinction between material transportation and message transportation is not in any theoretical sense permanent and unbridgeable.

This takes us very deeply into the question of human individuality. (98)

The reason this view takes us "into the question of human individuality" is that, for Wiener, "there is no absolute distinction between the types of transmission which we can use for sending a telegram from country to country and the types of transmission which at least are theoretically possible for transmitting a living organism such as a human being" (103). With this notion we have arrived at something like *Star Trek* before the letter—a fantasy of bodily transmission that would all but vaporize the liberal concept of the individual. If persons themselves may be sent (we would now say faxed) from place to place *as information*, then presumably they could also be "stored," as persons or data, in any number of material forms.

What is most odd about Wiener's discussion of these futuristic possibilities is how increasingly distasteful they seem to him. Once it becomes clear that his science fiction fantasy has become an argument for the feasibility of cloning, he ends it in a violent image of the "technical difficulties" of invading and reconstituting individual bodies:

Any scanning of the human organism must be a probe going through all its parts, and will, accordingly, tend to destroy the tissue on its way. To hold an organism stable while part of it is being slowly destroyed, with the intention of recreating it out of other material elsewhere, involves a lowering of its degree of activity, which in most cases would destroy life in the tissue. (*Human Use* 103)

Oddly absent from this account are the catastrophic consequences to individuality if the transmitted body were *not* destroyed at the site of transmission—a thought perhaps left out so that the violence of transmission can terminate a view of subjectivity too threatening to carry to its logical end. And this is precisely the rhythm that characterizes agency panic: a radical challenge to liberalism terminates not in a celebration of newness, but in retreat and disavowal.

Gravity's Rainbow offers a much more sustained and rigorous account of the problem Wiener articulates. As I have already demonstrated, the sending or receiving of messages with human bodies is an essential feature of the novel: spies tattoo messages under their mustaches (16); Thanatz reads the scars on Greta Erdmann's back (484); a Colonel's hair is a "perfect grating" on which various messages have been "written" (643); and Rollo Groast suggests that all bodily oddities may be part of a "clandestine drama for which the human body serves only as a set of very allusive, often cryptic programme-notes—it's as if the body we can measure is a scrap of this programme found outside in the street, near a magnificent stone theatre we cannot enter" (147–48). In short, the notion that the body could signify in unimaginable ways underwrites much of Pynchon's novel.

Slothrop's body, in particular, is a source of intense interest and anxiety because it appears to be a locus in which global information and individual sexual desire have been coordinated in a single, hidden, regulatory formula. The secret it holds promises to be *the* truth of the novel and much of *Gravity's Rainbow* is a narrative of the various tactics employed to discover and control this truth. Molly Hite has pointed out that this investigatory apparatus—indeed, nearly every element of the novel—falls into an "austere metaphysical binarism" (*Ideas of Order* 13). A number of critics have mapped this scheme in detail, suggesting that it offers a snapshot of the "full range of knowledge and beliefs" of a culture (Mendelson 162).[11] What such important mappings often overlook, however, is the way opposed approaches are coordinated in a single "regulatory" capacity, designed not only to frustrate the hermeneutical questions posed by the text but also to dramatize uncertainty about how to understand individual human agency in relation to social systems.

The two most prominent sciences applied to Slothrop's body are Pavlovian psychology and statistics, which attempt to account for the behavior of individuals and populations, respectively. Edward Pointsman and Roger Mexico, the respective practitioners of these two sciences, frequently debate the merits of each in explaining the Slothrop problem. While Pointsman expresses his faith in "true mechanical explanation"—"no effect without cause, and a clear train of linkages"—Mexico argues that "the next great breakthrough may come when we have the courage to junk cause-and-effect entirely, and strike off at some other angle" (89). As other readers have noted, the rather schematic antithesis embodied in these two men points to their function as surrogate readers standing in for radically different approaches toward the production of meaning. One of these methodologies, represented by Pointsman, is hermeneutic: a dizzying pursuit of clues, a peeling away of layers in search of a cause, a linear movement toward points of origin. The other, represented by Mexico, is rooted in poetics: an examination of maps, a search for explanatory schemes and metaphors, bidirectional movements from one set of coordinates to another. Pynchon is quite explicit about the roles of other characters in this binary reading scheme. As Franz and Leni Pökler argue, for example, we are told that Franz is "the cause-and-effect man," while Leni favors correlative explanatory schemes: "It all goes along together," she says. "Parallel, not series. Metaphor. Signs and symptoms. Mapping on to different coordinate systems" (159). Here, correlation is related to its linguistic counterparts, metaphor and paradigm, while causality is linked to metonymy and syntax. These relations suggest an interesting consequence. If correlative and causal models are indeed analogous to the semantic axes of language, then they cannot function independently of each other. Furthermore, to choose between rival readings would be like trying to choose between metonymy and metaphor, paradigm and syntax—an absurd proposition because, as linguists have shown, one cannot read unless both semantic functions are simultaneously at work.[12]

I want to suggest, then, that these competing methodologies function as elements of a single strategy: first a secret appears, then the two rival discursive approaches revolve around this central secret in apparent investigative competition, while, in fact, each requires and reinforces the other just as much as it requires that the secret remain a secret. And what is significant about the central secret of *Gravity's Rainbow*—Slothrop's odd relation to the rocket—is not only that it generates uneasiness about agency or signification, but that it is a *sexual* secret. As Michel Foucault has suggested, sex has long been "a general signification, a universal secret, an omnipresent cause" (*History* 69); it has become "the stamp of individuality," and thus "a means of access both to the life of the body and the life of the species" (*History* 146). This is what Pynchon's odd premise registers: Slothrop's most *individuating* feature is sexual in nature, and yet that feature appears to be coordinated with the life of an entire *population*. In other words, much like Prentice's erotic fantasy, Slothrop's sexual behavior begins to make visible the relations between individual bodies and social bodies. By using the very "stamp of individuality" as the medium in which information is moved across the globe, Pynchon throws into question where persons end and populations begin.

To put the matter somewhat differently, if, as Foucault suggests, sex has become the focus of diverse tactics applied to both individual bodies and whole populations, then in *Gravity's Rainbow* diverse tactics may be applied to a single person, whose most private acts, or private parts, already appear to be tied to the life of a vast population. These "tactics" are embodied in the two discourses that form the binary reading scheme I outlined above. Pynchon's binary scheme thus bears an uncanny resemblance to the "great bipolar technology" that Foucault claims reinvented the subject, using sex as a central site of discipline and regulation:

> On the one hand [sex] was tied to the disciplines of the body...On the other hand, it was applied to the regulation of populations...It fitted in both categories at once, giving rise to infinitesimal surveillances, permanent controls, extremely meticulous orderings of space, indeterminate medical or psychological examinations, to an entire micro-power concerned with the body. But it gave rise as well to comprehensive measures, statistical assessments, and interventions aimed at the entire social body or at groups taken as a whole. (*History* 145–46)

In Foucault's account, the individual body and the social body structure these two sets of interventions, respectively. Although the "body" in each case is different, the shared term is essential because it suggests that the disciplines and the regulations are essentially similar, that they are each part of a single strategy applied to analogous objects. The same is true in *Gravity's Rainbow*. While Pointsman focuses on the individual, material body of Slothrop, Mexico focuses on the figurative, social body, "Lady London." While Pointsman "imagines the cortex of the brain as a mosaic of tiny on/off elements," Mexico views London as a mosaic of rocket strikes spread across a ruled map (55). Neither science can do without the other. The true object of their mutual interest is a relation between the bodies each of them is studying. They appear then to constitute complementary aspects of a single strategy at work reconceptualizing the person.

But a strategy articulated *by whom*? This is a question repeatedly inspired by Foucault's work (and a question to which I will return). It is also what Roger Mexico begins to wonder one day while he and Pointsman walk along the cliffs of Dover, arguing. As Mexico recognizes the congruity of their "rival" activities, he begins to panic, imagining that he and Pointsman themselves are data on some ineffably large "cortex," a *bodily* site of information processing:

> They've paused in their walking. Roger stares back at [Pointsman]. The Antimexico. "Ideas of the opposite" themselves, but on what cortex, what winter hemisphere? What ruinous mosaic, facing outward into the Waste...outward from the sheltering city...readable only to those who journey outside...eyes in the distance...barbarians...riders....(89)

In this passage it is hard to tell whether the narration is coming from deep inside Mexico or is detached and speculative. In fact, the instability of the narrator's position dramatizes the central feature of agency panic: the difficulty of locating where actions originate and who or what controls them. Mexico's panic, like Prentice's, arises in a moment in which his material body seems to be nothing more than information in a much larger network. From his perspective, he and Pointsman are persons who hold diametrically opposed positions on the interpretation of certain data—"if ever the Antipointsman existed, Roger Mexico is the man" (55)—but, from the perspective eventually obtained here, they themselves are data, in binary form, on a larger "cortex," a massive body.

This latter perspective—the perspective of "eyes in the distance" gazing down and finding a binary data to be "readable" information—is the perspective of readers, the view that sees Pynchon's own austere binary scheme. But it is also the perspective of "Them." Agency panic, therefore, may be understood as a moment in which characters suspect that they are, in fact, characters, being constructed and observed by agents beyond their control. It is the suspicion that one's life may amount to the nightmare depicted in Peter Weir's *Truman Show* (1998), where the entire experience of an unsuspecting orphan (much like Slothrop) is fabricated and secretly recorded for the consumption of television viewers. As Pointsman ("the Antimexico") reads a mosaic of binary-coded neural switches on the surface of individual brains, and Mexico ("the Antipointsman") reads a mosaic of binary-coded rocket strikes on the surface of Lady London, we read a mosaic of binary-coded characters on the "cortex" of the novel, a "ruinous mosaic, facing outward into the Waste."[13] The object of study at each level is either a person or a personification—but the question is *which?* Each object is equally unstable, always threatening to reveal itself a mere cog in a larger, determining "consciousness."

This instability is a constant feature of *Gravity's Rainbow* and can be extreme. The novel later dramatizes the journey of skin cells to the epidermal layer *as if cells were persons* (148), and later still, suggests that Earth "is a living critter," that the globe itself has "a body and psyche" (590). In such moments the novel embraces what Dorion Sagan has termed the new biology's "radical re-rendering of the body": "a breakdown of the medically proper animal body" suggesting "correspondences among prokaryotic, eukaryotic, zoological and geophysiological (Gaian) levels. It now appears that a type of individuality has appeared at each of these levels" (363). In other words, it is difficult to read this novel and hold to an account of individual agency in which, as Max Weber puts it, "Action in the sense of subjectively understandable orientation of behavior exists only as the behavior of one or more *individual* human beings... since these alone can be treated as agents" (13). Rather, as systems theorist Niklas Luhmann has suggested, "cells and societies, maybe physical atoms, certainly immune systems and brains, are all individuals. Conscious systems have no exceptional status. They are a particular type" (116). *Gravity's Rainbow* regularly denies the conscious systems of individual persons such "exceptional status." But its characters and its narrator often take Luhmann's insight in a different direction. They retain the "exceptional status" of conscious systems by attributing consciousness to all kinds of systems, including atoms, cells, cartels, and economies.[14]

This response typifies the crisis of threatened agency in this novel and beyond it. A self-regulating (social) *system* appears to threaten a model of personhood in which the *individual* human body is the privileged site of autonomous, original, motivated social action; in an attempt to conserve the attributes of this model of individuality, individuals assign those attributes to the system as a whole, but they also recognize that the system may govern itself through aggregate effects and that the logic of individual motive and agency will not quite work to explain it. The result is panic about the difficulty of locating control at any one level of existence—the difficulty, in other words, in deciding what a person is.

Pornographies of Deduction

In *Gravity's Rainbow*, I have been suggesting, the scientific apparatus deployed to study Slothrop only produces, or reproduces at a higher level, the problems of agency it set out to study in the first place. One register of this pattern is the degree to which the scientific discourses applied to the novel's sexual secret are themselves continually eroticized, even treated as forms of pornography or "pornographies of deduction" (155).[15] Pointsman views "The Book" (a collection of Pavlov's letters) as "a rare work of erotica" (87–88). Mexico finds himself displaying "a pornography customer's reflex" to the acquisition of microfilms relevant to his work (35). And the technologically miraculous V-2 rocket is repeatedly likened to a phallus engaged with "Lady London" in intercourse so violent that it ends in "terminal orgasm" (223). In the peculiar case of Slothrop, the structural similarity between the ideologies of "external" observation common to science and pornography is obvious. The variety of experiments designed to expose, explain, and control Slothrop's body share in the very erotics that are their object—if only because their central dogma requires a methodological structure barely separable from voyeurism. Stephen Dodson-Truck, for example, eventually confesses that his task has been to watch Slothrop have sex with an operative named Katje: "My 'function' is to observe you. That's my function. You like my function? You like it? *Your* 'function'...is, learn the rocket, inch by inch. *I have...to send in a daily log of your progress. And that's all I know*" (216). In moments like this, the desire to measure erotic desire gets at the potential circularity of the project; Slothrop's desire is incited by the use of Katje so that it can in turn be measured by a hidden "recording eye" (216). And measurement "without passion" is not so easy; even the impotent Dodson-Truck admits that he masturbates about "half the time" during these keyhole observations (216).

But who is watching whom is the salient issue here, for as Dodson-Truck blunders through his confession, he and Slothrop are under the gaze of enormous "robed figures" on the horizon,

> hundreds of miles tall—their faces, serene, unattached, like the Buddha's, bending over the sea, impassive, indeed, as the Angel that stood over Lübeck during the Palm Sunday raid, come that day neither to destroy nor to protect, but to bear witness to a game of seduction. It was the next-to-last step London took before her submission...because sending the RAF to make a terror raid against civilian Lübeck was the unmistakable long look that said *hurry up and fuck me*, that brought the rockets hard and screaming...(214–15, ellipses added)

As the narrative shuttles between individual and population, between Dodson-Truck's surveillance of Slothrop and this supernatural surveillance of the world, it begins to present the war in sexual terms. Not only do the figures function by a masculinist rape logic—in this account Lady London begs for the violence of the German technological phallus—but they posit another observer who has no intention of acting ("to destroy or protect"), only of watching the sexual spectacle. This novel insists on locating geopolitical conflict in the body, whether it is the signifying body of Slothrop or the figurative "bodies politic" of the sort exemplified above. In each case, it employs a stock male fantasy, raising the bodies in question to the level of erotic spectacle—as though the secret of the war were the secret of sexuality itself and that secret might be gleaned by a voyeuristic fascination with the pornographized body. The fundamental premises of the book ensure that the desire to understand Slothrop's odd talent is the desire to understand male desire itself—to access the inmost reaches of an individual in an attempt to stabilize the plaguing problem of uncertain agency—and that to do so one must assume the position of an "external" observer: a scientist, a voyeur, a reader.

But I have already suggested how this novel complicates one's ability to assume such a position. In the passage above, as parallel local and global scenes unfold around him, Dodson-Truck, attempting to account for a hidden relation between local and global, feels himself subject to the same visual technology he employed to study Slothrop. At a moment in which he publicly recognizes the voyeuristic nature of his official "function," his position as sole overseer of Slothrop's body becomes unstable—and, more important, so does his masculinity. He nervously repeats the word "function" because he feels subject to a power structure that controls persons—or maybe even constructs them—with mathematical precision.[16] "We're all such mechanical men," he says. "I'm an impotent *man*" (216). These sexual spectacles reveal both his sexual inadequacy and his more general powerlessness in the terrifying and vague bureaucracy he serves. What I wish to emphasize, however, is that Pynchon here begins to fuse the idea of surveillance by an actual agent, human or divine, with a more structuralist vision of identity as a product of one's location, position, or function in a social network.

Slothrop's attempts to understand his own sexual desire reveal something of the same dynamic. When he runs into Margherita Erdmann, for example, he reveals that he has been given false identity papers naming him Max Schlepzig, Erdmann's old counterpart in the pornographic film *Alpdrücken*. "The name's just a random alias," he says, but she disagrees:

> Random....Another fairy-tale word. The signature on your card is Max's.... Don't you think I know that Latin *z*, crossed engineer-style, the flower he made out of the *g* at the end? You could hunt all the Zone for your "forger." They wouldn't let you find him. They want you right here, right now. (395, ellipses added)

Before he knows it, Slothrop finds himself engaged in a sadomasochistic encounter reminiscent of those in *Alpdrücken*. Although he has never met Erdmann before or seen her on film, he finds "somebody has already educated him" in how to torture her perfectly (396). What is in question, then, is *either* his autonomy *or* his individuality—just as was the case with Prentice. Simply by moving to a new *position* in the Zone, Slothrop finds himself behaving as though he were the person who occupied it formerly—in the most "personal" and apparently individual way. That is, he finds himself acting out—or being acted out by—a sexual fantasy of violent control.

In the story of sadomasochism derived from Hegel's account of master and slave, the fantasy of erotic domination is about the affirmation of individuality and agency. As one of Kathy Acker's many masochistic characters observes, razor blade in hand, "Since I'm now making blood come out of my own arm, I can't be nothing" (*Empire* 71). Jessica Benjamin has argued that such gestures are largely about the need for recognition as an autonomous agent—precisely the status Slothrop finds challenged here. But the paradoxical logic of recognition is that the more one demands recognition as an agent, the more one is dependent on another for that recognition. In other words, the contradictory dynamics of agency panic appear to be built into the fantasy of submission and domination. "In adult erotic domination," Benjamin says, "both partners are involved in controlling the other to conform to a fantasy...The aliveness and spontaneity that come from an unscripted relationship is missing" (293). The desire to "act out" one's agency has the paradoxical effect of undermining the possibility of individual agency. The more Slothrop asserts his control over Erdmann, the more he submits to a prescribed role in a pornographic film.

These dynamics help explain why Dodson-Truck, Prentice, Pökler, Erdmann, Slothrop, and many of Pynchon's other characters become so anxious about their autonomy in moments of erotic desire. Desires that should be the "stamp of their individuality" turn out to be precisely the opposite. Indeed, when *Alpdrücken* was first released, the narrator tells us, countless men (Pökler included) "carried the same image" home and *impersonated* Schlepzig, reenacting the film's violent intercourse with their wives (396). The film itself, by this account, supervised the mass-production of children. In such moments of "impersonation," Pynchon's characters often suspect their actions to be governed by cultural or discursive systems. In the case of *Alpdrücken*, the narrator suggests that male heterosexual desire is produced by women's lingerie—a conditioned stimulus that, like film, has an explicitly *mathematical* structure:

> It's easy for non-fetishists to sneer about Pavlovian conditioning and let it go at that, but any underwear enthusiast worth his unwholesome giggle can tell you there is much more here—there is a cosmology: of nodes and cusps and points of osculation, mathematical kisses... *singularities!* (396)

Here, the narrative expands on Dodson-Truck's earlier suggestion that mathematical "functions" could be embedded in social structures for the purpose of regulating individual behavior. Yet the specific mathematical form behind Slothrop's desire is the "singularity": the point in a function where the rate of change of one variable becomes infinite and thus, "the behavior of the function ceases to be mathematically expressible, except in a purely formal way" (Hayles, *Cosmic* 191). The graph of such a function can only be approximate: two curves rising asymptotically toward a point, but never meeting, leaving a textual absence at the singular point. Singularities exceed representation and are thus a mathematical version of the sublime—the aesthetic form said to provoke both elation and terror in its viewers. "*Singularities!*," says the narrator, "the change from point to no-point carries a luminosity and enigma at which something in us must leap and sing, or withdraw in fright" (396). When a subject's imagination is inadequate to conceptualize the social structures that have compromised his or her autonomy, we might say that sublime object and terrified subject come together in the sublime erotics of agency panic. In the case at hand, that panic is marked in part by the apparent transfer of individuality—another word for "singularity"—from a person to a regulatory formula. The mathematical specification of Erdmann's lingerie, and the erotic enigma it represents, appears to determine Slothrop's behavior with her, even as Slothrop himself becomes nothing more than the medium—indeed the absence—in which some hidden determinant expresses itself.

Mathematical formulas and letters, secret function and "Real Text"—these are the perpetual figures Pynchon offers for the structures and systems that might govern his characters' actions.[17] If they indicate Pynchon's attraction to the early promise of structuralism—the dream of locating the social codes and structures that would account for meaning, subjectivity, and human action—their ultimate elusiveness indicates Pynchon's refusal to embrace such totalizing hopes. This is part of the meaning of the singularity, which for all its apparent power, signifies nothing so much as nothing, absence. Writing about how a "symbol only of an absence"—in this case not a mathematical singularity, but a letter—can "determine" a series of subjects in relation to it, Lacan observes,

> between *letter* and *place* exist relations for which no French word has quite the extension of the English adjective *odd*. *Bizarre*, by which Baudelaire regularly translates it, is only approximate. Let us say that these relations are ... *singuliers*, for they are the very ones maintained with place by the *signifier*. ("Seminar" 38, ellipsis in original)

"*Singuliers*," because for Lacan "*bizarre*" does not get at the mathematical nature of individuation, the power of place within a structure to determine the subject.[18] Slothrop's *place* in the Zone appears to determine his actions throughout the novel, but now the mathematical model at hand allows us to specify what permits these continual impersonations: Slothrop himself is a singularity. His bodily oddity (his singular relationship to the rockets) represents a structure exceeding his ability to represent it adequately, and that structure, in turn, appears to be responsible for determining, or constructing, his person. But the direction of these intriguing relations is never clear because the nature of Slothrop's "nature" is eroticized absence—eroticized not only in that his body is studied pornographically and his most unique quality is sexual in nature but in that his sublime body keeps its own truth hidden so that a game of hermeneutical flirtation must forever be played in the process of unveiling it.

Statistical Oddities

Discourses of agency and determination usually rely on a strict rhetoric of inside and outside. Freud's bold pronouncement, "I believe in external (real) chance, it is true, but not in internal (psychical) accidental events" (*Psychopathology* 257), depends upon a careful separation of internal and external, psychic and physical—a separation marked by the border of the body. Such distinctions are not so easy to make in *Gravity's Rainbow*. Pynchon's novel deliberately confuses the relation between insides and outsides, even when these terms relate to the human body. One morning in Berlin, for example: "Everything's been turned inside out.... The civilians are outside now, the uniforms inside.... Old men with their tins searching the ground for cigarette butts wear their lungs on their breasts" (373, ellipses added). This radically embodied reversal of the metaphysical underpinnings of individuality is repeated throughout *Gravity's Rainbow*, and it is what allows Pynchon's characters to suspect their own "external" control without easily being labeled "superstitious" or "paranoid" in the pathological sense. Borders, fronts, lines, and boundaries are the structures most under question in this novel. Its mode of narration is "transmarginal," moving without transition from one character to the next and, as Molly Hite observes, effectively offering "multiple 'inside' perspectives with no 'outside' standard against which to measure them" (*Ideas of Order* 144). After an early obsession with rhetorical and symbolic oppositions ("ideas of the opposite" [89]), the narrative moves through the Zone (a place where "categories have been blurred badly" [303]), and into a state of extreme metaphysical confusion in which "Outside and Inside [are] interpiercing one another too fast, too finely labyrinthine, for either category to have much hegemony any more" (681).

This confusion helps explain the conflicted accounts of agency offered by Pynchon's characters. Prentice, for instance, when reading his letter, invokes the idea of *external* control, or "Them," despite the fact that he appears to understand the logic of an *immanent*, culturally-produced control. Similarly, Mexico finds that accidents with no clear cause tend to disable the very discipline that defines them as accidental:

Mexico thinks [the Slothrop problem] a statistical oddity. But he feels the foundations of that discipline trembling a bit now, deeper than oddity ought to drive.

> Odd, odd, odd—think of the word: such white finality in its closing clap of tongue. It implies moving past the tongue-stop—beyond the zero—and into the other realm. (85)

This is the paradoxical logic of a statistics whose ontological foundations have been shaken: it counts on there being a very small percentage of oddities or "singularities" by chance, but when they appear they nonetheless seem to imply a hidden cause, a secret regulatory function.

Slothrop finds himself confronting the same difficulties when trying, during a game of roulette, to understand if "something was done to him" long ago:

> He's been snuggling up, masturbatorily scared-elated, to the disagreeable chance that exactly such Control might already have been put over him.... All in his life of what has looked free or random, is discovered to've been under some Control, all the time, the same as a fixed roulette wheel—where only destinations are important, attention is to long-term statistics, not individuals: and where the House always does, of course, keep turning a profit.... (209, first ellipsis added)

It is significant that Slothrop's first sustained doubts about his autonomy come in a casino—a model of the way random individual events fall into regular patterns if allowed to transpire within a "fixed" structure or system. Inside the casino, events appear variable, uncontrollable. Outside, in the back office, however, balance sheets would suggest otherwise. Slothrop finds himself torn between these two views when using the casino as a model of his own experience. On the one hand, he feels that "their odds were never probabilities, but frequencies *already observed*" (208). On the other hand, he can only begin to understand the idea of his total determination, and of chancelessness, as a "disagreeable *chance*."

The structure of Slothrop's panic is significant: he can only understand his own person by invoking the idea of embodied, external control, "Them"—and yet he does so in a casino, which he fully appreciates as a mathematical model of normative regulation through "attention to long-term statistics, not individuals." This conflicted response parallels the responses of Prentice, Dodson-Truck, Erdmann, and others to the same kind of situation. In each case, an individual arrives at a crisis in trying to theorize power. It is unclear in these moments whether power is located in an individual or dispersed through the body politic; whether it is *external* to the subjects it governs or immanent in those subjects; whether it is selective and prohibitive or normative and regulatory.

Foucault has delineated these alternate forms of power in detail, arguing that while a prohibitive, monarchical power gave way, centuries ago, to normative forms of power, we still conceive of power in the old way, "we still have not cut off the head of the king" (*History* 88–89). In its modern form, according to Foucault, power is "a multiplicity of force relations" in constant motion and interaction, "always local and unstable" (92–93). It is "not in superstructural positions," but "comes from below" and "is everywhere" (93–94). Interestingly, this disembodied, mathematically modeled notion of power gives rise to an account of agency conflicted in much the same way as the accounts offered in *Gravity's Rainbow.*

> Power relations are both intentional and nonsubjective.... There is no power that is exercised without a series of aims and objectives. But this does not mean that it results from the choice or decision of an individual subject; let us not look for the headquarters that presides over its rationality... The rationality of power is characterized by tactics that are often quite explicit at the restricted level where they are inscribed... yet it is often the case that no one is there to have invented them, and few who can be said to have formulated them. (*History* 94–95)

The insistent language of intention in Foucault's writing, the constant reference to power's "tactics," "strategies," "aims and objectives," attributes to "power" the rhetoric of subjectivity, as if it constituted a higher form of consciousness, a "Them"—precisely the idea Foucault explicitly denies in this passage. In fact, Foucault's frequent assertions that power does *not* have at its apex "an element which is at least not purely bureaucratic," as Max Weber claimed (222), are necessary to counter the rhetoric of personification in his own narratives, in which power and resistance are treated as subjects, articulating "strategies" and "aims" whose effects are so discriminatory to certain groups that they *seem* to be intentional.

I want to stress that this sort of contradiction, in both Foucault and Pynchon, is not the result of a theoretical error. It is rather a product of narrative itself—of the desire, in both of these writers, to tell a *story* about power. This is so because a story requires agents, entities with desires and the means to fulfill them. Yet Foucault is careful to remind us that, in his narrative, power is a purely "nominalistic" agent, a construction or reification for the purpose of description alone. Equally important is that Foucault balances his narrative of power with a second, *structural* conception of power. This latter conception does not employ the categories of motive, cause, and effect, but rather articulates a spatial and *mathematical* vision of power. It represents power as a network of communications, tirelessly unfolding and reforming in vague mathematical spaces, "furrowing across individuals themselves," and "forming a dense web that passes through apparatuses and institutions, without being exactly localized in them" (*History* 96). This superstructural view of power reduces the human population to a mathematical grid, or *cortex*, on which the effects of power are visible as geometric structures. "Individual unities" appear only as areas on the grid across which the flows and counterflows of power move. From the point of view interested in these flows, the category of the individual drops out in favor of fields of abstractly-modeled information—functions, a "cosmology: of nodes and cusps and points of osculation" (*Gravity's Rainbow* 396). It is the careful interweaving of this view with the rhetoric of agency—the story of power's strategies and intentions—that keeps Foucault's account of power from becoming an expression of agency panic.

In Pynchon's work, by contrast, the sense that power might be centralized—that some "They" might be pulling the strings—is not simply nominalistic but is always a real possibility—never confirmed by Pynchon himself, but forever suspected by his characters. In the boundariless confusion of *Gravity's Rainbow*, when characters glimpse the possibility of a structurally organized power—a network of communications and cultural "functions"—they find themselves unable to accept the sort of advice Foucault offers. Faced with a power that seems "intentional," they assume a power that is also "subjective," even though it is never *clearly* visible as a subject. Their panic then turns endlessly on whether control comes from inside or out—or, to say the same thing another way, on where their persons are bounded. As the anxious narrator asks late in the novel, "What if They find it convenient to preach an island of life surrounded by a void? Not just the Earth in space, but your own individual life in time? What if it's *in Their interest* to have you believing that?" (697). Without stable boundaries, the notion of persons as discrete individuals becomes suspect and finally threatens to fall away, leaving what Thomas Schaub calls "a continuity" that transcends the individual, replacing the idea of "'self' as consciousness and memory" with "'self' as *intersection*" (*Pynchon* 49–50). What is so troubling about this "intersection" is the way it resists theorization, the way it appears simultaneously to be a vague mathematical grid and an immense *individual*.

Personalities Replaced by Abstractions of Power

There is a moment in Pynchon's *V.* in which Itague rebukes Kholsky: "Your beliefs are non-human," he says. "You talk of people as if they were point-clusters or curves on a graph." Kholsky replies, "So they are" (405). *Gravity's Rainbow* also works along such troubling lines. How else can one come to terms with Slothrop, whose primary mode of interaction with others is impersonation, whose person is ultimately distributed across a continent, and whose most salient feature is a set of points on a map of London, a graphic representation of that which seems to be his most internal, individual quality?

The notion that characters may be understood or even produced by mathematical models is nothing new. Mark Seltzer has described in detail how American realism-naturalism employs "the deindividualizing tendencies of statistics" to "provide models of individualization: models for the generic, typical or average man—what we might describe as the production of individuals as statistical persons" ("Statistical Persons" 90). Yet while the "statistical persons" of realism embody the social order by displaying an impossibly representative combination of average qualities in a single body, Pynchon's characters embody the social by being statistical impossibilities, freaks, oddities: a man whose erections appear to predict rocket strikes, a spy who experiences other people's fantasies, a man who can change the color of his skin, and so on. The "individuality," or uniqueness, of these characters depends almost entirely upon the way they violate the notion of the individual, material body as the basis for a separate, autonomous, inviolable personhood.

To put the same idea differently, these characters don't merely stand in for classes of persons as they might have in realist fiction; rather, numerous persons appear to stand in—or move through—these individual bodies. Take Pökler's daughter, Ilse, for example. After being conceived during a reenactment of *Alpdrücken*, she later only exists for Pökler as a film, visiting him montage-fashion, one day, one frame, a year: "The rapid flashing of successive stills to counterfeit movement" used originally "in the process of inventing calculus...had been extended past images on film, to human lives" (407, ellipses added). Ilse's yearly visits create the "illusion of a single child" (422), even though Pökler is not quite sure if the Nazis send the same girl each time. "Ilse, some Ilse, has persisted beyond her cinema mother, beyond film's end" (429), he thinks. Yet, from his point of view, her existence as an individual body is less certain than her existence as a montage of individual bodies, an illusion articulated by a calculus of personhood, by the very equations undergirding the technology of film. The same problems afflict Pökler himself, who eventually feels he is being abstracted from his material body into vaguer mathematical spaces:

> He would become aware of a drifting-away...some assumption of Pökler into the calculations, drawings, graphs, and even what raw hardware there was... each time, soon as it happened, he would panic, and draw back into the redoubt

of waking Pökler, heart pounding, hands and feet aching, his breath catching in a small voiced *hunh*— Something was out to get him, something here, among the paper. (405–06)

Here, the relation between mathematics and personhood is clear: Pökler imagines himself both to inhabit and to be invaded by the mathematics he has developed. This contradictory effacement of, and return to, the material body is marked most clearly by Pökler's "panic"; he "draws back" into his body just as an abstracting system of his own invention seems to pose a threat, to move outside his control.

In such moments Pökler glimpses one of this novel's recurrent suggestions: that it may be possible to understand human action as a function of mathematical formulas. This possibility underwrites the massive scientific study of Slothrop: the highly improbable statistical relation between him and the rockets implies the existence of a coherent system whose operations could theoretically be specified in the form of a mathematical expression. The search for such a system, through a mathematics of personhood, is largely conducted by Britain's White Visitation scientists, who run statistical analyses, make maps of brain activity, use personality tests like the "Minnesota Multiphasic Personality Inventory," and so on. One premise of their work is that *objective* study might offer a position *outside* the system of social relations from which the latter could be observed. It is for this reason that some of them experiment with spiritualism, hoping that a move beyond the physical world will afford them true objectivity. At a séance one evening, psychological operations man Milton Gloaming explains that by plotting the frequency of words uttered during séances he hopes to "develop a vocabulary of curves" for "certain pathologies," and in so doing, to categorize spirits for the purpose of control: "Schizophrenics for example," he says, "tend to run a bit flatter in the upper part then progressively steeper—a sort of bow shape...I think with this chap, this Roland, that we're on to a classical paranoiac" (32). The regulatory possibilities of a science that could redraw the lines around types of persons—healthy and ill, paranoid and rational—are immense. Or they would be, if Gloaming's project were not undermined by the contradictory relations of persons and bodies implicit in the séance. After all, this séance involves a bizarre "four-way entente" between "Roland Feldspath (the spirit), Peter Sachsa (the control), Carroll Eventyr (the medium), Selena (the wife and survivor)" (31). The control is a spiritual middleman who coordinates the spirit's use of the medium's body. In this psychic economy, Eventyr, Sachsa, and Feldspath are literally not themselves, and even "the control" is not in control of the séance. Instead, human agency is distributed between several "persons," along mathematical lines (from "beyond the Zero"). This poses a serious challenge to Gloaming's project. If the Medium is the message in any way, then his assumption that he's graphing single individuals is wrong.

As a number of readers have pointed out, the rationale for Gloaming's project—and for many other projects of his group—is what Weber called the "routinization of charisma."[19]

> It was widely believed in those days that behind the War—all the death, savagery, and destruction—lay the Führer-principle. But if personalities could be replaced by abstractions of power, if techniques developed by the corporations could be brought to bear, might not nations live rationally? One of the dearest Postwar hopes: that there should be no room for a terrible disease like charisma... (*Gravity's Rainbow* 81)

In essence a rationalization of rationalization, this plan proposes to complete the already-substantial shift, described by Foucault, from individual to discursive and structural forms of power. Interestingly enough, such rationalizations are the subject of Roland Feldspath's otherworldly advice at the séance Gloaming is studying:

> All these things arise from one difficulty: control. For the first time it was *inside*, do you see. The control is put inside. No more need to suffer passively under "outside forces"...A market needed no longer be run by the Invisible Hand, but now could *create itself*—its own logic, momentum, style, from *inside*....But you had taken on a greater, and more harmful, illusion. The illusion of control. That A could do B. But that was false. Completely. No one can *do*. Things only happen ...(30, ellipses added)

This account of control—which could be applied to a person as well as an economy—is distinctly different from the one that characterizes most episodes of agency panic. Rather than imagining agency to reside in an external personification, like the "Invisible Hand" of the market, Feldspath imagines a thoroughly rationalized, immanent sort of control. Despite this innovation, Feldspath's attempt to model control as *wholly* internal to a system leads to problems similar to those generated by agency panic's vision of wholly external control.[20] For Feldspeth, putting control "inside" the system only creates the "illusion of control"—and appears, at the same time, to deny the possibility of motivated action or agency altogether: "No one can *do*. Things only happen." What this account cannot conceive is the overlap between an economy and the individuals that constitute it—a relation made visible everywhere in *Gravity's Rainbow*. In other words, "putting" control inside a market would mean putting control inside the persons whose bodies, bodily needs, and individual desires make up and control that market at its most basic level.[21]

Gravity's Rainbow is full of characters, like Feldspath, whose notions of agency are inadequate to grasp how social structures might regulate the behavior of individuals without depriving them of all capacity for autonomous action. The novel itself dramatizes this problem in an ingenious fashion, using *uncertainty* about agency to illustrate both the ways in which human subjectivity is socially constructed and the ways individual bodies and actions in turn comprise and regulate "the social." Yet Pynchon also imagines these complex relationships in highly melodramatic terms. His topsy-turvy ontology of persons is at once radical—imagining new forms of "individuality" at systemic levels from the cellular to the social—and at the same time reliant on an all-or-nothing conception of agency. Slothrop is the best example of this logic of personation. He enters the novel as a kind of singularity, a locus representing something well beyond itself, but he is eventually disseminated across a continent. Before long, "it's doubtful if he can ever be 'found' again, in the conventional sense of 'positively identified and detained'" (712). As in Pökler's case, the abstracting mathematics behind this process takes material form. Slothrop begins to fall apart near a "colossal curved embankment" (509), a material Gaussian distribution curve in which he is a point so close to the margins that when the curve finally "herniates toward the excellent" he "will have already been weeded out" (508). Eventually, he is "broken down" and "scattered" (738) across the Zone, across the novel.

What is significant about this process is its enactment of postmodern transference, the imaginative reassignment of human qualities to the social level. Slothrop becomes so identified with the social order that he literally disintegrates. He is transformed into a geographical distribution similar to the map he once made of his most personal experiences. In this radical movement from singular locus to statistical distribution, from eroticized absence to scattered presence, from sublime body to disseminated persona, the novel finally reveals the way its central character impersonates, and is impersonated by, social structures. But this transformation only makes more visible the anxieties that underlie the novel's machinery of mathematical personation. To be a person in *Gravity's Rainbow* means to recognize, continually and with great nervousness, that your "personality" might not be yours, that it constitutes and is constituted by global control structures, and that as it moves in and out of your body, it marks certain lines of discursive production and regulation and moves information through immense but invisible networks.

3 Stalked by Love

Alien Invaders

In a comment about her 1972 novel, *Surfacing*, Margaret Atwood suggests that her protagonist's sense of being haunted, or hunted, by men can be understood as a ghost story, the sort where "the ghost that one sees is in fact a fragment of one's own self which has split off" (G. Gibson 29). In one sense, this remark seems to justify readings that have called that novel's narrator "paranoid" or "mad."[1] That is, if a woman's pursuer is merely a phantasm originating within her, then he seems to have been produced by the classic symptom of paranoia—the projection outward of internal (or psychic) conflicts. Yet Atwood's remark does not wholly endorse a psychoanalytic view, which might go on to pathologize and dismiss the protagonist's view of her own persecution, nor does it reject the possibility that, despite his psychic origins, the persecutor is real. Rather, Atwood eschews the psychoanalytic idea of "projection"—with its underlying assumption of psychic delusion—for the oddly material term "fragmentation," an expression suggesting that the persecutor is an autonomous, corporeal entity. While her remark places the idea of persecution in a psychological frame, it also suggests there is something useful, even logical, about a "paranoid" account of persecution.

Here, then, we have the same sort of thinking that marks the fiction of Heller and Pynchon. I begin with this example because the central relationship it supposes—between the potential existence of a male persecutor and the "fragmented" subjectivity of a female victim—makes possible a powerful *social* conception of violence against women, a crime that is too often viewed as a result of *individual* male behavior. I now want to explore this conception in a number of persecution narratives, including Freud's brief study of "female paranoia" and the more recent stalker, or "stalked by love," novels of Atwood and Diane Johnson.[2] Each of these narratives contains the two main features of Atwood's remark about ghosts. First, a woman claims she is being spied on, stalked, or otherwise persecuted by a male friend or lover; yet that persecutor never quite manifests himself clearly—and thus, the woman's claim *appears* paranoid to those around her. Second, she feels a grave insecurity about her identity and agency—a panicky sense that she cannot control her body or that she has fragmented into a desiring self and a "disobedient" body. The relation between these two features—feelings of persecution and problems of agency—is well documented in extreme cases of paranoid and schizophrenic illness.[3] But I am interested in how such relations arise outside a pathological context and how they depend upon gender. Indeed, I will show that the sheer difficulty of sorting out "paranoid" from "valid" interpretations is one of the factors allowing the psychoanalytic theory of paranoia to function as a "technology of gender"—Teresa de Lauretis's term for those gendered forms of social control exerted through institutions, discourses, and social relations (2–3).

My primary aim here, however, is not to critique psychoanalysis, but rather to examine the cultural functions of the stalker narrative itself. These functions depend heavily upon who is constructing such a narrative. Freud's story of stalking, for instance, has very different political implications than the story his female client tells him. Thus, my use of Freud's study alongside the novels of Atwood and Johnson has less to do with Freud's argument than with his female client's tale, which is strikingly similar to the stories related by Atwood's and Johnson's narrators. The significance of these narratives will be clearer if I first illustrate the cluster of effects I have been describing with an example from Atwood's first novel, *The Edible Woman* (1969), a text that insistently links male persecution to bodily crises of agency. As protagonist Marian MacAlpin's wedding day approaches, she begins to perceive her fiancé, Peter, as a threat. Early in the novel, for example, Peter describes gutting a rabbit in the idiom of sexual violence. He says, "I *whipped out* my knife...and slit the belly and took *her* by the hind legs and gave *her* one hell of a crack" (69, emphasis added). As he talks, Marian identifies with the rabbit. "Something inside me," she says, "started to dash about in dithering mazes of panic" (70). Immediately thereafter, she loses the capacity to govern and understand her own body. Finding "a large drop of something wet" on the table in front of her, she realizes "with horror" that it is a tear and says, "I must be crying then!" (70). Before long, Marian finds herself fleeing the scene. "I couldn't understand why...I was doing this," she remarks, running down the street. "After the first minute I was surprised to find my feet moving, wondering how they had begun" (72). And when Peter finally catches her, she realizes, "[he] must have stalked me" (74). In this moment of agency panic, certain parts of Marian's body seem off limits to her; at the same time, they seem to be governed by a familiar script in which heterosexual relations are understood on a model of male "stalking" or "hunting."

This is not an isolated episode. Similar crises of agency are linked, throughout *The Edible Woman*, to Marian's increasing fear that Peter "might be tracing, following, stalking her through the crisp empty streets" (245–46). As this potentially paranoid feeling grows, Marian begins to experience strange bodily problems. She frequently feels her body dissipating, "beginning to dissolve, like melting jelly" (43). She panics, for instance, when her body appears to be "the same, identical, merged with" the apparently uncontrolled and uncontrollable maternal bodies of her coworkers ("that liquid amorphous other") (167). More significantly, she develops an eating disorder, which she describes as if it were itself an autonomous agent: "The quiet fear was that this thing, this refusal of her mouth to eat, was malignant; that it would spread" (153). Here, Marian understands her inability to consume food as a form of cancer. This is a telling choice of models, not only because cancer is central to Atwood's later novel *Bodily Harm* (1981) but also because it is paradoxically uncontrollable and *hostile to* the body, while being at the same time *part of* (genetically *identical to*) the body. In other words, Marian feels that—like cancer—the agency governing her eating is not clearly internal or external to her identity. Her uncertainty about the origin and agency of her eating disorder is, in turn, analogous to her uncertainty about whether she is being stalked by a real (external) male stalker or merely "projecting" her (internal) fears outward. Indeed, the novel coordinates these rather different bodily threats because they contain the structural similarity I have been drawing out: each dramatizes a set of ontological confusions about whether a hostile agent is internal or external to the person it may be persecuting.

In essence, then, the uncertainty about ego boundaries found in cases of paranoia is also present in anorexia. In paranoia, the patient frequently feels victimized by a powerful, external agent. In anorexia, she often senses that her body is an "enemy" and her hunger "an alien invader" (Bordo, "Anorexia" 92–94). But in anorexia such self-divisions and agency problems are frequently gendered. Much like the sufferers of historically "female maladies," anorexics often speak of an inner male critic, a "'ghost' inside... 'a dictator who dominates me,'" or "a little man who objects when I eat"

(Bordo, "Anorexia" 101). Like Marian MacAlpin, then, real sufferers of anorexia frequently produce their own persecution narratives, albeit narratives in which the (male) persecutor seems internal, rather than external, to the body. Put somewhat differently, anorexic persecution narratives are like ghost stories in which the ghost is "a fragment of one's own self which has split off."

What is remarkable about *The Edible Woman* is that it contains not only an internal "dictator" or "ghost" compelling Marian not to eat, but also a male stalker, whose appearance (real or imagined) coincides with the protagonist's eating problem. This shadowy figure appears in all the narratives I will consider—always in the form of an anonymous man who is never visible as a single, material individual, yet who produces real, material consequences. These qualities, of course, are what allow readers like Freud to dismiss the stalker as a delusion. Yet they also allow Atwood and Johnson to construct a powerful and politically useful representation of social control. That is, the stalker figure offers one way out of the dilemma I have been tracing through postwar culture: how to conserve a sense of individual agency, identity, and volition, while still accounting for the way institutions, discourses, and practices shape individual experience. In order to accomplish this goal—in this case, to make visible the social sources of antifemale violence while also accounting for women's desires and choices—the stalkers in these narratives must have the ontological status of ghosts, present in the material world, yet never simply individual agents. Before I can explain this odd role, I must first illustrate how problems of agency and interpretation become intertwined in narratives of stalking, and to do so I would like to revisit an older narrative.

Female Paranoia

In 1915, Freud published a brief study about a woman who claimed to have been persecuted by her lover. The study, "A Case of Paranoia Running Counter to the Psycho-Analytic Theory of the Disease," is about a thirty-year-old woman who maintained that a male colleague at her workplace "had drawn her into a love-affair," then, with the intention of shaming or blackmailing her, "abused her confidence by getting unseen witnesses to photograph them while they were making love" (*Standard Edition* 263).[4] This "most attractive" and "distinctly feminine" woman had always lived quietly with her mother and had no previous romantic experience with men (263). She claimed that her colleague vigorously pursued an affair with her, despite her hesitation about it, until finally she acquiesced to his pleas and agreed to visit his bachelor rooms. There, Freud reports, "as they lay side by side...she was suddenly frightened by a noise, a kind of knock or click" (264). She immediately asked what this noise was and her lover reassured her that it had probably come from a small clock on the desk. As she later left the building, however, two unfamiliar men appeared to be whispering about her; one, she noticed, held a box. According to Freud, she then interpreted this series of puzzling events as follows: the box might easily have been a camera, and the man a photographer who had been hidden behind the curtain while she was in the room; the click had been the noise of the shutter; the photograph had been taken as soon as he saw her in a particularly compromising position that he wished to record (264–65). Shortly thereafter, she retained a lawyer. And the lawyer, believing her claim to be based on "an actual experience which had been correctly interpreted" (266), yet recognizing its "pathological stamp," decided finally to consult Freud (263).

What Freud finds puzzling about the case is that it appears to contradict his established theory of paranoia. According to that theory, which he developed from an analysis of Daniel Paul Schreber's *Memoirs of My Nervous Illness* ("Psycho-Analytic Notes"), persecutory delusions stem from homosexuality or "narcissistic object-choice" ("A Case" 265). Moreover, Freud had argued, the persecutor in such cases "is at bottom someone whom the patient loves or has loved in the past" ("A Case" 265). This latter claim seems true enough in "A Case of Paranoia." The problem is with the former claim. Freud's female patient displays "no trace of a struggle against a homosexual attachment" (265), and thus her case raises doubts about the supposed homosexual origin of paranoia. The "simplest thing," Freud admits, "would have been to abandon the theory" (266). In fact, he adds, "in psychiatric literature there is certainly no lack of cases in which the patient imagines himself persecuted by a person of the opposite sex" (265). Yet Freud dismisses such accounts. "It is one thing," he argues, "to read of such cases, and quite a different thing to come into personal contact with one of them. My own observations and analyses and those of my friends had so far confirmed the relation between paranoia and homosexuality without any difficulty" (265). This is a rather astonishing statement because Freud's earlier theory of paranoia is based entirely on the *reading* of Schreber's *Memoirs* and not on the sort of "personal contact" in the present case.[5]

Such disparities indicate how unwilling Freud is to reconsider either his theory or his diagnosis. Rather than altering either, he pores over the case until he sees "another way out" ("A Case" 266). Noting that hidden factors often lurk in the seemingly obvious, he decides a second interview is required to discover "any subsidiary details" previously omitted (266). During the second interrogation, Freud learns that his client had actually paid another, earlier visit to her suitor's apartment and that, after this first visit, she saw the man speaking to her work supervisor, a woman with "white hair like [her] mother" (266). Suspicious that the conversation was about her, she briefly imagined that her suitor and her boss were themselves romantically involved. These details save the day for Freud's original theory: he can now conclude that "the white-haired elderly superior was a substitute for her mother" and that the "*original* persecutor—the agency whose influence the patient wishes to escape—is here again not a man but a woman" (267).

There is, then, only the detail of the "click" to handle. But here things take an odd turn, and they do so, significantly, because Freud takes the liberty of assuming that the woman's account of her actions after hearing the click are "a mistaken memory" (270):[6]

> It seems to me much more likely that at first she did not react to the noise at all, and that it became significant only after she met the two men on the staircase. Her lover, who had probably not even heard the noise, may have tried, perhaps on some later occasion when she assailed him with her suspicions, to account for it in this way: "I don't know what noise you can have heard. Perhaps it was the small clock; it sometimes ticks like that." ...I do not believe that the clock ever ticked or that there was any noise to be heard at all. The woman's situation justified a sensation of a knock or beat in her clitoris. And it was this that she subsequently projected as a perception of an external object. (270)

Although Freud begins this study by remarking, "I consider it a wrong practice...to alter any detail in the presentation of a case" (263), here he freely supplements the details given by his client with speculations of his own. I mention this not because I wish to add to the already lengthy catalogue of Freud's inconsistencies, but rather to highlight his striking entrance into the original scene *as one of its characters*—the supposedly maligned male character—eager to supply his own speculative denials and excuses. Freud's comfortable slide into this role leads, almost directly, to the emergence of an all-too-familiar narrative in which a woman who claims to be disturbed by male sexual advances is told that, in reality, she was sexually aroused. The click, she is assured, is not the sound of a violator, but of her own throbbing clitoris. This explanation dismisses the possibility that the woman's claim might be rooted in justifiable anxiety about a new heterosexual relationship—the fear, for instance, that a communication between her lover and her supervisor might compromise her professional career. Yet such fears are hardly pathological. In *The Edible Woman*, to take one instance, Marian understands that upon her marriage she will have to "leave her job whether she want[s] to or not," because her supervisor "prefer[s] her girls to be either unmarried or seasoned veterans with their liability to unpredictable pregnancies well in the past" (168).

Despite such routine social expectations, Freud traces his patient's refusal to enter an inaugural heterosexual relationship to a deeply buried homosexuality. "Female homosexuality," according to Luce Irigaray, is for Freud "a phenomenon so alien to his imaginary economy that it could only be 'neglected by psycho-analytic research,' and even neglected in the therapy of the homosexual woman patient" (101). This neglect, however, may be precisely what allows Freud to use female homosexuality to "solve" so dramatically the mystery at hand. Freud's masculinist concept of lesbian desire seems to explain the patient's puzzling and "morbid" decision to turn away from a "cultivated and attractive" man, a man whose letters have made "a very favourable impression" on Freud ("A Case" 264–65). Indeed, the initial *lack* of a visible "struggle against homosexual attachment" in this case is what motivates Freud to uncover just such an attachment (265). In a thrilling piece of detective work, he traces the failure of a heterosexual relationship not to the dynamics of heterosexual relations but to an *external,* "homosexual" cause.

This is an interesting denouement, not only because it conforms so well to the conventions of the detective novel, but because in order to reach it Freud himself must replicate the essential gestures of the paranoiac. Not only does he dismiss a simple explanation in order to pursue clues that are initially invisible, but he traces the woman's problem to an *external, hidden* agent—someone not even the victim perceives as a persecutor. Moreover, when Freud speaks for his client's male lover, his theoretical speculations begin to mirror—or double—hers.[7] While the client attributes the click to the camera of a violating male spectator, Freud attributes it to her clitoral excitation. The appearance of these paired, but radically opposed, interpretations indicates the productive limit of a hermeneutical approach to the case: the "real" cause of the events appears to be permanently unfathomable. Even more significant, however, the presence of paired, but radically opposed, subjects is a hallmark of paranoia itself. As Leo Bersani suggests, "It is a peculiarity of the paranoid structure to combine opposition with doubling" (108)—for instance, in the figure of a double or "twin" who is also one's enemy and tormentor. In a sense, then, the work of analysis replicates the paranoid structure, with the persecutor's role falling to the analyst, who seems bent on opposing—indeed pathologizing—the odd speculations of his patient with equally bizarre and unverifiable counter-speculations of his own.

Freud himself often remarked on the similarities between paranoid and psychoanalytic claims.[8] Naomi Schor has used these comparisons and the case at hand to propose a gendered theory of interpretation. For Schor, this case is about a "paradigmatic" instance of "female paranoia" and "female theorizing" because it shows that "female theorizing is...riveted to the body, its throbbing, its pulsations" (210–11). To make this claim Schor must accept Freud's hypothesis—which she calls "audacious and quite possibly mad" (210)—that the camera click is indeed the sound of the patient's clitoris. Schor even proposes a "clitoral school of feminist theory...identified by its practice of a hermeneutics focused on the detail, which is to say on those details of the female anatomy which have been generally ignored by male critics" (216). Among the problems with this project is that Freud freely supplements and invents many details of "A Case," especially those details pertaining to the purported throbbing of the clitoris. At the same time, he ignores those details on which his patient most insists.

What *is* clearly paradigmatic in this case—indeed, what will recur in all the narratives I consider—is the female patient's association of persecution with the exposure of her body to male surveillance. She is frightened at the moment when her lover begins, as Freud puts it, "to admire the charms [of her body] which were now partly revealed" ("A Case" 264). Just as important (and this will become clear later), the persecution comes not only from her lover but also from *anonymous* male spectators, themselves hidden from view. In other words, the woman's original claim is tied to her feeling that she is a spectacle—a feeling that the scene is playing on her "*to-be-looked-at-ness*" (Mulvey 11). In John Berger's often-cited account of this effect (from which Atwood takes the epigraph to *Bodily Harm*), a woman must "continually watch herself" and be "continually accompanied by her own image of herself" until "she comes to consider the *surveyor* and the *surveyed* within her as the two constituent yet always distinct elements of her identity as a woman" (46).[9] Such self-divisions begin to indicate how a sense of being watched might be linked to pathologies of self-fragmentation, dissolution, and loss of bodily control—the symptoms of historically female maladies.[10]

For Freud, of course, the normal self already contains "surveyor and surveyed" in the form of superego and ego, respectively. Nonetheless, feelings of being watched, in his theory, are abnormal. In "The Uncanny," for instance, he argues that such feelings stem from an externalization of the critical agency called "conscience" (or "superego" in his later model):

In the pathological case of delusions of being watched, this mental agency becomes isolated, dissociated from the ego, and discernible to the physician's eye. The fact that an agency of this kind exists, which is able to treat the rest of the ego like an object—the fact, that is, that man is capable of self-observation—renders it possible to invest the old idea of a "double" with a new meaning and to ascribe a number of things to it—above all, those things which seem to self-criticism to belong to the old surmounted narcissism of earliest times. (235)

Here, Freud confidently maps the mental agencies onto what the subject believes to be an intersubjective or social relation. He concludes that the feeling of being watched results from abnormally zealous and unconscious self-monitoring, not from actual social experience. Yet if being observed constitutes a normal social experience for women, then Freud's purportedly gender-neutral theory of self-surveillance might mask the central issue in "A Case." It might, for instance, compel him to pathologize his patient's sense of being watched, rather than tracing her feeling to social relations in which it is "normal" for male identity to be strongly constituted by watching and female identity by being watched.

In one sense, the gender implications of Freud's theory are what his client's rival explanation of her experience contests. That is, the eventual *contest of interpretation* between analyst and client in the case concerns not only the ontological status of the persecutor (external or internal, real or projected), but also whether certain "normal" social relations might constitute persecution *for those able to perceive them*. This is so because cases of paranoia routinely negotiate whether a subject's feelings of being watched are in fact abnormal or whether they have some real social basis. Even the famously paranoid claims of Schreber, which seem excessive and even ludicrous at first glance, are not so easily deemed irrelevant to the larger social world. As Louis Sass notes, there is an "uncannily close...correspondence" between Schreber's "delusional cosmos" and Foucault's account of panoptic surveillance, in which one must "experience oneself *both* as the body that feels itself observed...and also as the watcher who feels like a pure and omniscient consciousness" (254, 252).[11] If this description of panopticism echoes Berger's account of female self-surveillance, then it helps to explain why Schreber repeatedly feels *feminized* by panoptic scrutiny—why, for instance, his sense of diminished agency is so tightly coupled to fears of being "penetrated" by cosmic rays and turned into the "bride" of God.

The similarity between Schreber's vision and Foucault's also helps to account for Atwood's tendency to dramatize gender relations through characters who seem deeply concerned, even "paranoid," about surveillance. Joan Foster, the heroine and stalker novelist of *Lady Oracle* (1976), for instance, understands her sense of being perpetually watched in the form of divine scrutiny imagined by Schreber: "Being told in Sunday school that God was watching you every minute of every hour had been bad enough, but now I had to think about all these other people I didn't even know who were spying on me" (106).[12] Marian MacAlpin no less strikingly locates her own fear of Peter and of heterosexual relations in the act that so terrifies Freud's female patient: *the clicking of a camera*. Shortly before her engagement party, as Peter tries to take a few photographs of her, she finds her body has "frozen, gone rigid." She rebukes herself, saying, "It's only a camera" (232), but she cannot stop equating camera with gun: "He had a camera in his hand; but now she saw what it really was.... 'No!' she screamed" (244). At the same time, she wonders if "the real Peter, the one underneath" (242) is as harmless as she once thought. She envisions a figure like him walking across the lawn with a cleaver in his hand. Eventually, when he attempts to photograph her again, she flees, more powerfully evoking the relation between being a spectacle and being a victim. "That dark intent marksman with his aiming eye had been there all the time, hidden by the other layers, waiting for her at the dead centre: a homicidal maniac with a lethal weapon in his hands" (246). As with Freud's client, Marian's "paranoia" is precipitated by a significantly increased commitment to a heterosexual relationship and manifests itself through analogies between spectator and violator, camera and weapon.

All of this is not to say that we must accept the *corporeal* presence of Marian's stalker or the client's "witnesses" ("A Case" 150). But neither should we follow Freud in dismissing these persecutors as the products of a deranged mind. In the stories at hand, they register the operation of a surveilling power that is (as Foucault says of its eighteenth-century forms) "all the less 'corporal' in that it is more subtly 'physical.'" This power is also "absolutely indiscreet, since it is everywhere" and "absolutely 'discreet,' for it functions permanently and largely in silence" (*Discipline* 177). The paradoxical nature of this power is embodied in Freud's term "*ungesehenen Zuschauern*" ("Mitteilung" 234), which has been translated as both "unseen witnesses" (*Standard Edition* 263) and "invisible witnesses" (*Collected Papers* 150). While the former translation suggests something materially present but hidden or overlooked, the latter suggests something ghostly or hallucinated. If we were to reconcile these different senses, we might say such "witnesses" consist not of an individual, corporeal spectator, or even a group of spectators, but rather of a *spectator function* that is built into normative male and female identity and that is both ubiquitous and "absolutely discrete"—quite physical, yet difficult to trace to a single corporeal persecutor. In their fear of cameramen, both Marian and Freud's patient theorize this form of control, suggesting that it is the kind of gendered social regulation Foucault might call "intentional and nonsubjective"; that is, it seems to have "perfectly clear" aims and objectives, though "no one is there to have invented them, and few who can be said to have formulated them" (Foucault, *History* 94–95). This paradoxical combination of apparently *intentional* yet *anonymous* malevolence, I will now suggest, is what explains the powerful conception of the stalker in the novels of Atwood and Johnson.

A Distrust of Surfaces

I have been arguing that, in Freud's hands, the psychoanalytic category of paranoia functions as a technology of gender, a feminizing tool. Ironically, in "A Case," the client's fear of male spectators is a form of resistance to feminization. But this resistance is converted into a paranoid delusion by the analyst, who suggests that her anxiety is not related to her entrance into a "normal" heterosexual romance but to abnormal, homosexual desires. The treatment of paranoia, then, replicates the oppositional, persecutory structure of paranoia itself. What is most contested in such a struggle is the boundary between the subject and the social order. While the patient believes that a persecutory agency exists in the external world, the analyst believes this agency exists only within the patient and is merely being projected outward. That is, the patient argues for a "small," hermetic and besieged self, while the analyst insists that the patient's boundaries are much larger than she thinks.

This sort of contest, and the problem of the subject it poses, is central to the postwar stalker novel. I now want to return to this genre, incorporating two tales of persecution remarkably similar in content to the one related by Freud, but remarkably different in their handling of the subject: Diane Johnson's *The Shadow Knows* (1974) and Atwood's *Bodily Harm*. The protagonists of these novels find themselves beset by increasingly threatening incidents. Like Marian MacAlpin and Freud's patient, they suspect that such threats may come from their husbands or lovers (past and present), but they have trouble confirming this sense and even suspect themselves of paranoia. Their interpretive distress turns, in part, on the uncertain agency of the threat to them. Is their persecution *personally* motivated, the product of someone's *willful* malice? Or is it an *unrelated* set of incidents—directed not at a specific woman but at *women in general*? One of the things at stake in these novels, then, is whether a woman's sense of persecution is best understood through sociology or psychology—through a general account of social conditions or a case history of individual (psychological) circumstances and personal relations.

Divorced, recently rejected by her married lover, and potentially pregnant, Johnson's narrator, N., is convinced that someone is trying to kill her. Her door is hacked up with an axe or knife (5); she receives repeated phone calls from a "phantom phone-caller" (11); someone puts a murdered cat on her doorstep (48); her car is covered with vomit and her tires slashed (142); and in the laundry room of her housing project, someone assaults her housekeeper and friend, Ev, precipitating an illness from which Ev dies. N. believes that these events are connected and intended to persecute her— and she alternately suspects her ex-husband, Gavvy; her ex-lover, Andrew; her ex-maid, Osella; her best friend, Bess; and various friends and acquaintances. As she puts it, "I suppose if you ask anyone who it is trying to murder them, they will straightway name loved ones without hesitation" (5). But she also admits, in the first line of the novel, "You never know, that's all, there's no way of knowing" (3). This is so, in N.'s view, because there is an absolute separation between the interiors and exteriors of persons. N., for instance, believes herself to be "riddled and shot through invisibly with desperate and sordid passions" that others cannot detect. "Not even I would think that, looking at me," she says: "Outside...I look like a happy moon" (8).

This familiar model of the individual suggests that a hidden interior self is the privileged site of identity and motive. While this model offers N. a rather consoling understanding of herself, it is less comforting when applied to others. At every turn it seems to prevent her from identifying her persecutor. When her ex-husband stops by and asks politely how she is doing, for example, she immediately suspects him but then finds that her idea of personhood keeps her from testing her suspicions. "You just don't know what's lurking in people's hearts," she thinks. "Though you don't know when people will turn bad on you, you don't know when they will turn good on you, either. Either way it makes you feel uneasy" (146).[13] N.'s uneasiness has its roots in the gothic romance. It is commonplace in that genre for a heroine to suspect that her lover is planning to do her bodily harm—to believe, as Joanna Russ once put it, that "somebody's trying to kill me and I think it's my husband."[14] "Every man I'd ever been involved with," says Joan Foster, the "costume Gothic" novelist in *Lady Oracle*, "had two selves: my father, healer and killer; the man in the tweed coat, my rescuer and possibly also a pervert; the Royal Porcupine and his double, Chuck Brewer; even Paul, who I'd always believed had *a sinister other life I couldn't penetrate.* Why should Arthur be any exception?" (292, emphasis added). This view of the male subject as a reservoir of secret intentions generates one of the insistent paradoxes of the "stalked by love" novel: the victim suspects those individuals closest to her because she can imagine them possessing malicious motives, but she can never confirm her suspicions because she believes any evidence of malice would be permanently unfathomable, masked by her violator's visible behavior. The idea that persecutory motives are at once *present and invisible* is a central feature of the Freud case discussed earlier. Because this view depends on a hermeneutics divorced from material evidence, it is easily labeled paranoid—not only by those who come under suspicion, like N.'s doubting friend Bess, but by analysts and readers as well.[15]

In *Bodily Harm*, Rennie Wilford finds herself subject to the same paradox. Recovering from a mastectomy and recently abandoned by her lover, she comes home to discover that someone has broken into her apartment, leaving a coiled rope behind. Afterward, like N., Marian, and Freud's patient, "she [can't] shake the feeling that she [is] being watched, even when she [is] in a room by herself, with the curtains closed" (40). Although she is "an expert on surfaces" (26)—a freelance writer focusing on fashion, trends, and "lifestyles"—she begins to suspect that something is lurking beneath the obvious surfaces of her world. Terrified, she leaves for the Caribbean island of St. Antoine on assignment to write a travel piece. There, however, she feels even more closely watched—and more seriously at risk—as she is drawn into the island's violent election politics. As in the cases cited earlier, she suspects her romantic interests: Daniel (her doctor), Paul (St. Antoine's dashing American gun-runner), and Jake (her ex-lover). But she also wonders if her fears are merely projections ("That scratching you heard at the window last night wasn't coming from the outside at all" [41]) in part because they are so coincidental with her cancer. "It's your own fear of death," she tells herself; "you're projecting onto some pathetic weirdo who's never going to bother you again" (40–41). In other words, the persecutor may be a man, but it may also be Rennie's own body, a "sinister twin" that has "turned against her," "a close friend" that has "betrayed" her (82).

As the novel develops, Rennie cannot escape the sense that the internal and external bodily threats to her are related. Not only do they appear at the same time, but they elicit similar moral judgments. When Rennie's friend, Lora, is sexually assaulted by her stepfather, Lora's mother tells her, "You're asking for it" (172); similarly, Rennie's mother believes that cancer, like rape, is "something you brought upon yourself" (82). Within the logic of the stalker novel, however, the most important similarity between cancer and a male lover-stalker is structural: both consist of a malignant interior masked by a benign surface. When Rennie examines her "good" breast for lumps, for instance, she worries despite her inability to turn up anything bad: "From the surface you can feel nothing, but she no longer trusts surfaces" (48). Eventually, the same skeptical view of exteriors leads her to suspect that "in some way that had never been spelled out between them [Jake] thought of her as the enemy" (211). Rennie's distrust of surfaces, then, is a version of N.'s uneasiness about "people's hearts"—and, more generally, of the paranoid tendency to believe in a persecutory agent hidden behind the *perceptible* surface of the world.

As I suggested above, this distrust of human exteriors is somewhat paradoxical. It hinges on a hermeneutics in which tangible evidence is misleading because the stalker has an impenetrable core of malicious motives. The paradox is that such a hermeneutics is guaranteed to fail because it posits a fundamental obstacle to its own operation: if persecutory motives are *utterly* secret, then one can *never* confirm their existence. Significantly, this conception of the stalker is different from the one that dominates late-twentieth-century legal discourse on stalking. While victims are occasionally stalked by an anonymous figure (Gilligan 322–23), statistics from law enforcement and victim assistance agencies suggest that this experience is atypical (Cordes; Gilligan; McAnaney et al.). Most victims know they are being stalked and know who their persecutor is.[16] The conception of anonymous stalking in the novels at hand, by contrast, stems from an apprehensive sense that *any* man could be a stalker—that stalking is, on the surface, inseparable from masculinity. Popular articles on stalking occasionally reflect this uncertainty when they provide tips on "how to spot a stalker," and thus imply the difficulty of doing so (Cordes; Malestic; Tuten and Sherman). Yet, unlike the stalked-by-love novel, such articles suggest that stalkers ultimately *can* be known by their telltale "signs." Indeed, journalistic and legal discourse on stalking routinely produces psychological profiles of the stalker, portraying him not as a mysterious "everyman," but as a highly individuated specimen—a ruthless sociopath, a habitual and obsessive abuser, or someone with a recognized sexual pathology (usually erotomania, borderline erotomania, or de Clérambault's syndrome) (Cordes 13; Malestic 24; McAnaney et al. 832–50; Tuten and Sherman 57).

Perhaps we ought to wonder, then, if the oddly self-defeating conception of the stalker at work in the novels at hand offers some other theoretical advantage or psychic consolation. For instance, there might be a theoretical advantage to being *unable* to pin one's persecution on an individual—because the problem of stalking may stem not from single, deviant individuals but from a larger complex of social institutions, narratives, and conditions. There might also be something reassuring about the conception of selfhood used to imagine the stalker himself. That is, the idea of a single, efficient persecutor might offer a strange sort of comfort to someone whose own self-control seems threatened by an array of social institutions. This second form of "reassurance," of course, would be diametrically opposed to the first; each would assuage an anxiety enhanced by the other. Yet agency panic arises because of such opposed psychic needs. It is an attempt to reconcile social theory with a conventional model of personhood.

Such attempts at reconciliation are plainly visible in the texts at hand. N., for instance, wants to think of both her stalker *and herself* as rational, motivated agents, each with a protected interior core of beliefs, motives, and desires. Yet she has extraordinary trouble conceiving of herself in these terms. Despite her claim to possess a strictly delimited hermetic interior, she is deeply anxious about the fuzzy boundary between her insides and outsides. After attempting to abort her pregnancy by getting an IUD, she discovers her door smeared with "some disgusting substance" (5): "it seemed to me," she remarks, "that [the door] was smeared with the murdered new life; fetal membranes and blood from inside me, that was my first thought" (9). This anxiety about the unstable borders between self and fetus, self and social realm, belies N.'s notion that her insides are safely sealed away and undetectable. It also indicates her uncertainty about whether she is reading her situation correctly. "It's as if you were flying along," she says, "in a craft from which all instruments are taken, all gauges and indicators, the thing that tells you whether you are upside down or not. Nothing outside to go by ..." (127). In such moments, N. cannot decide if the agency of her persecution—like the "disgusting substance" itself—is external or if it originates from within.

This form of uncertainty is the central dilemma foregrounded in cases of paranoia. It is no accident, therefore, that paranoia often looks like a struggle to maintain a clear sense of self. As Leo Bersani puts it,

> In paranoia, the primary function of the enemy is to provide a definition of the real that makes paranoia necessary. We must therefore begin to suspect the paranoid structure itself as a device by which consciousness maintains the polarity of self and nonself, thus preserving the concept of identity. (109)

Schreber, for instance, displays radical uncertainty about his boundaries, at times claiming to be infinitely small and at other moments asserting that he is coextensive with the universe. It is the appearance of God, as persecutor, in his thinking, that drives him back into a defensive posture and allows him to rearticulate the line between self and nonself. While paranoia may be too strong a term to describe the other cases I have been discussing here, Bersani's remark seems apt nonetheless. N., Rennie, and Marian, like Schreber, begin to fear persecution when they crave a strict idea of "self and nonself." Rennie becomes deeply anxious when she notices an inadequate separation between the interiors and exteriors of persons. She is disgusted at the sight of Lora's chewed fingernails: she "doesn't like the sight of ravage, damage, the edge between inside and outside blurred like that" (86). Similarly, Marian feels suffocated when she thinks about the "continual flux between the outside and the inside" of her fellow female office workers or realizes that their bodies (originally "outline and surface only") are always "taking things in, giving them out, chewing, words, potato chips, burps, grease, hair, babies, milk, excrement, cookies, vomit, coffee, tomato-juice, blood, tea, sweat, liquor, tears, and garbage" (*Edible Woman* 167). What Marian, N., and Rennie find unsettling in such moments, I am suggesting, is the way traffic across bodily borders threatens their view that persons are atomistic, self-governing entities, each with a protected core of unique desires, motives, and memories that cannot be controlled from the outside.[17] Because this atomistic model of the individual has masculine associations, it is telling that all three women most adhere to it when discovering the "unsettling" fluidity of the female body. Clinging to this hermetic, liberal view of self, in other words, seems to be a way of resisting femininity and feminization.

It becomes clearer why N., Rennie, and Marian want to conserve this model of individual agency and identity when we recall that each faces a crisis of bodily control closely associated with a heterosexual relationship. N.'s potential pregnancy, Marian's eating disorder, and Rennie's cancer are uncontrollable phenomena that complicate the distinction between self and nonself. Marian's eating disorder, for instance, manifests itself as a difficulty in distinguishing between consumption and self-consumption, or more generally, between her own (already alienated) body and other objects. She cannot eat a piece of cake because it feels "spongy and cellular against her tongue, like the bursting of thousands of tiny lungs" (207). As she peels a carrot, "the curl of crisp orange skin" reminds her of her own flesh, and she imagines the carrot screaming (178)—again identifying with whatever might move through her body.

Her response to these identity confusions is to reject food, thus blocking the disturbing flow of matter across the boundaries of her body.

Significantly, she understands this response in the language of vexed agency: "She was...irritated by her body's decision...but it was adamant; and if she used force it rebelled" (177–78). As I noted earlier, this contest of wills is typical in anorexia, where challenges to the patient's self-control ("my stomach wanted it") elicit both violent assertions of agency ("I will be the master of my own body") and fantasies of something like pure volition, willfulness untainted by bodily need—the "ideal," as one anorexic puts it, of "being without a body."[18] In such cases, the patient's struggle to determine the proper borders of her self—to decide whether her material body and its needs are part of her or hostile to her—is replicated in discussions about the cultural meaning of anorexia. It is not clear, for instance, whether a patient's refusal to eat is a sign of her extraordinary ability to control the one thing she still can control or a sign of her total domination by a destructive, culturally implanted ideal of female beauty. In other words, the disorder raises challenging questions about whether a patient's desire to refuse food is indeed *her* desire or whether it has come from without.

One problem with that debate is that its terms result from a misguided desire to attribute agency in an all-or-nothing fashion to either individuals or "society." Anorexia only seems to be a paradox—a pernicious form of social control *and* immense individual willpower—if we assume that individuals compete with (an abstractly conceived) "society" for their own control and that exertions of will cannot therefore produce normative, or "socially controlled" behavior. These assumptions rest on the idea that individuals are clearly bounded, autonomous entities. The problem with this popular view is its inability to account for activity that seems normative enough to be controlled by a larger social logic. Indeed, to preserve such a self-concept, Marian must adopt a fragmented sense of self by viewing her own body as "external" and threatening to her "self"—in an odd way, achieving the anorexic ideal of "being without a body." This logic is analogous to the logic of paranoia. Its function is to conserve a sense of core identity and self-control in the face of a threatening external assault on that control. What is most significant about the case at hand is the way Atwood links this threat to Marian's impending marriage and thus to a range of social controls exercised through that institution. Her eating disorder registers the bodily harm implicit in her consumption of normative femininity.

The same sort of unexamined commitment to heterosexual romance and femininity explains why Rennie's worries about a male persecutor are so tightly coupled to anxieties about the uncontrollability of her "insides." Rennie imagines her body "full of white maggots eating away at [her] from the inside" (83). She worries that her scar "will come undone in the water,

split open like a faulty zipper, and she will turn inside out" (80). This fear—
that "she'll see blood, leakage, her stuffing coming out" (22)—concerns the
potential "leaking" away of her agency and self-control. She is, for example,
haunted by the memory of her grandmother wandering around looking for
her own hands—an image coupling a failure of self-control with a failure of
identity. Eventually, Rennie begins to dream that, "There's something she
has to find. She stands up, in her bare feet, she's wearing a long white cotton
gown, it ties at the back, but this is not a hospital.... It's her hands she's
looking for, she knows she left them here somewhere, folded neatly in a
drawer, like gloves" (116). The hospital gown is significant because surgery
—the violent opening and refashioning of the body—is a powerful figure
for feminization in the novels of Atwood and Johnson. In Johnson's *Health
and Happiness* (1990), a woman's loss of bodily control leads to a seemingly
interminable stay in a hospital ("once she knew her body could act up on
her, how could she ever trust it again?" [146]), which in turn becomes the
site of both terror and a healing heterosexual romance: she is apparently
cured by "the intoxicating caresses of [the] famous physician" (259). Similarly, in *The Edible Woman*, doctors appear as one version of the "familiar"
yet anonymous "masked" man (135), and Marian's big makeover at a beauty
parlor is represented as an extensive surgical procedure intended to normalize her ("the doctor had set to work" on "the assembly-line of women
seated in identical mauve chairs under identical whirring mushroom-
shaped machines" [208–09]). Because surgeons are violators of bodily
boundaries *par excellence*, their appearance in these novels is a way to cou-
ple the heterosexual romance with the literal "invasion" and (re)construc-
tion of female subjects: "Surgery, she thought. Oh, definitely, surgery is the
thing" (*Health and Happiness* 260).

For Rennie, surgery is at once romantic—she is attracted to her surgeon
Daniel because "he knows what she's like inside" (81)—and terrifying: "her
body is down there on the table," she dreams, and "it's the heart they're
after...who can tell what they're doing, she doesn't trust them" (172–73).
This connection between heterosexual love and bodily violence ("it's the
heart they're after") also appears in Jake's attempts to reconstruct Rennie's
"exterior." Although Jake (like the Commander of *The Handmaid's Tale*) is
a professional "packager," not a surgeon, Rennie nonetheless imagines his
effect on her in the idiom of surgery. After realizing she is "one of the things
Jake [is] packaging" (104), for instance, Rennie cannot remember if he once
told her, "I want to be the one you open up for," or, "I want to be the one
who opens you up" (106). This confused memory again suggests that the
"interior" of the body is the site of identity and that involvement with Jake

might amount to something like a surgical violation of that protected space.

Jake virtually admits that he wants to reconstruct Rennie—a task that includes, for instance, the micromanagement of her posture during intercourse (106). This process "[begins] with the apartment" (104). Jake takes strict control over its appearance, decorating it with erotic pictures of women and choosing deep-pink sofas because they are "like thighs" (104). His tendency to equate women with physical property links him to the novel's pornographic artist, Frank, who makes furniture out of naked mannequins (208). Frank, in turn, is linked to a police exhibit of violent pornography that he calls "the raw material" (209) for his work. Rennie's visit to this exhibit—which is very much about surgical manipulation ("women being strangled or bludgeoned or having their nipples cut off" [210])—eventually convinces her that she herself is "being used" for "raw material" (212). Atwood thus establishes a series of connections between the violent opening of women's bodies and their domestication or "remodeling" into more feminine bodies.

The Edible Woman accounts for Marian's increasing feminization in virtually the same way. Marian understands Peter's recently constructed apartment to be the product of something like bodily consumption: "the clutter of *raw materials*... had disappeared, transmuted by an invisible process of digestion and assimilation into the shining skins that enclosed the space through which [she and Peter] were now moving" (225, emphasis added). Marian's view that construction proceeds via consumption is essential to her inability to consume. Being "constructed," in Marian's view, is like being consumed (being "an edible woman"). To follow the logic of the passage out, the body's assimilation of "raw materials" such as food is analogous to the social body's assimilation and processing of women into more socially acceptable, feminine subjects. For both Rennie and Marian, then, the "paranoid" tendency to imagine strict boundaries between self and environment is a way of conceptualizing resistance to "invasive" technologies of femininity—to the idea that one is "under construction," subject to what Gayle Rubin once called "a social apparatus that takes up females as raw materials and fashions domesticated women as products" (75).

"Through the pursuit of an ever-changing, homogenizing, elusive ideal of femininity," argues Susan Bordo, "female bodies become what Foucault calls 'docile bodies,'—bodies whose forces and energies are habituated to external regulation, subjection, transformation, 'improvement'" ("The Body," 14). If such bodies are habituated to continual "improvement," then they are habituated to feeling like "raw material." From one point of view, there is something odd about Bordo's formulation of this process: the phrase "*external* regulation" does not quite accord with the phrase "through the pursuit," which suggests an *internal* desire to pursue external regulations. Yet I have been arguing throughout this book that it is not possible to solve such paradoxes by simply "assigning" causality to either individual or social agents. The sheer difficulty of separating external controls from internal controls is part of what generates crises of agency in the first place. N., Marian, and Rennie attempt to reestablish strict boundaries between their insides and outsides because they suspect certain powerful regulatory mechanisms are *already* at work inside them. And this unsettling prospect is accompanied by another—the threat of an anonymous stalker. This second threat is equally confusing—seemingly external, but perhaps only a paranoid projection. Yet the confusion is what allows this figure to represent the causes of violence against women, for he seems to permit both a theory of individual action and a rival, sociological theory. It is to this representational advantage that I now turn.

Abnormally Normal

When Rennie tells Jake she feels like "raw material," she adds, "I feel I'm being used; though not by you exactly" (212). Rennie's sense that Jake is "not...exactly" the cause of her problems both implicates Jake and explains why her troubles do not disappear when she is with other men. The same sort of hesitation marks other stalked-by-love novels. While the genre seems full of instances in which women suspect their lovers of persecuting them, a closer look reveals that this is *not exactly* the case. Marian MacAlpin, for instance, suspects her fiancé of stalking her, yet cannot pin the blame on him in particular. In one telling instance, she decides that Peter is "not the enemy after all...just a normal human being like most other people" (271); the next moment, however, she confronts him, saying, "You've been trying to destroy me, haven't you" (271). Significantly, this rapid change of opinion occurs when Marian leaves the room and observes Peter from behind:

> But there was something about *his* shoulders. *He* must have been sitting with *his* arms folded. *The face on the other side of that head could have belonged to anyone. And they* all wore clothes of real cloth and had real bodies: *those* in the newspapers, *those* still unknown, waiting for *their* chance to aim from the upstairs window; you passed *them* on the streets every day. It was easy to see *him* as normal and safe in the afternoon, but that didn't alter things. (271, emphasis added)

From her position behind Peter, Marian detects a physical threat she does not normally see. He is frightening only when she loses sight of his individuating features and imagines that his face could belong "to anyone." This fantasy in turn conjures up the specter of an anonymous and generic male violence against women. Peter himself, then—in spite of his problematic treatment of Marian—is "not exactly" the problem. The passage transforms him into a representative of male violence through a set of striking grammatical maneuvers between individual and generic: the singular "he" abruptly becomes "they" and not until the end of the passage does it return to the singular "him." These hasty shifts signal Atwood's refusal to assign Marian's problem to an individual man. While Peter may be the agent of Marian's problems in the sense of factor or middleman, the causes of those problems lie in social relations extending well beyond him.

This method of understanding male violence is essential to all the novels I am considering. While N. attributes the attacks against her to "powers impersonal or personal" (116), Rennie, in *Bodily Harm*, imagines her stalker to be an impossibly "faceless stranger" despite her admission that "everyone [has] a face, there [is] no such thing as a faceless stranger" (41). Later, when she witnesses the brutal beating of a man from her prison cell, she finally realizes, "She's afraid of men and it's simple, it's rational, she's afraid of men because men are frightening. She's seen the man with the rope, now she knows what he looks like" (290). Here, as in *The Edible Woman*, the male violator is not simply an individual; Rennie calls him "the man with the rope" (the man who broke into her apartment) knowing full well that he is *not* that particular man. In making this substitution, Rennie recognizes the socially scripted nature of male violence, and only then is she able to see that her "paranoia" is what Adrienne Rich once called "*righteous* paranoia about men" (200, emphasis added).

The same blurring of individual and generic male bodies is critical in *The Shadow Knows*. "Sometimes," says N.,

> I scare myself with this idea: you are alone with someone you love and trust, whom you have always known, who you were a child with, maybe, and have seen each other cry... The two of you are away in the country, I imagine lying under a pasture tree surrounded by all the innumerable pleasures of exquisite days— fragrance, the grass to lie on, blue flies singing, your picnic lunch in a basket and the friend smiles over you at this moment of perfect repose, of perfect rapport; leans toward you smiling, and then his hands are around your neck, crushing your neck, but even when you are dying still you cannot see anything in the blue eyes that you had never seen before; they are the last thing you see, illimitably familiar and strange. (72)

This imaginary scenario depends upon the idea of the stalker I discussed earlier: his pleasant exterior *utterly* masks a hidden core of malevolence. The narrator's apparent familiarity with him is likewise misleading, perverted by his secret strangeness. Yet N. is not thinking of a specific individual with his own distinctive history and individual qualities. This imaginary stranger is "familiar" in theory only. He is a generic male character whose virtual anonymity is central to the operation of this fantasy. Indeed, while N. suspects Andrew and Gavvy of tormenting her, she is never able to imagine them murdering her in such a graphic way. She can only imagine a personally motivated attack on herself if she creates an attacker who is anonymous and deindividuated.

One of the reasons N. thinks of her persecution in these paradoxical terms is that she cannot decide whether it is rooted in personal motives or social structures. Although she imagines innumerable motives for her own murder, she is also acutely aware of the ubiquity of domestic violence. Thus, when Bess suggests that N.'s problems may be due to her low-income neighborhood, N. silently disagrees, thinking, "murder happens all over" (30). She has in mind a specific kind of murder, an instance of which has been related in the morning paper: "AGRICULTURE PROF KILLS WIFE, TOTS, SELF" (31). This item and a later story ("FATHER KILLS ESTRANGED WIFE, CHILDREN OUTSIDE CHURCH" [70]) eerily replicate her own situation as an estranged wife with four children, and thus they suggest a pattern of violence that cannot be explained simply through the category of personal motivation. Rather, such patterns are best understood through sociological observation, with its focus on statistical norms. Indeed, N.'s sociological insights continually disrupt her tendency to seek a psychological explanation for her persecution, an account focused on individual motive. Initially, for instance, she suspects that her tormentor is a "sane, everyday person" (16) who knows and hates her; yet later she wonders if he is an anonymous man who "may hate...females" in general (70). Such tensions increase when someone mails her "a photograph of an atrocity in Vietnam, a little thin woman lying dead, burned and bloody and smeared over, with dead children, bits of them, strewn around, and one tiny child left alive" (148). This threat is doubly disturbing because of the way it blurs the boundary between so-called "personal" and "political" forms of violence. An image of what is often called "motiveless" political violence here seems to be part of a highly motivated personal attack, thus challenging the conventional distinction between those categories. "It's funny," N. reflects, "that this impersonal photograph seen by millions of readers...pictures like this in the paper every day...could shock me worse than the [rejection] letter from Andrew" (148–49). Like the newspaper headlines, the photo takes N.'s persecution out of a purely psychological framework and places it in a social context. The result is a troubling agency dilemma, a question about how to account not only for the individual motives in cases like "PROF KILLS WIFE"—and N.'s own—but also for the statistical regularity of such cases.

Atwood's fiction addresses the same dilemma by creating analogies between individual bodies and statistical or "social bodies" and using these analogies to connect apparently isolated forms of abuse to larger patterns and norms. In *Bodily Harm*, Rennie's focus on appearances and bodily "surfaces" is analogous to her initial view of St. Antoine as a tourist spot; likewise, her mounting distrust of surfaces coincides with her growing awareness of violent island politics. Atwood establishes such connections by repeating words and phrases like "malignant" and "massive involvement," which describe the spread of cancerous rebellion in both Rennie's body (34) and the island's body politic (234). The resulting connection between individual and social bodies is essential to Rennie's growing political awareness, her sense that violence she might once have sorted into the categories "personal" and "political" is all driven by a gender politics formerly invisible to her. For instance, while she initially believes that her nationality has made her "exempt" from St. Antoine's "third world" political violence (203), she eventually sees that an equally political form of gendered violence drove her from the "first world" originally.

It is perhaps no surprise that the novel's action hero, Paul, dismisses Rennie's attempts to compare her experience to the "political" violence inflicted on St. Antoine's residents: "when you've spent years watching people dying," he says, "you don't have time for a lot of healthy women sitting around arguing whether or not they should shave their legs" (240). Yet Rennie becomes painfully aware of the regularity of female violation in the supposedly "exempt" first world, a brutality first apparent as she watches a snuff film in which a rat emerges from a woman's vagina: "What if this is normal," she thinks, "and we just haven't been told yet?" (210). When she asks Jake about this sort of pornography, he says, "Come on, don't confuse me with that sick stuff... You think most men are like that?" (212). Yet Jake routinely acts out his own rape fantasies with her, maintaining that they are part of "normal" heterosexual relations. Indeed, when hearing about Rennie's apparent stalker, Lora admits, "I'd rather be plain old raped... as long as there's nothing violent" (270)—something she can say because sexual assault is not "abnormal" in her experience. Atwood makes it painfully clear how widely accepted norms may mask violence by making it seem apolitical and unavoidable. Despite her cancer, for example, "Rennie looks quite well, she looks normal" (15), and despite a corrupt election and brutal political murders on St. Antoine, a Canadian diplomat proclaims that "the situation is normalizing" (294). When he asks Rennie to suppress the scenes of torture she has witnessed, she thinks, "The situation is normalizing, all over the place, it's getting more and more normal all the time" (296). This cynical remark testifies to her heightened awareness of political repression on St. Antoine, and her realization that violence may be made normal, acceptable, and thus invisible, in first world North America.

Perceptions of normality and their effects on individuals are central to the forms of violence I have been addressing here. When Marian experiences her eating disorder as a troubling "abnormality," her friends assure her that she is "marvelously normal" (207), even "abnormally normal" (206). These are puzzling terms of reassurance to say the least. Being "abnormally normal" means being something like a generic person—a woman feminized to the point where she has "no *particular* qualities," like the heroine of a gothic novel (Snitow 257, emphasis added).[19] It also means being something like a stalker, at least as he is imagined in these novels: a "statistical person," "anonymous" and generic, despite his capacity for violence.[20] Indeed, what is most striking about the stalker figure is his emptiness, his utter normality and deindividuation. These qualities may make him seem disappointingly vague, perhaps insubstantial or even imaginary. But they also indicate his most vital representational function: he embodies the social norms that threaten women.

Anonymous Effects

How does one begin to represent the control of individual female subjects? "In scenes of both reproduction and wounding," says Elaine Scarry, "the graphic image of the human body substitutes for the object of belief that itself has no content and thus itself cannot be represented" (198). Scarry has in mind the "agony of labor required in generating an idea of God and holding it steadily in place" (198), but I want to suggest that her claims might also apply to the work of representing those "complex political technologies" that Foucault has called "power." It is no accident that Foucault's concept of power has often been understood in recent cultural criticism as "a godlike agency which not only causes but composes everything which is its object" (Butler, *Bodies* 6)[21]—this despite Foucault's vigorous claims that when speaking of the "great anonymous, almost unspoken strategies" that make subjects, "one needs to be nominalistic"

(*History* 95, 93). If one needs to be nominalistic, then (to borrow Scarry's terms) one's "object of belief...has no content and thus itself cannot be represented." It is not hard to see how an object with "no content"—by which I think Scarry means no perceptible embodiment—would pose extraordinary representational problems. It is for this very reason that much postwar (social) theory has retained the rhetoric of human agency even as it dismisses liberal humanist theories of social action. The representation of abstract social relations is made a good deal easier when abstractions can be housed (however nominally) in a human figure or in human terms.

The narratives I have been investigating here operate on this principle, localizing social relations in a "graphic image of the human body," a stalker shadowy enough to represent the social. They construe male violence as if it were "both intentional and nonsubjective" (Foucault, *History* 94). The individual acts seem highly motivated, but their perpetrators are "not exactly" subjects. Rather, they are generic stand-ins for a more general cultural pattern. Consider, for instance, N.'s attempt to locate the individual responsible for persecuting her. As she stands outside her apartment, she says, "I partly noticed in my corner eye a figure—a man, I thought—but as I turned to look at him directly, he disappeared around the end garage.... [H]is shadow showed on the concrete, unmoving and waiting" (198–99). N. has the idea that she "should bravely walk down to the end and look around the corner and confront this lurker, maybe our murderer rendered harmless by daylight" (199), but then she hesitates:

> I had the idea, too, that if I confronted this quiet shadow, rounded the corner and our eyes would meet at last...then nobody would be there; he would vanish, it would prove to be a post or bush casting that shadow, and as long as I did not look at it, it was the murderer. (199)

The immateriality of this shadowy stalker is his most notable feature. N. understands that the agency of her persecution is "not exactly" a single individual, but that it is nonetheless helpful to think of him in these terms, even if she is only being "nominalistic."

Rennie understands her own violation in a similar fashion.

> Rennie is dreaming about the man with the rope, again, again. He is the only man who is with her now, he's followed her, he was here all along, he was waiting for her. Sometimes she thinks it's Jake, climbing in the window with a stocking over his face, for fun, as he once did; sometimes she thinks it's Daniel, that's why he has a knife. But it's not either of them, it's not Paul, it's not anyone she's ever seen before. The face keeps changing, eluding her, he might as well be invisible, she can't see him, this is what is so terrifying, he isn't really there, *he's only a*

shadow, anonymous, familiar, with silver eyes that twin and reflect her own. (287, emphasis added)

Again, the immaterial and generic nature of the persecutor is precisely what makes him "so terrifying." But another element is added, as well: this shadowy agency of violence is more explicitly rendered as a paranoid double, with features that "twin and reflect" Rennie's. That is, Rennie cannot imagine this shadowy agent to be clearly external *or* immanent to her. The essential conflict in paranoia—the uncertain demarcation of the subject—is a way of understanding controlling technologies, practices, and ideas that are responsible for one's persecution and yet a vital part of one's identity.[22]

Neither the paranoid dynamic nor the immateriality of the persecutor in these descriptions should indicate that there are no external, material effects of such persecution. On the contrary, the material effects of male violence in these novels are profound. N. is raped at the end of *The Shadow Knows*. The fact that she cannot pin this violent act on any particular man, however, counters the idea that such acts are the work of individual psychopaths. If the sense of an individual stalker registers the deployment of concrete tactics against one, then his immateriality and anonymity indicate the social strategies that coordinate such tactics—in effect accounting for the statistical regularity and generic profile of individual acts of violence against women. And if such representations remain fraught with suspicion and uncertainty, that is because a "paranoid" methodology may be the best way to make visible the violence involved in the production of "normal" heterosexual relations.

4 Secret Agents

Was I immersing myself, little by little, in a secret life? Did I think it was my last defense against the ruin worked out for me so casually by the force or nonforce, the principle or power or chaos that determines such things? . . . I sat at my desk in the dark, thinking of secrets. Are secrets a tunnel to a dreamworld where you control events?

—Don DeLillo, *White Noise* (1985)

Control is the key word here . . . The male, by remaining "hermetic," "closed up," maintains the integrity of the boundary that divides him from the world. (It is fitting that in the Western the ultimate loss of that control takes place when one man puts holes in another man's body.)

—Jane Tompkins, *West of Everything* (1992)

Lone Gunman and Social Body

"In modern North American history," writes Fredric Jameson, "the assassination of John F. Kennedy . . . gave what we call a Utopian glimpse into some collective communicational 'festival' whose ultimate logic and promise is incompatible with our mode of production" (355). For Jameson, the promise of this "collective experience of reception" (355) is incompatible with capitalism because "the logic of capital is . . . a dispersive and atomistic, 'individualistic' one, an antisociety rather than a society" (343).[1] Yet if the mass-mediated experience of Kennedy's assassination was "collective," what the mainstream media actually mounted for collective inspection was the epitome of capitalist individualism: the antisocial, "lone gunman" in the tradition of the American Western—not only in the figure of Lee Oswald but also in that of Jack Ruby. The Warren Commission's official government account of the assassination did much the same, concluding that "Oswald acted alone" and that "to determine the motives for the assassination …one must look to the assassin himself" (President's Commission 42). Their utopian promise aside, in other words, official representations of Kennedy's murder have hardly been "incompatible with our mode of production" and its underlying concept of individual agency.

What may seem to be at odds with capitalist individualism, however, is the widespread popular resistance to such representations. Americans increasingly believe that Kennedy was the victim of a conspiracy, and the conspiracy they have in mind would seem to provide the radical alternative to individual action. It is usually massive in scale and almost always an embodiment of collective power—whether that of organized crime, communism, or U.S. intelligence. The fact that the Kennedy assassination is still, to borrow Norman Mailer's words, "our own largest American mystery" (*Oswald's* 353) indicates a deep popular reluctance to accept the insistently individualist explanations of the murder offered by the government and the mass media. If there is a form of utopian collectivism anywhere in this affair, it would seem to be here, in the conspiracy theorist's relentless willingness to use the crime to imagine the causal power of large social systems and organizations.

But this is not the whole story, for despite its sociological vision conspiracy theory is rarely without individualist impulses and is often an attempt to reconcile these competing perspectives. The question, then, is why has this event become the postwar source of conspiracy theory par excellence? How can we explain the ceaseless and voracious national interest in it, the incessant production of discourse about it? Why has it been the subject of two federal investigations of breathtaking scope; numerous smaller investigations by state, private, and federal agencies; several thousand essays, articles, and books; scores of novels, films, and plays; countless news stories; endless reenactments, debates, and television news specials?[2] There are many ways to answer these questions, some of which are familiar and do not need rehearsal here. The most obvious is that the case has never been satisfactorily "solved." All of the contradictions and uncanny coincidences in the mountain of evidence about it continue to invite speculation about a secret historical agent—whether it is some vast and shadowy network of individuals or merely another hidden dimension of that paradoxical figure, Lee Harvey Oswald.

But it is not merely the endless hermeneutic difficulties of the case—its conundrums of historical agency—that have sustained American interest in it. It is also that the case dramatizes a pressing question about causality and that it does so through a strikingly simple and consistent structure: a *competition between lone-gunman and grand conspiracy theories.* Public discourse about Kennedy's murder routinely revolves around this pair of starkly opposed possibilities, one tracing the murder to an "atomistic," and often irrational, individual agent, the other positing a highly organized and powerful collectivity.[3] This explanatory rivalry is not the only epistemological structure that might have developed from the ambiguities of the case, and thus it is important to ask why it did develop. What do its categories of debate indicate, and what interests do they serve? Before I attempt to answer these questions, I want to make two observations. First, this rivalry mirrors a disciplinary debate about whether to account for social actions through a psychology of individuals and individual pathologies or a sociology of systems. Second, the lone-gunman–conspiracy debate overlaps a familiar set of questions about whether individuals are able to "act alone" or are governed by larger networks of "corporate" intention.

Given these homologies, it should be clear that my intention here is not to attempt yet another resolution to the lone-gunman–conspiracy debate, but rather to describe the cultural function of the debate itself. What I would like to suggest is that this debate is, at a certain level, not a debate at all. It operates by keeping in circulation two *apparently* rival, but actually complementary, notions about the relation of persons to the social order. In doing so, it conserves a traditional conception of agency in the face of extraordinary evidence to the contrary.

In order to substantiate this claim, I need to show what autonomous gunman and conspiracy accounts of Kennedy's murder have in *common.* I want to begin by considering the doubts of those who originally championed the lone-gunman theory. Consider, for instance, this telling caveat in Harrison Salisbury's otherwise approving introduction to the 1964 pocket edition of the Warren Commission Report:

> Few Americans will feel that [the *Report of the Warren Commission*] is the final word. Not, I submit, because the evidence is not toweringly clear. But rather because there is in each of our hearts some feeling, however small, of responsibility; some feeling that each of us had some share in the crime because we had a role in a society which made it possible; which gave birth to a young man who by a long, dreary, painful path became distorted into an assassin. (Salisbury xxix)

Salisbury's reluctance to believe that Oswald is wholly to blame stems from a familiar problem of agency, a difficulty in squarely locating the origin of individual actions. If we should feel a "communal share of guilt" about the assassination, then the notion of atomistic individualism behind the Commission's lone-gunman theory may be *too* atomistic. Examined closely enough, in other words, the murderer's motives and actions appear to flow not just from "the assassin himself" but also from the social body that "gave birth" to him. In the strictest sense, Salisbury suggests, individuals never truly act alone. What is significant about this view is that Salisbury sees the alternative to his lone-gunman view as the most radical of options, a *wholly social* explanation. If Oswald cannot be blamed entirely, then "society" in general must be at fault. Like Milo Minderbinder's Syndicate in *Catch-22*, the Kennedy murder turns out for Salisbury to be an event in which *everyone* "has a share."

This moment of ambivalence in one correspondent's otherwise rousing defense of the Warren Report would be of little interest if it did not betray a conceptual problem of agency that is hard-wired into Kennedy assassination discourse. That problem becomes more clear when we juxtapose Salisbury's account to an apparent rival, such as Oliver Stone's *JFK*, the popular 1991 conspiracy film about the assassination. Stone's film, which is based on the much-criticized theories of New Orleans prosecutor Jim Garrison, insists that the Warren Report was part of a government cover-up and that the assassination was planned by a network of individuals at the highest levels of the military–industrial complex. Such a vast yet cohesive network is a typical feature of postwar conspiracy theories. Paradoxically, it possesses the *singularity* of will and coordinated action of a *single* individual. Its intentions are uniform; it never "leaks" information; and it functions with the coherence of a single body. In imagining the conspiracy this way, Stone assigns to a social system (the conspiratorial network) those qualities traditionally understood to epitomize individuals in a market economy.

There is thus an uncanny similarity between the dominant approaches to this notorious postwar event. If the Warren Commission's lone-gunman theory triggers guilt about the lone gunman being a patsy for the social, then grand conspiracy theories such as Stone's tend to conserve—albeit in a collective "body"—the classic attributes of the individual agent. While disagreeing over who (or what) counts as an agent, both assassination theories agree about the qualities an agent must possess. To be more specific, both accounts register a *desire for* but a *difficulty with* the notion of agency articulated by liberal individualism. While lone-gunman accounts tend to conserve this model at the level of the individual, conspiracy theory conserves it, paradoxically, at the level of the social.

In what follows I will be tracing some of the challenges the assassination poses to this model of individualism and agency, and I will be doing so primarily through Don DeLillo's novel *Libra* (1988), a text that offers an unusually sophisticated vision of Kennedy's murder. *Libra*'s strength is that it interlaces two narratives, one of Oswald's development from boy to assassin, the other of a complex, ever-changing conspiracy against the President, developed on the fringes of the CIA. The two narratives unfold simultaneously, in alternating chapters, until both stories converge in the attempt on the President's life. This structure replicates the explanatory rivalry I have been describing. In doing so, it dramatizes both the cultural appeal and the inadequacy of possessive individualism. The rugged male individuals of *Libra* are perpetually anxious—or paranoid—about their capacity for autonomous action, afraid that they might be inhabited or controlled by cultural determinants. In response to these fears, they attempt to seal themselves off from social controls or to confirm their autonomy through violence. Before delving into this subject, however, I must first indicate how the hermeneutical difficulties of the case are connected to the questions of agency I have been sketching thus far.

Archaeological Details

The Kennedy assassination is often said to mark a loss of innocence for America. It has been repeatedly associated with a decline in public confidence in the U.S. government. In the words of *Libra*'s narrator, it was "the seven seconds that broke the back of the American century" (181). This sense of trauma stems from many factors, but one of the most important has been the inability of the federal judicial system, deployed massively in the investigation of this single crime, to produce evidence that would align motives and acts, causes and effects, in a convincing way. Above all, the official investigation into Kennedy's death produced a crisis of knowledge—a crisis epitomizing the condition of knowledge and history in postmodernity because it turns on an unbridgeable gap between historical events and historical narrative. If the Warren Commission told a story that, according to Anthony Lewis, "often achieves a genuine literary style" (xxxiii), it still could not convince many Americans that it had accurately represented historical events. The massiveness of the official investigation itself, the very scope of the inquiry, its willingness to "answer, specifically, every...theory and rumor" (Lewis xxxii), indicates an uncertainty, or even paranoia, about how far causality might extend—about how to separate a single incident from the unwritten mass history of everyday life. The "almost archeological detail" of the Commission's investigation (Lewis xxxii),

the 26,550 interviews and re-interviews conducted by the FBI and Secret
Service, the 30,000 pages of reports submitted to the Commission, the encyclopedic twenty-six volumes of Commission testimony (President's
Commission 8), and the four million pages of documentary evidence still to
be released by the government (Kurtz lvi)—all of these things constitute a
body of evidence that begins to resemble the story of the social body in
general, something remarkably diffuse and scattered, yet interconnected
through the violent destruction of that other "social body," the President. In
short, the investigation itself registers the same misgivings that Salisbury
and others express about the "social origins" of the murder.

This is the crisis of historical agency in which *Libra*'s Nicholas
Branch finds himself. Branch is a retired CIA analyst who has contracted
to write the Agency's "secret history" of the assassination and is thus a figure
representing some of DeLillo's own difficulties reconstructing the event.
Branch has been working on his history for fifteen years as of
1988, but "the truth is he hasn't written all that much" because "it is impossible to stop assembling data. The stuff keeps coming" (59). What prevents
him from writing his history is not simply the proliferation of "evidence"
but also a growing uncertainty about what counts as evidence—and
thus, about what might count as a cause. Though the assassination itself
lasted only seven seconds, the investigation seems to endorse the idea that
innumerable occurrences and persons might have determined those seven
seconds.

> Branch has unpublished state documents, polygraph reports, Dictabelt record-
> ings from the police radio net on November 22. He has photo enhancements,
> floor plans, home movies, biographies, bibliographies, letters, rumors, mirages,
> dreams… Everything is here. Baptismal records, report cards, postcards, divorce
> petitions, canceled checks, daily timesheets, tax returns, property lists, post-
> operative x-rays, photos of knotted string, thousands of pages of testimony…
> Documents. There is Jack Ruby's mother's dental chart, dated January 15,
> 1938. There is a microphotograph of three strands of Lee H. Oswald's pubic hair.
> (181)

Any narrative that could place all of this documentary material in a
causal relation to the murder would either be incomprehensibly vast, or
paranoid, or both. Branch knows this. He is "writing a history, not a study
of the ways in which people succumb to paranoia" (57), yet he cannot dismiss the potentially paranoid notion that there is a hidden connection
between all the evidence. "He wants to believe [Oswald's] hair belongs
in the record," for instance (182). Like a true paranoid, he suspects that

"Everything belongs, everything adheres...It is all one thing..." (182). Yet, because he cannot identify the logic that connects the evidence, he cannot decide whether it contains important clues or is simply worthless "trivia" (182).

Branch thus finds himself in an epistemological crisis of the sort Didion describes in "The White Album." Wanting to mine the evidence for the hitherto hidden key to the case, yet overwhelmed by the sheer volume and ordinariness of the data, he is unable to produce his history. His problem is not just that he cannot "solve" the mystery once and for all, but that the production and management of documents overrides the interpretive impulse that justifies gathering those documents in the first place. The CIA's anonymous curator continually sends Branch the results of ballistics tests conducted on "human skulls and goat carcasses, on blocks of gelatin mixed with horsemeat," on cadavers, and on a "gelatin-tissue model 'dressed' like the President" (299). Branch feels that the CIA is "saying in effect, 'Here, look, these are the true images. This is your history....'" (299). If this is so, then the "true images" of the event are no longer images of the President or his potential assassins, but of wounded bodies in general. And what these images document is not simply the death of the nation's leader, or the culpability of various suspects, but *the immensity of the investigation itself.* The ceaseless collection of historical "evidence" has begun to simulate the event which it is supposed to document—thus unsettling the relation between evidence and event, representation and referent. "The notes are becoming an end in themselves. Branch has decided it is premature to make a serious effort to turn these notes into coherent history. Maybe it will always be premature. Because the data keeps coming.... The past is changing as he writes" (301). The question haunting Branch is what constitutes a coherent history. Should the historian interpret documents or merely collect and manage them?

To put this dilemma in more general terms, Branch is caught between traditional historiography and what Michel Foucault has called "archaeology." The most immediate difference between these two forms of historiography is their "position in relation to the document" (*Archeology* 6). Traditionally, Foucault explains, documents were transparent indices of past events, tools of a history whose fundamental goal was "the reconstitution, on the basis of what the documents say, and sometimes merely hint at, of the past from which they emanate" (6). But more recently, he claims, history has become archeological, focused not on the "secret origin" (25) to which documents might refer (i.e., historical events) but on documents themselves:

The document, then, is no longer for history an inert material through which it tries to reconstitute what men have done or said, the events of which only the trace remains; history is now trying to define within the documentary material itself unities, totalities, series, relations.... In our time, history is that which transforms *documents* into *monuments*. (7)

Branch is forever poised between these two methods, wanting to write his history but consumed by the organizing of documents—the archaeological work "in which society recognizes and develops a mass of documentation with which it is inextricably linked" (*Archaeology* 7). If "all historical narratives contain an irreducible and inexpungeable element of interpretation" (51), as Hayden White suggests, then the archaeological method is diametrically opposed to traditional historiography. Archaeology "is not an interpretive discipline: it does not seek another, better-hidden discourse. It refuses to be 'allegorical'" (Foucault, *Archaeology* 139). Likewise, it refuses to posit "secret," unlocatable origins and to view individual intentions as the causes of historical actions. It abandons the "sovereignty of consciousness," the notion that everything "formulated in discourse was already articulated in that semi-silence that precedes it" (*Archaeology* 12, 25). Above all, archaeology refuses to seek causes beyond what is immediately tangible or visible.

This is an interesting methodological boundary because the "reflex of seeking other orders behind the visible," as the narrator of *Gravity's Rainbow* reminds us, is "also known as paranoia" (Pynchon 188). This interpretive reflex is what Branch alternately embraces and resists as he hesitates between traditional history and archaeology.[4] "There is no need, he thinks, to invent the grand and masterful scheme, the plot that reaches flawlessly in a dozen directions" (*Libra* 58). On the other hand, he wonders how he can "forget the contradictions and discrepancies" (300), the connections, plots, or schemes that seem to lie just beyond the all-too-visible evidence. As he analyzes the violent deaths of relevant witnesses and agents, he looks for "patterns and links" then finds himself doubting them as "cheap coincidences." Ultimately, the narrator tells us, "He wants a thing to be what it is" (379). This is a strange, and telling, desire. While expressing a wish for clarity, it also indicates a distrust of the tangible—a potentially paranoid sense that hidden motives or causes lie just beyond what things seem to be. Yet it is significant that Branch does not merely wish things to be what they *seem*; he wants things to be *what they are*—a tautological formulation that both acknowledges and disavows his own paranoid sense that "things" (i.e., pieces of evidence) are always signifying a hidden historical truth.

"Paranoid thinking," writes Leo Bersani, "hesitates between the suspicion that the truth is wholly obscured by the visible, and the equally disturbing sense that the truth may be a sinister, invisible design *in* the visible" (102). This formulation is helpful in mapping Branch's thinking, which hesitates between the idea that the evidence is utterly misleading—masking a secret, historical agent—and the idea that the evidence reveals this secret agent, but that some new form of vision or disciplinary understanding is required to see it. I have substituted the word "agent" for Bersani's "truth" because I want to return to the initial terms of this chapter by indicating how Bersani's distinction might depend on the way a historical agent is imagined. In traditional historiography, says Foucault,

> the historical description of things said is shot through with the opposition of interior and exterior; and wholly directed by a desire to move from the exterior ... towards the essential nucleus of interiority.... Thus the nucleus of the initiating subjectivity is freed. A subjectivity that always lags behind manifest history; and which finds, beneath events, another, more serious, more secret, more fundamental history, closer to the origin, more firmly linked to its ultimate horizon (and consequently more in control of all its determinations). (*Archaeology* 120–21)

A traditional, "interpretive" history, in other words, has an investment in the idea of an initiating subject, an agent that *originally* and *ultimately* determines events. While this agent may be "an individual subject," or "some kind of collective consciousness," or even "a transcendental subjectivity" (122), it is conceived on the model of *individual subject*—and, more exactly, on the model of the liberal subject. Archaeology, by contrast, does not hope to write "the history of an individual or anonymous consciousness, of a project, of a system of intentions, of a set of aims" (122).

We may thus distinguish between traditional history and archaeology—and between Branch's rival impulses—on the basis of their conceptions of historical agency. It is important to note, however, that Foucault's later work qualifies the archaeological project by conceding that "there is no power that is exercised *without* a series of aims and objectives" (*History* 95, emphasis added). Foucault goes to great lengths to remind us that such aims are *not* merely articulated by individuals or even by groups with some clear "headquarters" (95). But even though he wishes to write "without reference to a cogito" or "a systems of intentions" (*Archaeology* 122), he is unable to dispense with the rhetoric of intentionality when describing the operations of a socially dispersed power. This is a telling shift, one that both makes Branch's ambivalence more understandable and suggests how difficult it is to create a *narrative* of historical events without a language of human agency. I will return to this dilemma later. For the moment, however, it does not greatly diminish the distinction I have been setting out: while traditional interpretive historiography attempts to locate an ultimate cause in a central subject or "headquarters," archaeology finds causality dispersed in a "network" (*History* 95) of institutions, discourses, and laws beyond the intentional control of any individual or group.

It would appear on initial inspection, then, that in the case of Kennedy's murder these historiographical differences mirror the differences between lone-gunman and conspiracy theories—the lone-gunman theory depending on an individual agent of history, and conspiracy theory allowing for a network of actors. Yet this is not quite the case. First, conspiracy theory routinely moves beyond visible evidence to posit a hidden cause. Second, while popular conspiracy theories do attempt to theorize dispersed forms of social power, they also tend to invoke the account of agency that Foucault so vigorously resists: they posit a set of intentions that can be traced to a clearly located "headquarters."[5] As the narrator of *Libra* explains:

> If we are on the outside, we assume a conspiracy is the perfect working of a scheme. Silent nameless men with unadorned hearts. A conspiracy is everything that ordinary life is not. It's the inside game, cold, sure, undistracted, forever closed off to us. We are the flawed ones, the innocents, trying to make some rough sense of the daily jostle. Conspirators have a logic and a daring beyond our reach. All conspiracies are the same taut story of men who find coherence in some criminal act. (*Libra* 440)

Libra's General Edwin Walker espouses a florid theory of this sort. He believes that important national events are determined by the "Real Control Apparatus," a network of powerful men "we can't see or name," men who "know each other by secret signs" and "work in the shadows to control our lives" (283). The "Apparatus," as Walker imagines it, "paralyze[s] ... our individual lives, frustrating every normal American ambition, infiltrating our minds" and controlling our actions (282). Like other examples of "the paranoid style," this one suggests that individuals are less than agents, that human action is governed by a higher, collective power (the Real Control Apparatus). For Walker, this determining "apparatus" (whose acronym, RCA, seems more than coincidental) is not visible in the communicational fabric of American society, but is hidden *behind* it. It is a "plot we can't uncover" (283), a coherent organization with clear intentions and a "headquarters" that could be found *if* only we knew where to look.

In the case of the Kennedy assassination, it is important to see that such theories develop not only from attempts to explain who killed the president but also from a desire to *theorize social controls* more generally. Consider, for instance, the view of conspiracy outlined by suspected conspirator David Ferrie in *Flying into Love* (1992), D. M. Thomas's fictional account of the assassination:

> There are two kinds of conspiracy, he reflects. There's the kind that is kept to just two or three reliable people; it appears to be impenetrable; but if someone finds just one clue the whole thing unravels. The other kind involves dozens of people, most of whom don't know each other and don't know *of* each other. They know only the small part they've been asked to play. The whole thing is messy, there seem to be innumerable clues; but almost all of them turn out to be red herrings, and they simply draw people deeper into a maze that has no exit. This conspiracy is of that kind. (17)

Here, Thomas develops an opposition between centralized and decentralized conspiracies. The latter model, which is said to describe the Kennedy case, seems designed to explain how the causes of an event could be socially dispersed. The "conspirators" in this sort of scheme would never "breathe together," the literal meaning of "conspire," but would instead play only the small, prearranged parts they have been "asked" to play. But the problem is: asked *by whom*? If these "conspirators" have been enlisted by some more secret agent, then this model of conspiracy is no different from the first; it merely consists of a more centralized "inner circle" of conspirators within a larger network of unwitting actors.

If, on the other hand, no central conspirator or group is directing all of the actors (that is, if even the *plotters* "don't know *of* each other"), then this second theory describes the operation of a social system. After all, a social system is a network in which separate actors "play parts" that, through no centralized intention or planning, produce all kinds of *apparently* intentional effects. Ferrie's mistake, then, lies in his appeal to conspiracy theory instead of social theory—the latter of which would explain the production of social patterns through an analysis of communications, institutional forces, and ideological constraints and *without* recourse to a monolithic actor, set of intentions, or "headquarters." To call such patterns the results of "a conspiracy" is to employ the wrong explanatory metaphor.

This form of misapprehension, which I will call the *theory of social conspiracy*, can be recognized by way of its central contradiction. While it attempts to theorize broad sociological effects and sweeping systemic operations, it nonetheless posits an invisible headquarters, "center of operations," or mysterious "higher power" that plans, manages, and brings such effects to fruition. This theory has been widely marketed to U.S. audiences in films and television programs and, due to the influence of the Kennedy affair, has been particularly influential in postwar assassination films. Prominent post-Kennedy assassination films such as *JFK*; *Seven Days in May* (Frankenheimer, 1964); *Winter Kills* (Richert, 1979); *The Parallax View* (Pakula, 1974); and *Blow Out* (De Palma, 1981) all depend upon this quasi-supernatural view of conspiracy. Of the films preceding Kennedy's murder, interestingly enough, most posit traditional conspiracies, where a few individuals plot murder for fairly clear reasons. Only Frankenheimer's *Manchurian Candidate* (1962) suggests the same terrible conspiratorial scope and power found in later films—and it does so largely because it traces a political assassination to communist infiltration and "thought-control." Its central villain is the apparently all-American wife of U.S. Senator and vice-presidential candidate Johnny Iselin (who is modeled on Joseph McCarthy). As the film eventually reveals, however, Mrs. Iselin is a communist agent plotting to assassinate the presidential candidate and control the White House through her ineffectual husband. She thus seems to be the center of a traditional conspiracy. Yet, like other agents in the genre of social conspiracy, she is only effective because she is backed by an invisible network of "silent, nameless men." It is this larger network that has brainwashed her son, turning him from a rugged war hero into a robotic, "other-directed" assassin.

The model of "social conspiracy" encourages the form of historical inquiry Foucault describes as traditional: it is "shot through with the opposition of interior and exterior" and is certain that a "secret... nucleus of interiority" (*Archaeology* 120–21), or "inside game," will make "rough sense" of historical events. It also assumes a "coherence" between individuals so taut that they act as if they were one person. In the case of Stone's *JFK*, for instance, a network of business interests, military brass, and intelligence agents murders Kennedy with clear motives in mind: they want to stop the downsizing of the military by involving America in the Vietnam War. This sort of "grand and masterful scheme" (*Libra* 58) is a kind of "master narrative," the disappearance of which is often said to be a defining mark of the postmodern. It is a totalizing explanation, an account that *theorizes a social system* (the closed system of the institution or conspiracy) but that does so *on a model of the possessive individual*, a subject whose clearly conceived intentions wholly determine its subsequent actions. Stone's massive conspiracy, for instance, depends not only upon informational relays between many separate persons but on the seamless coherence of those relays and the strict separation of inner from outer, such that information never "leaks" out of the system's "body." The theory of social conspiracy thus recuperates the "decentered" subject in a sense, assigning to the collective agency of the conspiracy the supposedly lost qualities of the individual: self-presence, individual unity, autonomy, and a protected "interior" as the site of identity. It operates through the rhetoric of postmodern transference.

Branch implicitly distrusts this sort of theory. "He has learned enough about the days and months preceding November 22," the narrator tells us, "to reach a determination that the conspiracy against the President was a rambling affair that succeeded in the short term due mainly to chance" (441). As I will demonstrate later, this rather humdrum view of the assassination is supported by the plot of *Libra* as a whole, which suggests that, despite a conspiracy, no one individual, agency, or system controls all of the events in the case. This is not the whole story, however. Branch cannot accept this view without entertaining serious reservations because he cannot dispense with the idea that intentions (strategies, aims, objectives) lie behind all historical developments. He is not in bad company in this regard; I have already noted a similar tension in Foucault's work. But while Foucault's recuperation of intentions is a rhetorical strategy at work in a *structural* view of causality, Branch's reservations take the form of intermittent panic about a monolithic historical actor. Immediately after his confident assertion of a "chance"-based solution to the case, Branch reviews the "worrisome omissions" in the record, and before long he is entertaining his recurrent suspicion that the CIA is "mocking him" (299), that "someone is trying to sway him toward superstition" (379), that they are "withholding material from him" (442), that there is "something they aren't telling him" (442). In these moments, the CIA becomes Branch's version of Pynchon's "Them"—a shadowy corporate agent with its own intentions and vast powers of control. He wonders, for instance, "if the Agency is protecting something very much like its identity—protecting its own truth, its theology of secrets" (442). As his panic increases, a grand conspiracy does not seem so far-fetched: he "has a theory," for instance, "about the Oswald doubles who were active for almost two months" (377). Finally, he tends to attribute agency to social structures such as the CIA, while simultaneously imagining humans as puppets of a larger agent: "To Nicholas Branch, more frequently of late, 'Lee H. Oswald' seems a technical diagram, part of some exercise in the secret manipulation of history" (377). Such suspicions may be inevitable given Branch's historiographical dilemma. But what is significant about them is their connection to an intentionalist view of social systems. Indeed, Branch's agency panic is a testament to the remarkable appeal of liberalism in theorizing complex social and institutional effects—an appeal all the more remarkable in that Branch himself clearly recognizes its inadequacy.

A Cardboard Cutout

I have been tracing interpretive dynamics in which the appearance of coincidence or pattern induces a sense of anxiety about the determining power of social systems or agencies. But how does this dynamic function in *Libra* as a whole? There are plenty of coincidences and doublings in *Libra*, odd repetitions, uncanny reappearances, moments of déjà vu. Moreover, the narrative structure of the novel operates on a principle of coincidence and doubling. It balances a narrative of the individual assassin, Oswald, with a narrative of conspiracy. The ingenuity of this design is its replication of the agency crisis I have been discussing. The novel's dual narratives prevent readers from knowing whether Oswald's motives for shooting at the President are "his own" or whether they are "constructed" by the conspirators. By intertwining lone-gunman and conspiracy plots, and refusing to identify either as the sole "cause" of the assassination, DeLillo is able to explore how individual action is influenced by social formations—one of the overriding concerns in his fiction.[6]

Before the conspirators know anything about Oswald, they build their plot upon an *imaginary* assassin, creating masses of fake documents— newspaper clippings, purchase orders, telephone calls—all in order to "put someone together, build an identity, a skein of persuasion and habit, ever so subtle...a man with believable quirks" (78). The rich interior of this handmade assassin, according to his creator, Win Everett, is to be revealed in a slew of false documents that will "show the secret symmetries in a nondescript life" (78) and convey a sense of "lingering mystery...a purpose and a destiny" (147). When the conspirators discover Oswald, he is more like their imaginary character than they can believe. As Dave Ferrie tells Oswald, "Lee Oswald matches the cardboard cutout they've been shaping all along. You're a quirk of history. You're a coincidence. They devise a plan, you fit it perfectly. They lose you, here you are. There's a pattern in things" (*Libra* 330). One of the questions such a coincidence raises is whether Oswald is indeed a "cardboard cutout," someone whose most definitive actions have been scripted, or programmed, in advance—not simply by a group of conspirators but by "a society...which gave birth to...an assassin" (Salisbury xxix). As I suggested earlier, this question structures much thinking about the assassination. It is also one of the questions that recent cultural criticism has taken most seriously—continually positing the subject's external construction in response to earlier notions of transcendent, autonomous subjectivity.

It is no accident, then, that the same question haunts DeLillo's Lee Harvey Oswald. Oswald continually senses that he is "a zero in the system" (106). He often believes that powerful "historical forces" are arranging his life—causing uncanny coincidences, making sure he gets secret messages from radio and television, even controlling his actions. Of course, these beliefs are true in a rather mundane sense. "Coded messages," for instance, bombard us through radio and television in the form of advertisements. But Oswald does not understand such hidden messages to be directed at whole populations; rather, he believes they emanate from a unified, intentional subject and are directed *at him personally*. He is like the "public agent" of William S. Burroughs who declares, "I . . . don't know who I work for, get my instructions from street signs, newspapers and pieces of conversation" (*Soft Machine* 31). When a pair of movies about assassinations comes on television, Oswald understands them as "secret instructions entering the network of signals and broadcast bands" (370). "They were running a message through the night into his skin," he believes; "They were running this thing just for him" (370).

Similar views have been central to some of postwar America's wackiest conspiracy theories. Lincoln Lawrence's *Were We Controlled?* (1967), for instance, argues that an implant in Oswald's head, triggered by posthypnotic suggestions, caused him to kill the President. In *Assassination by Consensus* (1966) William Smith hypothesizes that a mastermind influenced Oswald through "psychic displacement"—a view reiterated in William Bowert's *Operation Mind Control* (1977). In the context of such bizarre theories, the occasional speculations of DeLillo's Oswald seem almost commonplace. And in a sense they *are* rather commonplace. One of the reasons Oswald, like so many Americans, can view mass communications as the products of a unified and controlling subject is that he sees agency as a *property* that is assigned, in an all-or-nothing manner, to himself or to "society" conceived as a totality. His "paranoia" about control is only an extension of the popular belief that social messages (advertisements, movies, television shows) issue from a monolithic force, from which one should struggle to free oneself.

Oswald's *extreme* commitment to this view—which is best evidenced in his desire to resist social controls—leads him into repeated, often violent, attempts to test his own agency. The point of these efforts, he reminds himself, is to show that "they didn't own or control him" (336), that it is "strangely easy to have a say over men and events" (163). Before making his attempt on the life of General Edwin Walker, for example, Oswald attends a rally and smiles at Walker while gripping a .38 revolver in his pocket, "just to do it, to get this close and show how simple, how strangely easy it is to make your existence felt" (373). In such moments, Oswald construes antisocial violence as an antidote to his agency problem. By killing the well-known General Walker, Oswald could show that he is not historically inconsequential.

This familiar form of masculine agency recovery is one of DeLillo's obsessions. "Violence is a form of rebirth," says Murray Siskind in DeLillo's *White Noise* (290), virtually quoting Richard Slotkin's classic description of masculine self-making as "regeneration through violence." A Lebanese terrorist in *Mao II* (1991) understands violence similarly as a way to gain "self-respect" and "identity" when one's own self-determination seems to be in question: "terror is what we use to give our people their place in the world. What used to be achieved through work, we gain through terror" (235). Not coincidentally, human labor is what guarantees autonomy in the theory of possessive individualism. The striking replacement of work by terror in this passage, then, begins to reveal how a fierce commitment to individual autonomy—the opposition of self to "society"—may lie behind violent, masculinist "solutions" to the threat of social control. This is certainly the case in the so-called "Unabomber manifesto," whose version of violent resistance to "oversocialization" (F.C. 25) and "the COLLECTIVE power of industrial society" (198) is rooted in a celebration of rugged individualism and "wild nature" (183). While such violence can be an effective form of resistance to a dominant political order, it is misguided when directed at the social order *in general*. Oswald's desire to make his existence felt, for instance, leads him to shoot at *both* arch-conservative Edwin Walker *and* the considerably more liberal Jack Kennedy—a pair of acts incomprehensible unless one presumes that collectivity itself, even in the form of political affiliation, is a danger.[7]

In his account of serial killers, Mark Seltzer observes that "maladies of agency and pathologies of will or motive" are often connected to "what might be called an addiction to self-making or self-transformation" ("Serial Killers" 97). Like outbursts of violence, in other words, attempts to remake oneself may stem from anxieties about agency. For Oswald, remaking, like murder itself, seems to offer a solution to the problem of social control. Even as Win Everett is "putting together a man with scissors and tape" (145), Oswald is constructing and reconstructing himself. He perpetually shifts his alliances and reconstructs his own motives—as if to preempt their external construction. Part of his fantasy in defecting to Russia, for example, is that "he could almost believe he was being remade on the spot" (113). In Russia, a KGB agent decides whether to have Oswald "rebuilt so to speak, given a new identity," but Oswald attempts to ward off this form of construction by imagining himself to be "a real defector posing as a false defector posing as a real defector" (162). In this dizzying account of his own identity, Oswald understands his own motives to be diametrically opposed. The logic here is reminiscent of Heller's Yossarian. By avoiding alignment with *any* collective set of strategies (such as national motives), Oswald hopes to remain a free agent. But rather than guaranteeing his freedom, this attempt to resist control only seems to *undo* his identity, making his actions self-canceling and thus irrelevant.

A similar unraveling of identity occurs in each of Oswald's attempts to establish an identity free of external control—and it occurs because his panic impels him to resist identification with *any* collective organization or action. Once back in New Orleans, for instance, Oswald distributes pamphlets for his "Fair Play for Cuba Committee." Before long, however, he turns FBI informant and attempts to infiltrate an anti-Cuban group by posing as a Castro-*hater* who is infiltrating local *pro*-Castro organizations. "The charm of the thing," says the FBI agent, is "you can carry on your [pro-Castro] politics in the open" (311). That is, Oswald can simultaneously do the following: (1) openly campaign for Cuba; (2) betray Cuban sympathizers to an anti-Castro group; and (3) provide the FBI with information that will hurt the same anti-Castro group. "It goes round and round," says Oswald (311). It goes round and round because the arrangement is a miniature economy, a circuit of exchanges in which Oswald is a conduit channeling information to both sides but providing neither with a real advantage. The paradox of his attempt to resist collective identification—and thereby to avoid being "controlled" by others—is that Oswald really does become "a zero in the system," a mere "relay" whose actions are self-canceling. As anti-Castro organizer Guy Bannister puts it, Oswald "has his work, we have ours. It amounts to the same thing" (142). Bannister's description is telling because it focuses on the output of the *system* of exchanges, discounting individual motive and action. Ironically, the notion that a system produces more significant actions than the individuals who constitute it is what fuels Oswald's panic and what he attempts to resist by becoming a "double agent."

Oswald's most revealing form of resistance to external controls is his attempt to write his own history. Because he wants to imagine himself instrumental in "something vast and sweeping" (41), but dislikes the feeling of "being swept up, swept along" (322), he begins to establish a historical record of himself, "a collection of documents" (235): news clippings, government reports, original writings and photographs, even his FBI informant number. He collects these things "just to have for the record, to build up the record" (232). The most famous is the photograph of himself wearing a pistol and holding a rifle, something which, the narrator suggests, carries him "into the frame of official memory" (279). As Roland Barthes suggests, a photograph "is authentication itself" (*Camera Lucida* 87)—a historical marker, a monument to one's historical presence. Of course, this is not always the case in the universe of conspiracy, where photographs sometimes authenticate the fictions of those who dare to rewrite history for their own political reasons. In Stone's version of the story, for instance, the photograph in question is a falsification intended to frame Oswald. *Libra*, however, offers a more complex vision in which Oswald is constructed as a patsy, but also constructs himself as the rugged individual agent of history. His monumentalization of himself in documents is a kind of archaeology before the event—an attempt to compete with those other secret historical agents who, he suspects, could easily have "superimposed his head on someone else's body. Forged his names on documents. Made him a dupe of history" (418). For Oswald, then, the work of historical self-construction is part of the endless business of beating social determinants to the punch, writing history before it writes you.

The reason these efforts are endless, perpetually failing to convince Oswald of his autonomy, is *not* that DeLillo makes him a social construct, in the crude sense of that term. On the contrary, as I have shown, Oswald is highly autonomous from one point of view. The reason he is sometimes seen as an "effect" or "production" of the social order is that his relentless self-reconstruction leaves him with no "core" of stable motives, beliefs, or commitments.[8] Oswald's problem lies in his overcommitment to an ideology in which selfhood is guaranteed *only* by the possession of an impenetrable and unique interior. This hyperatomistic version of the possessive individual is guaranteed to fail because it requires one to possess what Eve Kosofsky Sedgwick calls "*pure* voluntary"—a will purified of *all* potential determinations ("Epidemics" 586). As Sedgwick demonstrates, human volition will always seem "insufficiently pure" if one believes it possible to avoid social determinants altogether; in fact, she argues, given such an impossible ideal, even assertions of the will begin to resemble socially scripted behaviors (584). Yet this impossible ideal is precisely what drives Oswald. Forever nervous about the way social pressures seem to control him, he "purifies" his interior until there is little left to purify. Agency panic spurs his endless undoing.

The Secrets of the Masses

"Happiness," the real Lee Harvey Oswald wrote in his "Historic Diary," "is not based on oneself, it does not consist of a small home, of taking and getting. Happiness is taking part in the struggle, where there is no borderline between one's own personal world, and the world in general" (President's Commission 368). DeLillo uses this statement as the epigraph for part I of *Libra*. But his own Oswald is not always so sanguine about the effects of collective identity. Oswald's occasional fantasies of mass struggle and "historical action" are fraught with anxiety about the erosion of his own individuality and usually elicit a longing for privacy, secrecy, or individual integrity. He expresses this desire by repeatedly assuring himself, "There is a world inside the world" (13). This mantra becomes his way of redrawing the borderline between his "personal world" and the "world in general"—the borderline the Diary statement calls into question. It imagines a boundary that protects his inner self, "the true life inside him... his leverage, his only control" (46). This fantasy of self-enclosure concisely evokes the major tenets of possessive individualism, in which individuals are defined in opposition to "the world in general," are constituted by economic exchanges ("taking and getting"), and are individuated by what they "possess" in a protected interior. The Diary statement, on the other hand, privileges the collective and public over the private. Taken together, Oswald's contradictory desires indicate his uncertainty about how to guarantee his status as a meaningful social actor without compromising the fantasy of a self-contained reservoir of desires, difference, and self-control—a masculine fantasy epitomized in *Libra* by the keeping of secrets.

More specifically, Oswald's frequent invocation of a private "world"— his need for "a secret name" (47), his sense that "nobody knew what he knew" (46)—represents an attempt to stop up the leakiness of his person, to separate what is "his" from what is external or social. As the young Lee Oswald's social worker notes, Lee "feels almost as if there is a veil between him and other people... but he prefers this veil to remain intact" (12). One of the things Lee is hiding behind his veil is a "secret" engagement with Marxist literature. Although he checks this material out of the public library and renews it frequently, he believes "the books themselves were secret. Forbidden and hard to read" (41). His own unimportance seems "transformed" by these secret texts, so that he is part of "something vast and sweeping...a sweeping history" (41). "The books," he believes, "made him part of something. Something led up to his presence in this room, in this particular skin, and something would follow" (41). Significantly, Lee's interest in Marxism lies less in its revolutionary possibilities than in its promise to explain his own determination (the reasons he is "in this room," "in this particular skin"). Likewise, Oswald is less interested in mobilizing a revolutionary proletariat class than in being the heroic individual agent of history. Thus, he indulges in vague fantasies of heroic action, of nights "struggling with secret and feverish ideas," developing "a secret name," and moving "through the city in the rain, wearing dark clothes" (41). Critical to such fantasies is his view that secrecy is an antidote to social determination. Though the books tell him he is "locked into a process, a system of money and property that diminished [his] human worth every day" (41), their secret status seems to promise his liberation. "The books were private," he believes, "like something you find and hide, some lucky piece *that contains the secret of who you are*" (41, emphasis added). This odd notion that a library book is "private" or that the "secret" of one's identity might reside in a document that is mass-produced—for the masses, about the masses, only consumed in private—is akin to Oswald's paranoid suspicion that some television broadcasts carry "secret instructions" to him (370). Both ideas involve a misrecognition of generic, social (indeed, socialist) messages for private communications and sources of individual identity. Typical of Oswald's engagement with Marxism, this misunderstanding stems from a form of individualism in which secrets form a last barrier of defense against social influences.

This masculinist view of selfhood—which dreads any "penetration" of the self by a "domesticating" social order—compels all of *Libra's* male agents to equate secrecy with autonomy and self-control. "Do you know what [Kennedy's] charisma means to me?" asks Guy Bannister. "It means he holds the secrets.... Strip the man of his powerful secrets. Take his secrets and he's nothing" (68). Many of *Libra's* characters view the CIA, that "theology of secrets" (442), as an agent in its own right. As Win Everett remarks, "Secrets build their own networks" (22). The association of secrets with agency explains why so many of *Libra's* agents use false names; retaining their true identity in secret is emblematic of the traditional "masculine reserve" and "hermetic" self-enclosure that epitomizes "male integrity" (Schwenger 43–45). Consider, for instance, the terms in which Win Everett worries about his daughter Suzanne. He asks himself, "Don't secrets sustain her, keep her separate, make her self-aware? How can she know who she is if she gives away her secrets?" (26) This odd speculation—that one could lose self-knowledge by "giving away" one's secrets—articulates the deepest and most illogical assumption of possessive individualism. It implies that selfhood is a form of physical property. As such it must be zealously guarded, for if exposed to society, it may be lost forever.

The limitations of this view become clear later in the novel when Everett's wife, Mary Frances, worries that Suzanne is becoming *too* self-enclosed ("so preoccupied lately, so *inner*" [222]). What Suzanne is doing in secret, Mary Frances knows, is listening to "Weird Beard," a Dallas disc jockey whose cryptic pronouncements are meant to encourage individual resistance to social controls:

> You're out there in the depths of the night, listening in secret, and the reason you're listening in secret is because you don't know who to trust except me. We're the only ones who aren't them. This narrow little radio band is a route to the troot.... We need this little private alley where we can meet. Because this is Big D, which stands for Don't be Dissimilar.... We're the sneaky little secret they're trying to uncover.... Weird Beard says, Eat your cereal with a fork. Do your homework in the dark. And trust your radio before you trust your mother. (266)

The notion that the airwaves are "a private alley" involves a striking failure to see what Jameson calls "the collective experience of reception" (355). Yet this failure is what allows Weird Beard's listeners to imagine themselves as nonconformists. Most of *Libra*'s characters make this mistake. Even Oswald's KGB contact suggests that "The masses need radios so they won't be masses anymore" (197), as if the private experience of reception somehow transformsed mass communications into private communications and sources of individuality. Likewise, Weird Beard suggests that individual autonomy lies in individual difference—resistance to the social conformity of Dallas ("Big D, which stands for Don't be Dissimilar"). But his instructions on how to be different ("Eat your cereal with a fork") are a *mass* communication. Only because they are received in private do they seem to be secret—and hence individual rather than generic.

DeLillo repeatedly demonstrates that, in modern consumer culture, our most "private" individual qualities, our deepest "secrets," may be no more individual than the "individual wrap" we require on our consumer products.[9] *Libra*'s Beryl Parmenter, for instance, believes that "no message she could send a friend was more intimate and telling than a story in the paper about a violent act" (261). For her, as for so many of DeLillo's characters, the violent act carries with it an aura of uniqueness and intimacy—so much so that it seems a "private alley" of communication despite being rendered in the mass medium of the newspaper. DeLillo insistently presents such contradictions in order to undermine the view that violence is a form of resistance to social controls. Even at their most violent, for instance, the rugged male individuals in *Libra*'s CIA conspiracy reenact classic roles from popular scripts. Wayne Elko models himself after the characters in *The Seven Samurai* ("In which *men outside society* are called on to save a helpless people from destruction" [178, emphasis added]). Guy Bannister frequently reminisces over his participation in the shooting of John Dillinger at the Biograph, where *Manhattan Melodrama* was playing. The weekend before the assassination Oswald watches two films about attempted presidential assassinations, *Suddenly* and *We Were Strangers*. He is arrested while viewing *War is Hell* and avoids being shot by Wayne Elko only because Elko wants to coordinate the killing with a climax on screen. These conjunctions make clear that while the rugged male individualism and "inner reserve" of the lone gunman in the tradition of the Western appear to embody individual agency, they are themselves generic formulations, perpetually recirculated in popular narratives.

Ultimately, DeLillo suggests, the spectacular violence that so regularly punctuates American public life represents a last-ditch effort to conserve a fantasy of pure opposition to the influences of mass culture. "After Oswald," thinks Branch,

> men in America are no longer required to lead lives of quiet desperation. You apply for a credit card, buy a handgun, travel through cities, suburbs and shopping malls, anonymous, anonymous, looking for a chance to take a shot at the first puffy empty famous face, just to let people know there is someone out there who reads the papers. (181)

The underlying argument here has become somewhat commonplace. It suggests that when individuals see the mass media as a powerful agent and themselves as "zeros in the system"—not visible in the circuit of powerful images—they may resolve their dilemma by killing someone, thus "recovering" the scarce commodity of their agency and seeing the confirmation of that recovery when they appear on the nightly news.[10] Yet the passage also makes a telling reference to Thoreau's famous pronouncement in *Walden* that "the mass of men lead lives of quiet desperation" (7). This allusion suggests that a pure opposition between self and society—the guiding ethos of Thoreau's experiment in self-reliance—*still* governs the desire to "run 'amok' against society" (or, as Thoreau preferred, to let it "run 'amok' against me" [155]). Unlike the narrator of *Libra*, however, Thoreau never said that the mass of men were *required* to "lead lives of quiet desperation." They might instead have followed his program for distinguishing socially implanted desires from the "gross necessaries of life" (10)—thereby moving toward a condition of "*pure* voluntarity" (Sedgwick, "Epidemics" 586). And they might have followed this program by retreating to the atomistic privacy of a cabin in the woods or by going to that other antisocial locale in *Walden*—the jail.

These solutions are part of what appeal to figures like the Unabomber—America's newest cabin-dwelling advocate of civil disobedience. They also appeal to the secret agents of *Libra*. Above all, Nicholas Branch observes, these violent individuals are "men in small rooms" (181)—what Jameson calls the dispersed, "atomistic" subjects of late capitalism. Their antisocial behavior hardly amounts to a triumph of Thoreauvian self-reliance. It is rather an index of anxiety about the very possibility of self-reliance, a final effort to conserve this supposedly endangered ideology in the face of ubiquitous and seemingly omnipotent mass-communication and control systems. According to the Unabomber's manifesto, for example, some individuals "have gone so far as to rebel against one of modern society's most important principles by engaging in physical violence. By their own account, violence is for them a form of 'liberation.' In other words, by committing violence they break through the psychological restraints that have been trained into them" (F.C. 30). The slogan for this view might read: "say 'no' to power; say 'yes' to violence." But the problem with such a view, as DeLillo's work makes clear, is that the model of liberation through violence *is itself* a generic, mass-mediated construction. "Killing in America," remarks the narrator of *The Names* (1982), is "the logical extension of the consumer fantasy.... Pure image" (115). Just like contemporary market exchanges (the traditional guarantee of selfhood in possessive individualism), murder offers a fantasy of autonomy that is ultimately no more original or "liberated" than any of the other social controls individuals fear "have been trained into them."

Central Intelligence

One conspicuous response to agency panic, I have been suggesting, is a violent attempt to conserve individual identity and volition. It is important to see how this response is connected to the secondary component of agency panic—the belief that a social entity or a network of communication may itself be an agent, "a collective actor," as Jameson puts it, "virtually a human being in its own right" (347). What unites these components is a powerful desire to understand control as the property of a central intelligence, a clearly bounded locus that directs the actions of more peripheral agents. This desire has been powerful not only in social theory but also in theories of human consciousness, where the philosopher Daniel Dennett has called it "Cartesian materialism" (*Consciousness Explained* 107). From the perspective of a Cartesian materialist, the "brain is Headquarters, the place where the ultimate observer is" (106). Yet, in a statement that echoes Foucault's view of social power, Dennett explains, "there is no reason to believe that the brain itself has any deeper headquarters, any inner sanctum, arrival at which is the necessary or sufficient condition for conscious experience. In short, there is no observer inside the brain" (*Consciousness Explained* 106).

Agency panic may be understood as variation of Cartesian materialism: it cannot dispense with the notion of *centralized* control. Thus, in response to evidence that human behavior is not controlled entirely from within, it simply transfers the site of control to an external, "social" headquarters. Consider, for instance, the form agency panic takes in DeLillo's *The Names*—the story of a cult that murders arbitrarily chosen victims so that its members can test their capacity for unconditioned action. In the throes of anxiety about his own autonomy, one cult member remarks, "For thousands of years...the world was where we lived, the self was where we went mad and died. But now the world has made a self of its own. Why, how, never mind. What happens to us now that the world has a self?" (297). The answer to this question depends upon what one means by "self"—whether it is merely a way of describing the sum of myriad individual actions or a global, unified "subject" with its own motives and identity.

The latter view is crucial to the theory of "social conspiracy." The popularity of this theory helps to explain why secretive organizations—particularly the Central Intelligence Agency—have become such powerful symbols of the social order. As Norman Mailer recently put it, "Of all government bureaucracies, the CIA probably bears the greatest resemblance to an organism" (*Oswald's* 480). DeLillo's nervous CIA agents view the CIA as a monolithic, humanoid entity. They speak of its "identity" (442), motives, and divine power. Win Everett describes its information-gathering technologies this way:

> These systems collect and process. All the secret knowledge of the world....I'll tell you what it means, these orbiting sensors that can hear us in our beds. It means the end of loyalty. The more complex the systems, the less conviction in

people. Conviction will be drained out of us. Devices will drain us, make us vague and pliant. (77)

This passage typifies the logic of agency panic. It suggests that large intelligence-gathering systems not only threaten to drain humans of loyalty, conviction, and individual will but also acquire that which most guarantees personhood in the theory of possessive individualism—secrets.

Yet DeLillo's account of the CIA and the conspiracy against Kennedy does not embrace such melodramatic views. In large measure, this is because DeLillo details the operation of a large intelligence system, showing how institutional constraints might influence individual decisions without possessing something like subjectivity themselves. Early on in *Libra* he describes the command structure of a typical CIA operation. Fourteen high-ranking officials, including presidential advisors, meet; after an hour and half, eleven of them leave and six new agents enter; two hours later, seven leave and four enter; later still, five leave and three enter. This hierarchy is not designed in the interests of efficiency, as is a corporate pyramid. Rather, fourteen "executives" give general guidance to four "workers," whose activities are a secret to their superiors. This inverted pyramid structure ensures that the Agency will not do the will of any one person and that no single individual has control of or even knowledge of the entire structure. This is especially true of those we might expect to be in charge:

> The DCI, the Director of Central Intelligence, was not to know important things. The less he knew, the more decisively he could function. It would impair his ability to tell the truth at an inquiry or a hearing, or in an Oval Office chat with the President, if he knew what they were doing in Leader 4 [a lower level anti-Castro task group]....The Joint Chiefs were not to know....The White House was to be the summit of unknowing. (21–22)

This bureaucracy is not rationalized so as to place ultimate control of the organization in the hands of its leader. Instead, the very name of the low-level planning group—"Leader 4"—suggests the serial replication and dispersal of leadership functions in this organization.

In other words, there is no center to DeLillo's Central Intelligence. Unlike most popular conspiracy theories, DeLillo's story suggests that the plot against Kennedy develops because the CIA has no central command and control. Its operatives design their own national policy and make sure their superiors are "insulated from knowing" it (21). This CIA, although called "The Company" by its agents, does not consist of "organization men" who sacrifice their individuality for a corporate will; it consists rather of renegades and free agents who are regularly subcontracted and often act on their own. While the sum of these acts may appear to reflect an intention of the Agency, there is in fact a *lack* of collective will among those who plot Kennedy's murder in *Libra*. The original plan of conspirator Win Everett is to shoot at but *miss* Kennedy, thus shocking the nation into renewed fear of Cuban communism. Once he gives the operational details of his plot to a subgroup, however, they convert the mock-assassination into a real attempt on the President's life. Everett's paranoia compels him to see this change as the result of a secret motive force ("Plots carry their own logic. There is a tendency of plots to move toward death" [221]). But DeLillo's story does not endorse such a reading. He rejects the theory of "social conspiracy" for a more systemic, Foucauldian view of power in which there is no monolithic center or "headquarters" governing the system.

Ultimately, the latter view of power makes it illogical to kill the President—if by killing him one imagines government will be dramatically altered. As a character in Kathy Acker's *Empire of the Senseless* explains, "killing someone, anyone, like Reagan or the top IBM executive board members, whoever they are, can't accomplish anything" (83). In Foucault's view, likewise, power is no longer centralized and prohibitory—emblematized by the monarch's power to cut off heads—but is instead dispersed, institutional, and discursive. Yet, he claims, we have not come to terms with this shift in power: "we still have not cut off the head of the king" (*History* 88–89). There is no better example of this failure than *Libra*'s Mafia boss, Carmine Latta, who believes, "You cut off the head, the tail doesn't wag" (174). This is a "sentimental view of power," observes Frank Lentricchia, a return to "a world whose fortunes are inseparable from the fortunes of such powerful individuals" (204).[11] Yet this individualist view of power is as popular with DeLillo's characters (including Kennedy himself, who obsessively plots the destruction of Castro) as it is with conspiracy buffs such as Oliver Stone, whose allusions to *Julius Caesar* attempt to reinvigorate the Kennedy Camelot myth and to remind us that, in Kennedy's murder, we "lost a king." Indeed, it is no accident that Stone's movie offers *both* a reductive, social conspiracy theory *and* a transcendental, "great man" notion of political power, for, as I have been suggesting all along, these two views are opposite sides of the same coin.

Libra, by contrast, advances a more complex and less nervous story of conspiracy. It does not endorse the fantasy of social conspiracy theory and its monolithic historical agent. Nor, on the other hand, does it offer the stripped-down narrative of the ultimate individual, the lone (and possibly lunatic) gunman. It renounces these neat, but reductive, accounts of causality for the less thrilling possibility that actions may *not* be governed by *"pure voluntarity,"* an all-or-nothing portioning of agency, that they may instead be governed by a web of motives, exchanges, decisions, ideologies, and habits, all of which are influenced by the structure of social systems. This resolution may be less comforting than one that depends on the purely self-possessed individuals of market capitalism or the purely constructed subjects of postmodernism. *Libra* powerfully suggests, however, that such accounts grossly oversimplify the causal origins of complex events. They hinge upon a fantasy of individual autonomy that blinds us to the influence of social systems on our behavior. And, in the end, they may not be just reductive, but dangerous.

5 The Logic of Addiction

The panic of the alcoholic who has hit bottom is the panic of the man who thought he had control over a vehicle but suddenly finds that the vehicle can run away with him. Suddenly, pressure on what he knows is the brake seems to make the vehicle go faster. It is the panic of discovering that *it* (the system, self *plus* vehicle) is bigger than he is... He has bankrupted the epistemology of "self-control."

Gregory Bateson, "The Cybernetics of 'Self'" (1972)

Bad Habits

"Addiction," remarked social psychologist Stanton Peele in 1975, "is not, as we like to think, an aberration from our way of life. Addiction is our way of life" (*Love and Addiction* 182). By all accounts, this view has gained remarkable popularity in America. Not only are estimates of traditional substance abuse significantly higher, despite declining narcotic and alcohol consumption, but treatment is being mandated for, and sought by, dramatically larger numbers of Americans. More significantly, medical institutions have adopted increasingly flexible definitions of addiction, creating vast numbers of new addicts and whole new categories of addiction.[1] The most striking feature of America's general discourse on addiction, in other words, is just how general it has become: Americans now account for all sorts of ordinary human behavior through the concept of addiction.

In part, this impulse stems from the work of addiction specialists such as Peele, whose *Love and Addiction* advanced the thesis that "addiction is not a special reaction to a drug, but a primary and universal form of motivation" and that "there are addictive... ways of doing anything" (48, 59).[2] The increasing popularity of this view would be unremarkable if it signaled merely a growing belief that the compulsion to repeat certain behaviors is a normal human tendency, rather than a sign of disease. But many Americans seem to have adopted Peele's thesis while also retaining the idea that *any* habit, drive, or compulsion indicates a lack of self-control so dangerous it merits medical attention. In his encyclopedic story of America's addiction to addictions, *Infinite Jest* (1996), David Foster Wallace catalogues some of these "exotic new" maladies. At a rehab center, his narrator explains, one learns:

> That sleeping can be a form of emotional escape and can with sustained effort be abused... That purposeful sleep-deprivation can also be an abusable escape. That gambling can be an abusable escape, too, and work, shopping, and shoplifting, and sex, and abstention, and masturbation, and food, and exercise, and meditation/prayer.... That most Substance-addicted people are also addicted to thinking, meaning they have a compulsive and unhealthy relationship with their own thinking.... That it is possible to abuse OTC cold and allergy remedies in an addictive manner.... That anonymous generosity, too, can be abused. (200–05)

The bizarre logic of this view—the contradictory sense that addiction is utterly normal *and* dangerously pathological—explains why so many Americans now claim to be addicted to behaviors that once epitomized individual autonomy. As Eve Kosofsky Sedgwick has suggested, the relatively new illnesses known as "exercise addiction," "workaholism," "shopaholism," "sexual compulsiveness," and "codependency" or "relationship addiction" all stem from a sense of insufficient free will. "Under the searching rays of this new addiction-attribution," she observes, "the assertion of will itself has come to appear addictive" ("Epidemics" 584).[3] Paradoxically, the compulsion to sort addictions from freely willed acts increasingly erodes the distinction between those terms; this erosion, meanwhile, feeds the frenzy to separate will and compulsion once and for all. In other words, the national tendency toward addiction-attribution stems from what I have been calling agency panic.

The question, then, is not just how to account for the growth of addiction as an explanatory concept in America, but how to account for the more pervasive anxieties about agency and personhood that encourage its growth. To begin, it is worth observing that basic human activities such as shopping, sex, and work can only appear to be unwanted "addictions" if one makes several assumptions about persons. First, one must believe individuals *ought to be* rational, motivated agents in full control of themselves. This assumption in turn entails a strict metaphysics of inside and outside; that is, the self must be a clearly bounded entity, with an *interior* core of unique beliefs, memories, and desires easily distinguished from the *external* influences and controls that are presumed to be the sources of addiction. Finally, one must view control as an indivisible property, something that is possessed either by the individual or by external influences. Only in the context of these assumptions can *any* less than perfectly willed behavior seem to be the product of dangerous external controls. It is the continuing popularity of these assumptions that has encouraged Americans to view drugs, in the words of one observer, as "a power deemed capable of tempting, possessing, corrupting, and destroying persons without regard to the prior conduct or condition of those persons—a power which has *all-or-none effects*" (Blum 327, emphasis added). Addiction discourse, like other postwar discourses of agency, is governed by a refusal to abandon the assumptions of possessive individualism, despite an anxious sense that they fail to explain the unsettling compulsions that seem to be turning us into a nation of addicts. Indeed, the matter can be put more pointedly. The apparent existence of multifarious, powerful addictive threats shores up and revivifies the embattled national fantasy of individual autonomy.

One of the most telling pieces of evidence for this thesis is the degree to which addiction has come to be seen as a national epidemic of depleted self-control. Americans, Peele observes in *Diseasing of America* (1989), "seem to feel that they are more out of control of their lives than they have felt in the past.... The addiction industry expresses the sense of loss of control we have developed as a society" (232–33). *Diseasing of America* rails against the growth of the "addiction treatment industry" and its disease-based conception of addiction, yet ironically it was Peele's earlier hypothesis ("anything can be addictive") that helped to legitimate the growth of an addiction culture. After all, *Love and Addiction* argues that we live in an "addicted society" and that "our vulnerability to addiction" is a direct result of our "transition to the modern age" (151). This assertion, with its subsequent focus on "lost...internal self-assurance" (151), virtually repeats David Riesman's narrative of the fall from rugged individualism (or "inner-direction") to postindustrial uniformity (or "other-direction"). And addiction literature is not the only source of anxieties about the American tendency toward addiction, for addiction has epitomized waning individuality in an array of cultural criticism. It is instructive to see, for instance, how readily the Unabomber's narrative of dwindling human autonomy—itself a recapitulation of popular critiques of "postindustrial society"—invokes models of addiction to account for the dangers of technological rationality:[4]

Imagine an alcoholic sitting with a barrel of wine in front of him. Suppose he starts saying to himself, "Wine isn't bad for you if used in moderation. Why, they say small amounts of wine are even good for you! It won't do me any harm if I take just one little drink…" Well you know what is going to happen. Never forget that the human race with technology is just like an alcoholic with a barrel of wine. (F.C. 203)

Such warnings help to explain the all-or-nothing logic that leads the author to recommend a regimen of *total abstinence* from advanced technology—a remedy that, in his view, would require a strict diet of masculinist self-reliance, a return to the individualist frontier, and (of course) "regeneration through violence."

It would be possible to cite any number of links between addiction and more pervasive anxieties about agency, but I want to focus my attention on the postwar American writer whose work most obsessively draws such connections—William S. Burroughs. Burroughs not only writes about his lifelong preoccupation with drug addiction, but he uses the concept of addiction to represent other postindustrial conspiracies against human agency and uniqueness. The characters of his fiction are usually addicted to junk, but as early as *Naked Lunch* (1959) they are also addicted to commodities, images, words, human contact, and even control itself. They are also the subjects of sadistic forms of mass control, Pavlovian conditioning, and medical or psychological torture. In short, their existence represents a terminal case of agency-in-crisis.[5] While these characters and scenes have often been read as representations or products of an intoxicated imagination, I will show that they have widespread cultural roots. Indeed, some of the most bizarre control scenarios in Burroughs are taken, virtually unmodified, from more sober and popular nonfiction texts. My intention in these pages, then, is not so much to illuminate Burroughs himself as to unravel the mystery of a highly individualist culture that believes itself beset by threats to individual autonomy.

I want to begin this task by examining the problems of subjectivity created by Burroughs's disease-based model of addiction—his view of addiction as "virus." According to this model, addictive substances are agents powerful enough to erode human subjectivity. Not only do they exhaust the addict's will, but they become "characters" of a sort, part of a phantasmagorical landscape where it is difficult to tell one person from another and even harder to tell persons from nonpersons. The fluid and uncertain subjects of these scenes are often labeled "schizophrenic" and "postmodern," but they are a direct result of attempts to conserve a traditional model of individualism. Burroughs's nervousness about the erosion of individual autonomy stems from the same contradictions that have produced the contemporary culture of addiction: only by assuming that individuals should owe *nothing* to the "outside" for their actions and identity can Burroughs sustain a panic-stricken vision of the individual as a total addict and the world as a hostile place full of controlling agents.

Control Addicts

In the preface to *Naked Lunch*, Burroughs claims that his novel is a study of the "junk virus" (vi)—though it is never quite clear whether this term refers to addictive drugs themselves or the larger drug economy in which they move. A 1957 letter to Allen Ginsberg explains further that the "Real theme of the novel is Desecration of the Human Image by the control addicts who are putting out the...addicting virus" (*Letters* 365). Neither of these remarks gives an accurate description of *Naked Lunch*, but both hint at the anxiety about agency that runs through it. First, Burroughs views junk less as an inert *commodity* (something that must be bought and consumed by active agents) than as a parasitic *organism* (something that invades and controls the bodies of unwitting individuals). Second, while he imagines a worldwide conspiracy producing the junk virus, he views the conspirators themselves as "control *addicts.*" This tautological concept—the "control addict"—embodies precisely the tendency identified by Sedgwick, in which assertions of will or control are understood as addictions. But it extends the general implications of that tendency even further. The more radical idea of an *addiction to control itself* liquidates the concept of control altogether—at least insofar as control is a property of human beings.

For Burroughs, this line of thinking leads to a series of novels in which ideas of control are absolutely central and, at the same time, utterly vexed. In 1955, he explained to Ginsberg that in the "vast Kafkian conspiracies" of *Naked Lunch*, "agents continually infiltrate to work on other side [sic]...; more accurately, agents rarely know which side they are working on" (*Letters* 269).[6] If the first part of this explanation gives the impression of conspirators who are rational, motivated individuals, the second part contradicts that impression by portraying them as pawns in a larger, more obscure plot. This reversal reopens the questions of control that the remark seemed designed to resolve: who governs and controls the conspiracies afoot, and who or what counts as an agent? In a text where the very *conspirators* are unaware of the plots they conspire to carry out, something has gone haywire in the idea of personhood. It is in *this* sense that *Naked Lunch* is about "the desecration of the Human Image." The novel's addicts and "agents" alike are all under the sway of powerful external controls, and individuals who cannot control themselves are not persons—at least not in the discourse of possessive individualism.[7]

Junk, on the other hand, *is* something like a person in Burroughs's work. One reason junk addiction is dehumanizing, for example, is that in the junk-junkie relationship only junk retains human attributes. The addict, says Burroughs, "needs more and more junk to maintain a human form" (vi)—as if junk were an injection of humanity itself. "Junk is the ideal product," he adds, because "the junk merchant does not sell his product to the consumer, he sells the consumer to his product" (vii). This passage relies on the same reversal of human agency found in Marx's discussion of commodity fetishism: junk merchants are instruments of their powerful commodity, and junkies are merely objects to be sold.[8] As long as a product "is a value in use, there is nothing mysterious about it," says Marx. "But, so soon as it steps forth as a commodity, it is changed into something transcendent....it stands on its head, and evolves out of its wooden brain grotesque ideas..." (81–82). In Burroughs's junk economy, junk takes on human qualities for two reasons: first, because it "steps forth" into something like pure exchange-value—it is "quantitative and accurately measurable...like money" (vii); and second, because while it has no *productive* use (it is *junk*), its use-value to the addicted consumer is infinite. It is "the mold of monopoly and possession," says Burroughs, because it reduces the body to a single and "*total need*," which "knows absolutely *no limit or control*" (vii, emphasis added). In Burroughs's world, junk produces a terminal capitalist subject, a "grotesque" consumer whose needs and desires have all been replaced by one simple but overpowering bodily need. As the narrator of *Junky* (1953) puts it, "Life telescopes down to junk, one fix and looking forward to the next" (22).

Burroughs represents the telescoping effect of junk in shocking, bodily terms. His addicts literally have "grotesque" bodies and "wooden brains"—body parts that have mutated so as to do nothing but detect and consume junk. Willy the Disk, for instance, has "a round, disk mouth lined with sensitive, erectile black hairs. He is blind from shooting in the eyeball, his nose and palate eaten away sniffing H, his body a mass of scar tissue hard and dry as wood." Willy "only functions at night" when his "blind, seeking mouth" leads him anywhere there is junk (7). Not all of Burroughs's junkies are so fantastically embodied, but almost all have a modified natural body. They have "undreaming insect eyes" (58), "black insect laughter" (51), and bizarre, nonhuman organs specially suited for sensing what Burroughs calls the "silent frequency of junk" (7). They are forever extruding "rancid ectoplasm" (19) and undifferentiated cellular material in biologically primitive attempts at consumption.

Why does Burroughs represent the addict in this way? As I have already suggested, within the discourse of possessive individualism, addicts do not meet the criteria for personhood because they are not wholly autonomous, rational agents. In representing the addict, Burroughs merely literalizes this notion. Not only do his addicts' desires telescope down to the solitary desire for junk, but their bodies follow suit. As William Lee, the sometimes narrator of *Naked Lunch*, puts it, "The addict regards his body impersonally as an instrument to absorb the medium in which he lives" (67). This view of the body as a technology for finding and consuming junk helps account for Burroughs's phantasmagorical representations of addicts as limited insectoid creatures with special sensory organs for detecting junk. "You know how old people lose all shame about eating…?" asks Lee. "Old junkies are the same about junk… all their guts grind in peristalsis while they cook up, dissolving the body's decent skin, you expect any moment a great blob of protoplasm will flop right out and surround the junk" (5). This final suggestion is not just a figure of speech; in Burroughs's bodily economy of addiction, junkies *do* extrude protoplasm because they *are* simpler lifeforms—usually single-celled organisms and insects. Junk, in other words, makes the *human* body unnecessary—except as an increasingly efficient (and grotesque) tool for locating junk.

To be more precise, junk consumption generates a dynamic of embodiment and disembodiment in Burroughs. Grotesque embodiment only occurs when junkies become sober and desire more junk. When high, by contrast, the addict is virtually disembodied and utterly lacking in desire. As Burroughs explains, the intoxicated junky is a "terminal" subject, with "metabolism approaching absolute ZERO" (*Naked Lunch* xiv) and "flesh that fades at the first silent touch of junk" (8). Again, Burroughs renders these notions bodily. Lee, for instance, lives in "varying degrees of transparency" (71) and (like Burroughs himself) becomes known in Tangier as "The Invisible Man." On a three-day high, his flesh becomes "so soft that he [is] cut to the bone by dust particles" (70). Like other junkies, he often has an "anonymous, grey and spectral" (15) look about him. When he shoots heroin into a friend's arm, the friend's "misshapen overcoat of flesh" turns "colorless in the morning light" and falls "off in globs onto the floor" (70). If this bodily matter resembles the "ectoplasm" so often extruded by Burroughs's *sober*, junk-hungry addicts, that is precisely what it will become when the high wears off. Ectoplasm, of course, is not only undifferentiated cellular matter, but also the material residue of a ghost. And the *intoxicated* junkie is a quasi-immaterial, spectral subject—a ghost.

This strategy of literalization helps to explain the phantasmagoria of Burroughs's surreal junk universe. It also depicts, in a graphic way, the paradox of bodily control inherent to addiction. The addict, in Burroughs, is always taking junk to resist reembodiment and the problems it brings. When Lee senses his own impending incarnation, for instance, he shoots up again in order to "refuel the fires that burned through his yellow-pink-brown gelatinous substance and kept off the hovering flesh" (70). The reason Lee and others want to prevent the return of their "hovering flesh" is not that they don't want bodies. In fact, the opposite seems true. As one addict says, "I am a ghost wanting what every ghost wants—a body" (8). Yet the problem is that the body of the addicted junky can only return in an undesirable form, because (in Burroughs's bodily economy) addiction *means* possession of a grotesque and uncontrollable body. In the junk-starved addict, Lee observes, "viscera and cells, galvanized into a loathsome insect-like activity, seemed on the point of breaking through the surface" (*Junky* 58). Oddly enough, then, while junk creates the initial problem, junk is also the antidote to it. "The *pharmakon*" (drug, poison, magic charm), notes Jacques Derrida, "will always be understood both as antidote *and* as poison" ("Rhetoric" 7). For Burroughs, junk intoxication is the only way the junky can avoid hideous reembodiment.

Addiction thus emerges as a paradox of embodiment: addicts who wish to have a functional and controllable body must kick the junk habit yet, in going off junk, they find themselves imprisoned in a grotesque and uncontrollable body; they can only ward off this obscene instrument of consumption by staying high, yet staying high means surrendering the body to junk—which then intensifies the initial problem. The addict's dilemma, in other words, is whether to risk a struggle with his or her own body in order to regain control of it. Crucially, then, Burroughs's representation of the addict's dilemma presumes a Cartesian dualism in which the "self" or spirit remains the site of identity, while the body is external to the self—mere matter controlled from without. As Jean Cocteau puts it in *Opium: the Diary of a Cure* (1929), "It is not I who become addicted, it is my body" (73). In this view, addiction results in "smaller" subjects who are embattled, struggling against a controlling environment that includes even their own bodies. This is not the only way to theorize addiction, and thus its central feature is quite telling: it willingly splinters the subject to retain the idea that control is a property, parceled out *either* to oneself or to one's environment but never a mixture of the two.

The Junk Virus

If addiction offers a radical challenge to personhood—a challenge Burroughs envisions at the most basic, bodily level—this challenge is all the more severe given its pervasiveness. As is the case in contemporary America, narcotics are not the only kind of debilitating addiction in Burroughs's fiction. The junk economy operates because of a complex system of mutually reinforcing addictions. "Selling is more of a habit than using," admits one dealer. "Nonusing pushers have a contact habit, and that's one you can't kick. Agents get it too" (*Naked Lunch* 15). The narcotics agent in *Naked Lunch* who gets this "contact habit" is Bradley the Buyer. Bradley is famous for being the "best agent in the industry," but the better he gets the more he comes to look like a junky: "He can't drink. He can't get it up. His teeth fall out... The Buyer takes on an ominous grey-green color" (15). Before long, he assumes the familiar protoplasmic form of the addict and his unruly amoeba-like body engulfs the district supervisor of narcotics (18). Eventually, when he is caught "digesting the Narcotics Commissioner," a court rules that he has "lost his human citizenship" and condemns him for being "a creature without species" (18). Here again, Burroughs specifically represents the addict as a nonperson. Even more significant, however, is that "addiction" of Bradley's sort afflicts individuals at every level of the junk economy—including makers, sellers, and even law enforcement "agents."

This representation has a good deal in common with the concept of addiction currently popular in America. Bradley the Buyer, moreover, possesses a personal quality that more clearly reveals the implications of popular views of addiction. "Fact is," says the narrator, Bradley's "body is making its own junk or equivalent. The Buyer has a steady connection. A Man Within" (15). This notion—that Bradley is producing an addicting substance *within his own body*—calls into question the traditional notion of addiction, which suggests that an external substance has taken control of the subject. In order to understand Bradley's situation, we must resort to one of two alternative explanations. The first would require us to view his body as wholly external to (or separate from) his "self," the sort of Cartesian dualism I mentioned earlier. This solution would retain a traditional concept of addiction—the all-or-nothing logic that locates control either in the self or in a source outside the self—but it would do so only by redrawing the line between self and world so that the body is no longer considered a part of the self. The second explanation, on the other hand, would view the tendency toward addiction as *internal* to the subject. This explanation would jettison traditional notions of addiction, and in doing so would challenge liberal assumptions by viewing dependencies as an essential part of subjectivity. That Bradley's body produces an addicting substance, in other words, might only indicate that he is human—that, like all humans, he possesses the capacity for addiction. The fact that Bradley eventually loses his "human citizenship" indicates how reluctant Burroughs is to endorse this second solution.

The rivalry between these two ways of accounting for less-than-clearly-willed behavior has troubled many accounts of subjectivity. As Avital Ronell observes (45), addiction is one of the human tendencies most disruptive to Heidegger's ontology of Being. The problem with addiction, for Heidegger, is that it is neither clearly internal nor external to Being. On the one hand, it seems to transfer the essential qualities of Being to external sources. The addict, says Heidegger, is "'lived' by the world" (196). On the other hand, Heidegger concedes that addiction is internal to Being—so close in nature to other *essential* drives (like the urge to live) that it "is not to be rooted out" (196). This is precisely the problem that governs the contemporary rhetoric of addiction, which seeks endlessly to "root out" addictions—only to discover that they have grown, multiplied, changed shape, and taken root everywhere.

It is also the problem at work in Burroughs's fiction, which insistently represents addiction as *virus* and *parasite*, entities that can be viewed as both internal and external to the self. "Like any good parasite," remarks Derrida, the *pharmakon* "is at once inside and outside—the outside feeding on the inside. And with this model of feeding we are very close to what in the modern sense of the word we call drugs, which are usually to be 'consumed'" ("Rhetoric" 6). In fact, the problem I have been tracing here may be reformulated as a difficulty in conceptualizing parasitism. If one accepts the assumptions of liberal humanism, the parasite must be regarded as an external invader of an integral self. On the other hand, poststructuralist approaches—particularly deconstruction ("a discourse 'on parasite' and in the logic of the 'super-parasite'" [Derrida, "Rhetoric" 6])—have held that parasites occupy a complex position between inside and out, neither wholly supplementary nor essential to the subject. In this view, technologies (including drugs) cannot simply be viewed as hostile invaders of a bounded self. The "natural, originary body does not exist," says Derrida, "technology has not simply added itself, from outside or after the fact, as a foreign body," but "is 'originarily' at work and in place in the supposedly ideal interiority of the 'body and soul'" ("Rhetoric" 15).

Burroughs frequently presents scenarios that demonstrate this view. A tape recorder, he once wrote, "is an externalized section of the human nervous system   you can find out more about the nervous system and gain more control over your reactions by using the tape recorder than you could find out sitting twenty years in the lotus posture..." ("Invisible Generation" 213). In moments like this, Burroughs pressures traditional assumptions about the person in the most radical fashion imaginable. Yet he often does so in the mode of *panic*—and thus tends to romanticize a traditional view of the individual, a fantasy of the autonomous self isolated from *any* threat of external invasion or control. Much like the disease model of addiction, his writing presents junk as a "possessing" demon, a destructive "evil virus" with extraordinary powers of control (*Naked Lunch* vii). And, as I have already suggested, junk is not the only such danger for Burroughs. Indeed, it will be easier for me to demonstrate the exceptional nature of his anxieties about control by focusing on his attitude toward a technology that few contemporary Americans would view as a danger—writing.

Like Derrida, Burroughs explicitly views writing as an "organism" (Derrida, "Plato's" 79) and a *pharmakon*—a technology that supplements human memory. Yet Derrida and Burroughs understand the implications of this view differently. Derrida's account of the druglike quality of writing comes in his analysis of Plato's *Phaedrus*. In Plato's text, writing is presented to the king as a way of extending the human capacity to remember events. The king, however, rejects this offering on the grounds that writing will act as a "drug" of sorts, a technological supplement making human memory unnecessary. One of the many problems with the king's position, according to Derrida, is that it "implies that the living being is finite" and projects a fantasy in which the "perfection of a living being would consist in its having no relation at all with any outside" ("Plato's" 101). This fantasy—the dream of a self hermetically sealed from the external world—is central to the contemporary American logic of addiction. In fact, Derrida has recently connected it to both prohibitionist *and* liberationist rhetorics of drugs ("Rhetoric" 14–17). What is significant for our purposes, then, is the extreme way in which Burroughs embraces this view. Like Plato's king, he views writing and other forms of communication as dangerous supplements to human memory and self-control. "The word is now a virus," warns the narrator of *The Ticket That Exploded* (1967). "The word may once have been a healthy neural cell. It is now a parasitic organism that invades and damages the central nervous system" (49). This panic-stricken account of control suggests that, like drugs, communications are enemies of the self. Like other postwar treatments of agency, this one has a historical component: while language was once a "healthy" part of our internal control system (a "neural cell"), it is now a threatening competitor, an alien presence that damages our capacity for self-control.

The most notable feature of this view is its melodramatic rendering of the idea that communications can influence human identity and action. No doubt, ideological effects can be disturbing when revealed, yet the *general* effectivity of messages, covert and overt, should hardly come as a surprise. Social relations would be impossible if communications did *not* influence human behavior. Indeed, communications can only seem dangerously parasitic if one has an exceptionally romantic ideal of selfhood—an expectation of radical human autonomy and a nostalgia for the days when messages were in harmony with the self, instead of bent on its destruction. As Derrida suggests, such a view mistakenly associates the "perfection of a living being" with an absolute isolation from "any outside."

This ideal, I will show, governs much of Burroughs's writing. And because it is made impossible by basic social activities, it continually leads to expressions of agency panic. How else, for instance, can we explain the famous "cut-up technique," the strategy of arbitrarily chopping up and reassembling written and spoken passages by which Burroughs sought to break the controlling power of "the word"? This method of resistance—which Burroughs developed into a full political program in his essay "The Invisible Generation" (1967)—presumes that any text (even one's own) can be a dangerous instrument of control. The point of using cut-ups is to reintroduce the accidental into what appears determined and determining, thereby short-circuiting the power of social messages.[9] When hearing a cut-up, Burroughs explains, it is "as if the words themselves had been interrogated and forced to reveal their hidden meanings" ("Invisible Generation" 206). Broadly employed, this technique could no doubt disable all kinds of external influences. Yet, if we follow the idea to its logical conclusion and keep in mind that all messages are suspect, it is clear that a successful program of cut-ups would effectively isolate the individual from communications and thus social relations in general. The cut-up promotes a form of hyperindividualism—a defense of atomistic selfhood against a "penetrating" and controlling social order. If the technique's fundamental exhortation—"everybody splice himself in with everybody else" ("Invisible Generation" 212)—seems to generate a fragmented, postmodern subjectivity, it does so only to defend the individual (and individualism itself) from social systems that humans have "no control over."[10] In this world of powerful control technologies, *everyone* is an addict, "lived by the world," because messages of any sort constitute mind-altering drugs that undermine the individual's self-control. The "subject," a doctor tells Lee, "is riddled with parasites" (*Soft Machine* 89). The goal for Burroughs is to exterminate them. "When it comes to bedbugs," writes the one-time exterminator, the "only thing is to fumigate" (*Exterminator!* 6).

Cellular Panic

Here, then, is the problem confronting Burroughs. When he attempts to understand addiction or control on the model of the parasite, he generates an uncontrollable proliferation of agency problems. His response to these problems is agency panic. Rather than accepting the less strictly bordered, and less rationally centered, subject implied by his own representations, he worries in hysterical terms about external invasion and control of the self. At the same time, he attributes agency to nonhuman entities and depletes it from humans until it is no longer clear who, or what, counts as an agent. The result is a view of the world in which subhuman components and large social organizations appear to behave like rational, motivated individuals, while human beings are merely "soft machines":

> The soft machine is the human body under constant siege from a vast hungry host of parasites...What Freud calls the "id" is a parasitic invasion of the hypothalamus...What Freud calls the "super ego" is probably a parasitic occupation of the mid-brain where the "rightness" centres may be located and by "rightness" I mean where "you" and "I" used to live before this "super ego" moved in...(Appendix, *Soft Machine*, 1968 ed., qtd. in Miles 120)

What might once have been considered components of the self are here regarded as independent agents, parasitic entities no longer integral to the subject. This view imagines something like the decentered, fragmented subject of postmodern theory, the vision of "deterritorialized" schizophrenic desiring machines advanced by Deleuze and Guattari. Yet Burroughs's view does not really do away with centered subjectivity. Rather, it leaves intact a smaller core of rationality (or "rightness") by way of what I earlier called a Cartesian splitting of the subject. Burroughs thus salvages a vestige of autonomous subjectivity, removing from it both that which is determined (the superego or conscience) and that which is irrational (the id).

But this view has a second effect: it populates the world with entities that once constituted the self but are now autonomous. In one sense, this newly spawned hoard of "parasites" presents a major challenge to individualism. Yet it also depends upon that concept because these entities themselves behave as if they were rational, autonomous, bounded individuals. Consider, for example, Burroughs's belief that "kicking a habit involves the death of junk-dependent cells and their replacement with cells that do not need junk" (*Junky* 23). In this "cellular equation," each cell of the body is imagined as a tiny addict or nonaddict, and addiction becomes a matter of "cellular decision" (*Junky* 151) and "cellular panic" (*Naked Lunch* 57). At the same time, the individual addict becomes a sort of social body, a miniature version of the junk economy. What might once have been called the addict's attributes—qualities like decision making and emotion (panic)—have been transferred to his or her component parts. Addiction thus occurs not at the level of the human being but at the level of the cells, which are themselves *miniature individuals*. This bizarre view epitomizes the logic of addiction, which has always personated the world with powerful substances (e.g., "the demon rum") while construing humans as powerless.

Because this view also has much in common with posthumanist models of the subject, it is important to see where Burroughs departs from posthumanism. Postmodern biology provides a good example of the latter because, as Donna Haraway has shown, it privileges "biotic components" over the traditional, integrated organism.[11] In the new biology, she explains, "what counts as a 'unit,' a one, is highly problematic, not a permanent given" because "single masterly control" of the biological organism has given way to a "postmodern pastiche of multiple centres and peripheries" ("Biopolitics" 212, 207). This conception of subjectivity is similar to what Deleuze and Guattari have called "the body without organs," a fantasy of subjectivity that resists the totalizing concept of the organism. It is also similar to recent views of the mind as a "society" of independent agents.[12] Like postmodern biology, these theories attribute traditionally human qualities to biotic components or "organ-machines": Deleuze and Guattari speak of intelligent blood cells and "the molecular unconscious" (*Anti-Oedipus* 283). As a result, their subject "is not at the center, which is occupied by the machine, but on the periphery, with no fixed identity, forever decentered" (20). Within such posthuman theories, "even the most reliable Western individuated bodies...neither stop nor start at the skin" (Haraway, "Biopolitics" 215), and "individuality is a strategic defence problem" (212).

When this postmodern view is coupled with a vestigial form of possessive individualism, the result is often agency panic. In Richard Dawkins's version of evolutionary theory, for instance, "selfish" genes are privileged over whole organisms, which Dawkins describes as "partially bounded local concentration[s]" (264) and "machines for the production of single-celled propagules" (254). Because the "parasite genes" (210) have their own "selfish" desires (e.g., they would " 'like' to reduce capital investment" in the total organism), Dawkins foresees an "evolutionary 'arms race' " (39). What is most striking about his theory is that its conservation of intentionality—albeit at the level of the gene—generates a rhetoric of invasion and self-defense, an anxious sense that the individual is under attack and needs protection. In Dawkins's scheme, Haraway notes, " 'We' can only aim for a defended self... Within 'us' is the most threatening other—the propagules, whose phenotype we, temporarily, are" ("Biopolitics" 217).

This is just the sort of biotic struggle Burroughs imagines. But we can now specify the conflict that animates it. On the one hand, Burroughs exhibits a radical, posthumanist tendency to question whether humans are self-governing agents. On the other hand, he exhibits a humanist refusal to modify the traditional model of the agent, which he applies to other, nonhuman entities. The result is a defensive—or paranoid—conception of the world as a place full of motivated, parasitic entities whose capacity to control individuals, should they gain entry, is total and complete. "I live," Burroughs admits, "with the constant threat of possession, and a constant need to escape from possession, from Control" (*Queer* xxii). In such a world, individuals are not responsible for their actions, which can always be traced to a larger entity. Thus, to explain the 1951 "accident" in which he put on a "William Tell act" with his wife and shot her in the head, killing her instantly, Burroughs claims he was possessed by an evil entity.[13]

> My concept of possession is closer to the medieval model than to modern psychological explanations, with their dogmatic insistence that such manifestations must come from within and never, never, never from without. (As if there were some clear-cut difference between inner and outer). I mean a definite possessing entity. And indeed, the psychological concept might well have been devised by the possessing entities, since nothing is more dangerous to a possessor than being seen as a separate invading creature by the host it has invaded. (*Queer* xix–xx)

In this passage, Burroughs suggests that the difference between the inside and outside of persons is not clear-cut, but then insists vigorously that he was subject to invasion and external control. It is no accident that this contradiction arises as he accounts for the act that epitomizes the misogyny running through his writings, because the very terms of the description are already gendered.[14] Nothing worries Burroughs so much as relinquishing an atomistic, masculinity for a more fluid, socially connected subjectivity. It is as if, once employed, the logic of parasitism becomes immediately intolerable and induces a state of panic in which *any* sign of diminished voluntarity seems to indicate a *complete* transfer of agency from self to social order.

Burroughs so needs to believe this transfer is real that he deems psychology itself a trick of the "possessing entities." Psychology, of course, has always taken the opposite route, deeming possessing entities a trick of the psyche. "When human beings began to think," writes Freud,

> they were, as is well known, forced to explain the external world anthropomorphically by means of a multitude of personalities in their own image; chance events, which they interpreted superstitiously, were thus actions and manifestations of persons. They behaved, therefore, just like paranoics, who draw conclusions from insignificant signs given them by other people...(*Psychopathology* 259)

On the surface, this account diametrically opposes the one offered by Burroughs. Freud explains compulsion and coincidence via the paranoid mechanism of *projection*, while Burroughs explains these events via the *introjection* of external agents. On a deeper level, however, these accounts are similar. Both posit a core of rational will that is subject to a determining agency. They disagree only about the location of that agency. As Freud puts it, anthropomorphism "*is nothing but psychology projected into the external world*" (258). And if Freud believes that there are no accidents in the unconscious, Burroughs believes that "there are no accidents in the junk world" (*Naked Lunch* x) and, more dramatically, that "there is no such thing as a coincidence" ("On Coincidence" 99).

Ultimately, however, Burroughs so radically projects psychology into the outer world that the world *in general* seems to possess a psyche—and a psyche whose most consistent quality is malice. He believes in magic, and magic, he says, "is the assertion of *will*, the assumption that nothing happens in this universe...unless some entity *wills* it to happen" ("On Coincidence" 101). He thus defends the "so-called primitive" tendency to blame *all* apparent accidents on a malicious agent (102). In his antipsychology, all events are motivated because the qualities of the subject (motive, desire, understanding) reside *everywhere*. This is the logic of postmodern transference writ large. "Take a walk around the block," Burroughs advises his writing students.

> Come back and write down precisely what happened with particular attention to what you were thinking when you noticed a street sign, a passing car or stranger or whatever caught your attention. You will observe that what you were

thinking just *before* you saw the sign relates to the sign. The sign may even complete a sentence in your mind. You are getting messages. Everything is talking to you. ("On Coincidence" 103–04)

If a sign can complete one's thoughts, and thinking is done only by persons, then the "person" having thoughts in the passage is not a human individual. It is a much larger communication system, extending well beyond the individual's borders. This radical conception of subjectivity, however, cannot last for long. Soon enough, it induces the familiar panic response ("the students become paranoid" [104]), which is a defensive attempt to consolidate the self by separating it from external "messages."

The pattern I have been describing—in which a radical challenge to individualism elicits an anxious defense of individualism—typifies the paradoxical logic of addiction. By some accounts, in fact, addiction is sustained by this habit of mind and can be cured if the addict learns to *accept* a feeling of compromised autonomy rather than retreating into hyperindividualism. The notion that a larger system is controlling one's actions, for instance, is essential to twelve-step programs, which function in part by converting the source of the addict's paranoia into the very gateway to recovery. In his "cybernetic" theory of addiction, anthropologist Gregory Bateson suggests that the Alcoholics Anonymous program works because it correctly understands the self as part of a larger system, which the alcoholic is "powerless" to control. Indeed, Bateson argues, the reason alcoholics drink in the first place is to surrender to such a "systems view" of themselves, thus giving up the more popular but "absurd" idea that they are autonomous agents with the capacity for self-control. In a state of intoxication, the addict's "entire epistemology changes." "His self-control is lessened" and he is able to "see himself as and act as *a part of* the group" ("Cybernetics" 329). Unfortunately, drinking only provides this feeling temporarily. To overcome the need for alcohol, the addict needs to develop a "systems-based" or "cybernetic" view on a more permanent basis. Here, as in postmodern biology,

> the "self" as ordinarily understood is only a small part of a much larger trial-and-error system which does the thinking, acting, and deciding. This system includes all the informational pathways which are relevant at any given moment to any given decision. The "self" is a false reification of an improperly delimited part of this much larger field of interlocking processes ("Cybernetics" 331).

A person, in other words, is not a material individual, but a socially dispersed system of communications.

A similar conclusion might be drawn from the writing exercise Burroughs gives his students. Yet Burroughs cannot stop there. Like Bateson's alcoholic, he relinquishes this postmodern or "cybernetic" epistemology for the "epistemology of self-control." And he does so, I believe, because he does not share Bateson's positive view of communicative systems. For Bateson, such systems are akin to the "higher spiritual power" of Alcoholics Anonymous. "There is," he writes, "a larger Mind of which the individual mind is only a sub-system. This larger Mind is comparable to God and is perhaps what some people mean by 'God,' but it is still immanent in the total interconnected social system and planetary ecology" ("Form" 461). For Burroughs, though, social systems are a continual source of terror: "Brainwashing, psychotropic drugs, lobotomy and other more subtle forms of psychosurgery; the technocratic control apparatus of the United States has at its fingertips new techniques which if fully exploited could make Orwell's *1984* seem like a benevolent utopia" ("Limits of Control" 117). In a world where the "higher powers" are in the business of mass-producing mindless, pliant subjects, a surrender to external control seems less like a cure to addiction than the cause of it.

Reconditioning Centers

Nothing makes Burroughs's view of technological systems more clear than the "control addicts" who populate his novels. These individuals are usually scientists with a strictly instrumental view of persons, and they are often in the employ of shadowy governments who want to use postindustrial technologies for purposes of mass social and political control. The most famous control addict, Dr. Benway, operates a "Reconditioning Center" for the Freeland Republic. His center uses sadistic techniques—including drug "therapy," compulsory psychoanalysis, and torture—to restructure the identities of his subjects. One of his prized products, for instance, is the "latah," an individual who compulsively imitates human actions upon command and thus exhibits the "Automatic Obedience Processing" Benway's scientists seek to perfect (*Naked Lunch* 28).

The most telling feature of these reconditioning "routines" in Burroughs's writing is how many of them concern sexual identity. Benway frequently uses violent psychotherapy to redirect human sexual desires. "You can make a square heterosex citizen queer with this angle," he says (27). Burroughs's interest in Pavlovian "sexual conditioning," like Pynchon's, lies partly in its depiction of a subject whose "deepest" self and "most personal" desires are open to external control—a subject epitomized by the addict. "Admittedly," he writes, "a homosexual can be conditioned to react sexually to a woman, or to an old boot for that matter. In fact, both homo- and heterosexual experimental subjects *have* been conditioned to react sexually to an old boot, and you can save a lot of money that way" ("Sexual Conditioning" 87). The humor of this remark belies Burroughs's other interest in the nightmare of sexual conditioning: his own experience during psychoanalytic treatment. Like his friend Ginsberg—and like an addict—he was treated for homosexuality, was "cured," and turned, however briefly, to a heterosexual lifestyle.[15]

An uneasy connection between addiction and homosexuality haunts Burroughs's work. These two identities—addict and homosexual—have long been associated with one another, not only because they emerged at the same historical moment but because they have historically been viewed as expressions of "unnaturalness."[16] As Sedgwick notes, that the two are now associated with HIV seems horribly to have "ratified" the connection between them and marked them "as unnatural, as unsuited for survival, as the appropriate objects of neglect" (589). It is all the more uncanny, then, that Burroughs should bring together the categories of homosexuality, addict, and "virus" so forcefully. Consider, for instance, the explanation he gives for his first two novels, the very titles of which evoke the twin identities he struggled with throughout his career: *Junky* and *Queer*. In the retrospective preface to *Queer*, he explains how junk addiction functions as a "cure" for homosexual desire: "Lee on junk is covered, protected and also severely limited. Not only does junk short-circuit the sex drive, it also blunts emotional reactions to the vanishing point, depending on the dosage.... When the cover is removed, everything that has been held in check by junk spills out.... And the sex drive returns in full force" (xii–xiii). The opening lines of the novel clarify this relation between junk and homosexuality in stark economic terms. "The first time he saw Carl, Lee thought, 'I could use that, if the family jewels weren't in pawn to Uncle Junk'" (1).

This dynamic explains more fully why Burroughs views addiction as a way of "keeping off the flesh" and its (homosexual) desires. What is odd about this view, however, is that it associates junk not with the lost autonomy of addiction, but with a newfound self-control. "While it was I who wrote *Junky*," Burroughs explains,

> I feel that I was being written in *Queer*. I was also taking pains to ensure further writing, so as to set the record straight: writing as inoculation. As soon as some-

thing is written, it loses the power of surprise, just as a virus loses its advantage when a weakened virus has created alerted antibodies. So I achieved some immunity from further perilous ventures along these lines by writing my experience down. (*Queer* xiv)

Both writing and junk use offer Burroughs a paradoxical form of self-control: they ward off uncontrollable sexual urges, which are here conceptualized as an invading virus. As a result, Lee in *Junky* is "integrated and self-contained," while in *Queer* he is "disintegrated" and "unsure of himself" (*Queer* xii)—or, to put it differently, in *Junky* he is a liberal subject while in *Queer* he is a "postmodern" or decentered subject. Junk use appears then to be a self-defeating method for preserving a liberal selfhood against an enervating and penetrating homosexuality—a conception that only underscores the masculinist biases of liberal individualism. We may now further specify the paradoxical logic of addiction as Burroughs experiences it: not only is junk an evil addicting substance, but it is also a welcome relief because it short-circuits the internal virus of "uncontrollable" sexual desire. Like any good *pharmakon*, it is both poison *and* antidote. The paradox is that Burroughs cannot become an "integrated and self-contained" self without the use of an *external* technology. We have thus arrived at another conundrum of selfhood, a splintering of the addict into a host of smaller components, each of which may be called on to regulate the crises of self-control generated by the others.

It is within the context of this ever-receding and ever-embattled internality that Burroughs understands mass cultural technologies and psychiatric "cures" as the ultimate invaders of the self. In one scene from *Naked Lunch*, a doctor claims to have turned a former homosexual into a "healthy" subject. His lab technician, however, challenges this claim. "What I'm getting at, Doc," says the technician, "is how can you expect a body to be healthy with its brains washed out?... Or put it another way. Can a subject be healthy *in absentia* by proxy already?" (139). To the technician, the idea of health is incompatible with the normalizing efforts of techno-medicine. What Burroughs suggests, in other words, is that reconditioning cannot produce a healthy subject—not only because its violent methods and normalizing ideology are unhealthy but because there will literally be no subject left when the process is complete. "It is highly questionable," he writes, "whether a human organism could survive complete control. There would be nothing there. No persons there. *Life is will* (motivation) and the workers would no longer be alive, perhaps literally" ("Limits of Control" 118).

One version of the subject whose brains have been washed out—who is "*in absentia* by proxy," so to speak—is the addict. Indeed, for Burroughs, nothing captures the effects of postwar technocracy so well as the addict. This is why drug addiction and other technological controls are intertwined throughout his writing. As Benway remarks wistfully, "Pending more precise knowledge of brain electronics, drugs remain an essential tool of the interrogator in his assault on the subject's personal identity" (*Naked Lunch* 25).

Given such connections, it should come as no surprise that Burroughs represents the effects of mass culture in a bodily fashion because this is also how he represents addiction. Consider his description of the "political parties of Interzone," the global village he modeled on Tangier. Each of these "political parties" represents a radically reimagined idea of individuality, and except for Factualism—the party Burroughs aligns himself with—all of them are hostile to liberal selfhood. The Liquefactionist party, for instance, favors "the eventual merging of everyone into One Man by a process of protoplasmic absorption" (146). The Divisionists, by contrast, "cut off tiny bits of their flesh and grow exact replicas of themselves in embryo jelly" (164). While these practices are diametrically opposed, their effects would be largely the same: they would destabilize the traditional self in the same way as posthuman biology and Burroughs's animistic theory of addiction.

Yet the Senders' party offers the clearest index of how Burroughs feels about mass culture and technology. According to Lee, they are the most dangerous party. Their goal, as one Sender proclaims, is to reestablish a Mayan form of telepathic control. Their system, however, will draw on new technologies to achieve "control of physical movement, mental processes, emotional reactions and *apparent* sensory impressions" of persons "by means of bioelectric signals injected into the nervous system of the subject" (162). "Shortly after birth," the Sender explains,

> a surgeon could install connections in the brain. A miniature radio receiver could be plugged in and the subject controlled from State-controlled transmitters.... The biocontrol apparatus is prototype of one-way telepathic control [sic]. The subject could be rendered susceptible to the transmitter by drugs or other processing without installing any apparatus...Now one sender could control the planet. (163–64)

Here, the link between drugs and electronic culture is explicit, much as it was in popular postwar descriptions of television as "the plug-in drug." The

Senders' bizarre human engineering project is designed to produce an entire population of addict-subjects.

But what is most bizarre about this fantasy of control is that it was presented as a serious possibility at the 1956 National Electronics Conference in Chicago. The speaker was an electrical engineer named Curtiss R. Schafer, of the Norden-Ketay Corporation. His subject was "biocontrol," the great achievement of which, according to Schafer, would be "the control of unruly humans" through electronics—an idea Schafer based on the (cybernetic) premise that since "planes, missiles, and machine tools already are guided by electronics,... the human brain—being essentially a digital computer—can be, too" (Packard 239–40). Burroughs has appropriated the scenario from Vance Packard's *Hidden Persuaders*. In Schafer's words,

> The ultimate achievement of biocontrol may be the control of man himself.... The controlled subjects would never be permitted to think as individuals. A few months after birth, a surgeon would equip each child with a socket mounted under the scalp and electrodes reaching selected areas of brain tissue.... The child's sensory perceptions and muscular activity could be either modified or completely controlled by bioelectric signals radiating from state-controlled transmitters. (Qtd. in Packard 239–40)

Schafer ended, Packard observes dryly, with "the reassuring thought that the electrodes 'cause no discomfort'" (240).

It is no accident that Packard's central claim is that psychologically savvy advertisers had begun to turn consumers into addicts of a sort—an association already implicit in the historical concept of the consumer. He describes the "hooks" of the admen as "*prescriptions* for our secret distresses" and "*cures* for our hidden aversions," and he views hapless consumers as "adult-children" (239), highly susceptible to what Riesman terms "other-direction" and what Ellul calls "involuntary psychological collectivization" (406).[17] In one description of a typical motivational experiment, Packard argues that even product labels can tranquilize shoppers, stripping them of self-control. As some shoppers walked by a surreptitiously videotaped supermarket display, he explains,

> Their eye-blink rate, instead of going up to indicate mounting tension, went down and down, to a very subnormal fourteen blinks a minute. The ladies fell into what Mr. Vicary calls a hypnoidal trance...Interestingly many of these women were in such a trance that they passed by neighbors and old friends without noticing or greeting them. Some had a sort of glassy stare. They were so entranced as they wandered about the store plucking things off shelves at ran-

dom that they would bump into boxes without seeing them and did not even notice the camera. . . . (107)

Confronted by the magically intoxicating packages, these consumers become something less than willful agents ("in this generation," says one adman, echoing Marx's account of commodity fetishism, "the products say 'buy me, buy me'" [107]). The subliminal seduction is so powerful that when these tranquilized "babes in consumerland" sober up, they often find they do "not have enough money to pay for all the nice things they [have] put in the cart" (107–08).[18]

No doubt, then, one reason Burroughs found *The Hidden Persuaders* so attractive was that it implied the connection between mass psychology and drugs so central to his own writing. Burroughs strengthens this connection when he turns the real electrical engineer and biocontrol advocate, Curtiss R. Schafer, into *Naked Lunch*'s Dr. Curt "Fingers" Schafer, the Lobotomy Kid. To Dr. Schafer, "The human body is scandalously inefficient. Instead of a mouth and an anus," he asks, "why not have one all-purpose hole to eat *and* eliminate?" (131). "Why not one all-purpose blob?" replies Dr. Benway (131).

This brings us back to where we began, because the all-purpose blob is the model of the junkie, the figure whose protoplasmic body has been rationalized so as to have but one purpose—the consumption of junk. Dr. Schafer is busy perfecting just such a subject. His self-described "Master Work" is "*The Complete All American Deanxietized Man*" (103), an individual whose nervous system has been "reduced" to relieve him of human feelings such as angst. To his horror, however, just as Schafer unveils this new and improved individual for his colleagues it turns into a "monster black centipede" (104)—again solidifying the link between the insectoid subjects of junk addiction and the similarly "empty" subjects of mass culture.

These scenarios, finally, explain why Burroughs chooses the single-celled organism and the insect as the models for the addicted subject. Tony Tanner has suggested that "matter returning to lower forms of organization" is Burroughs's "version of that entropy which is such a common dread among American writers" (118). This interpretation is helpful if we recall that the postwar literary interest in entropy stemmed from the writings of Norbert Wiener, which characterize entropy as an "evil" tendency because it moves us "from a state of organization and differentiation in which distinctions and forms exist, to a state of chaos and sameness" (*Human Use* 11–12). Wiener, moreover, explicitly associates insects with fascism and mass culture. Like the totally "conditioned" (51) subjects of fascism, he claims, the insect is a "cheap, mass-produced article, of no more individual value than a paper pie plate to be thrown away after it is once used" (51). This is what Burroughs suggests about the addict-subjects of postwar technocracy. Indeed, what could describe Burroughs's work better than Wiener's argument that while we have the technical capacity to "organize the fascist ant-state with human material," to do so would mean "a degradation of man's very nature" (52). Wiener develops this defense of human uniqueness for the same reason that Burroughs so often defends the "Human Image": his central thesis casts such doubt on human uniqueness and autonomy that it quickly becomes intolerable and must be counteracted by an impassioned humanism. The larger point of Wiener's text, after all, is that "if we could build a machine whose mechanical structure duplicated human physiology, then we could have a machine whose intellectual capacities would duplicate those of human beings" (57). Only in the context of this daring, materialist thesis does Wiener feel compelled to prove, at considerable length, the rather absurd point that "the human individual...is physically equipped, as the ant is not, for...the most noble flights" (51–52).

Such a humanist retreat repeats the gesture I have been tracing throughout *Empire of Conspiracy*. In Burroughs, the gesture is dramatic because his model of pervasive addiction offers radical challenges to humanism. Burroughs finds himself so deeply enamored of liberal humanism that his own attacks on it continually propel him into a state of panic. It is in this sense that his writing dramatizes the tensions in the contemporary culture of addiction. It depicts persons as "soft machines," addict-subjects "lived by" a world of technologies that have themselves appropriated the qualities of rationality, integrity, and self-control supposedly lost to human beings.

Epilogue: Corporate Futures

Postmodern Constructs

The stories of postmodernism that have been unfolding over the past decade or so have frequently included, among their central elements, a psychopathological model of historical change: the modern period, so the story goes, was dominated by expressions of alienation and paranoia, while the postmodern period has been characterized by fragmented, schizophrenic forms.[1] This idea, which is sometimes openly asserted and other times merely assumed, mirrors earlier postwar narratives of the shift from "inner-direction" to "other-direction," "Protestant ethic" to "social ethic," or, more generally, individual autonomy to mass control. I have already suggested that there is reason to be suspicious of accounts that theorize such a dramatic historical change in human subjectivity. It seems important to add that even the notion of a radical shift in *models* or *ideas* of subjectivity is problematic. There is little reason to imagine that modern paranoia suddenly "gave way" to postmodern schizophrenia as a dominant concept of subjectivity. Rather, both of these extreme forms of subjectivity continue to coexist in postmodern texts. As a result, I have been arguing, they must be understood as part of a debate about personhood. The tensions between them can be understood as analogues of the long-standing conflict between social constructionist and liberal models of self. Or they can be seen as reflections of the competing disciplinary assumptions of sociology and psychology. But if we must adopt the language of cultural psychopathology, it is vital to notice that the most "schizophrenic" texts discussed thus far— those of Pynchon and Burroughs—are also the ones with the greatest commitment to paranoia as both a theme and an approach to the world. If this fact means anything, it is that the postmodern movement away from a cen-

185

tered, autonomous subject has often been accompanied by a corresponding and paradoxical desire to conserve that self—to worry about its disappearance, to romanticize its importance, and to compensate for its loss, even if the "compensation" comes in the sometimes disturbing form of postmodern transference.

This is not to deny that postmodern narrative has been deeply influenced by assaults on the ontological priority of the individual as an integrated, total unit. Theorists such as Deleuze and Guattari, who advocate a view of subjectivity in which "the enemy is the organism" (*A Thousand* 58), seem so in tune with recent science fiction that Scott Bukatman suggests that they themselves "are cyberpunks" (326). Nonetheless, the fact remains that for many postwar and postmodern writers, the prospect of an egoless, or "anti-oedipal," mode of being has hardly seemed a promising form of resistance to fascism, instrumental reason, or modern social institutions. To imagine the end of subjectivity as we have known it—to view persons as products of social and discursive structures, or collections of smaller biotic components, or "desiring-machines" with no stable locus of central control or identity—has often been seen as a form of surrender, an acceptance of one's incorporation into the very structures that seemed so threatening in the first place. It is no accident that even the advocates of such radical subjectivities model them on the experience of "madness." As R. D. Laing observed in *The Politics of Experience*, a text that would significantly influence Deleuze and Guattari, "We defend ourselves violently...with terror, confusion and 'defenses' against ego-loss experience" (87). That such "paranoid" defenses stem from a confrontation with schizophrenic ego-loss indicates the extent to which these two extreme mental states are interrelated. If we must speak in the language of postmodern theory, then "modern" paranoia seems, paradoxically enough, to have become a response to "postmodern" schizophrenia. Reports of the liberal subject's death, it turns out, have been somewhat exaggerated.

This is not to say that liberal individualism is alive and well, only that it continues to have broad appeal despite its inadequacies. The reason for its resilience, even in postmodern texts, has partly to do with the difficulty of *embracing* its radically "deterritorialized" alternative—a self without borders, or a "body without organs." From the perspective of liberal theory, to embrace such a view would be to abandon the source of one's agency. And this is the other reason for liberal individualism's tenacity: it has taught us to believe that agency is a "property" *only* of self-contained, autonomous entities, whether they are individuals or social systems. To view oneself as less strictly bordered—that is, to adopt a self-concept derived from systems theory or poststructuralism—would be to recognize oneself as too "leaky" or "open" to contain the scarce, magical, and easily dissipated property called "agency."

Thus, in postwar culture, even those who can imagine a less centered human subject rarely abandon its accompanying conception of agency as the property of a centrally housed, integrated subject. Instead, they displace it into new hosts—into the miniature forms of "intelligent" biotic components, "talking" cells, and "selfish" genes, or into more massive agencies, "intelligent" systems, and "autonomous" social networks. The desire to find some kind of integral, bordered, and *willful* entity is everywhere in our culture. Even sophisticated social theory often describes the effects of complex communications, rules, institutional structures, and social exchanges as if they were the result of an intending subject at work. And popular conceptions of social control rarely bother with the complexities of social action. They simply transpose the liberal subject into a giant body, a powerful system with all of its unity, intentionality, and internality intact.

Nowhere is this tendency more visible than in representations of the corporation. The corporation is the ultimate monolithic collective actor, the postmodern superindividual par excellence. Its status as such is one of the reasons Gaddis makes "the JR family of corporations" the de facto protagonist of his novel—a collectivity whose "character" might be said to consist of the fragments of communication made on its behalf by innumerable agents throughout the novel. But if Gaddis's corporation gathers its coherence and power from a complex web of human interactions, laws, and institutional constraints—the totality of which cannot be seen by any one person in the web—popular conceptions of the corporation are rarely so nuanced. Regardless of their complexity, visions of the corporation's imaginary coherence derive from its incomparably singular motive. Unlike the government and the media, the corporation is constitutionally compelled to produce profits for its stockholders; all of its decisions revolve around that fiduciary responsibility. It is, as Ambrose Bierce once quipped, "an ingenious device for obtaining individual profit without individual responsibility" (48). Indeed, in America corporations *are* individuals in the legal sense. They are afforded constitutional protection as economic actors even though none of their individual stockholders can be held liable for their actions. In *Gain* (1998), Richard Powers traces the emergence of this legal position.

> If the Fifth and Fourteenth Amendments combined to extend due process to all individuals, and if the incorporated business had become a single person under

the law, then the Clare Soap and Chemical Company now enjoyed all the legal protections afforded any individual by the spirit of the Constitution. And for the actions of that protected person, for its debts and indiscretions, no single shareholder could be held liable. (159)

When the head of Clare discovers Bierce's definition, he cannot understand the joke because the definition accords with "the absolute letter of the law" (159).[2]

It is no accident, therefore, that corporations are so frequently imagined to possess an extraordinary internal unity and frightening, godlike power. They seem less like systems comprised of human decision makers with limited knowledge and more like self-motivated agencies, repositories of secret intentions, with the capacity for astonishing control of consumers and workers. This is one reason why product liability actions continually reveal to us the darkest of corporate intentions and, in doing so, increasingly banish the possibility that our lives may be governed by either individual action or what used to be called "accident" and "chance."[3] The United States judicial system is striding briskly toward a position in which "nothing happens in this universe...unless some entity *wills* it to happen" (Burroughs, "On Coincidence" 101). In an age of agency panic, it seems especially important to believe that where there is injury, there must be will, and the will we seek these days is often corporate: immense, ruthless, and irresistibly powerful.

It is not hard to see how we got here. As I observed in Chapter 1, early postwar narratives often understood the corporation and its demands for uniformity as a significant threat to the viability of individualism. These texts also suggested that postindustrialism reduced individuals (even corporate heads) to mere "switching elements" in a larger "cybernetic" collectivity that would make human action irrelevant. The symptoms of this social condition were to be detected not in corporations themselves, but in persons, who seemed to be exhibiting a wide array of disturbing behaviors, including compulsive shopping, "group think," and "other-direction," to name but a few. To combat this problem, some of these texts offered a fantasy of resistance to incorporation into larger social organizations and thereby rallied support for the model of individualism that is central to capitalism and that continues to underwrite conservative ideas of self-reliance, government deregulation, and anti-socialism.

This cold war discourse still informs late-twentieth-century representations of the corporation. It is visible even in narratives that have been understood as models of postmodern subjectivity. I want to conclude, therefore, with a brief look at several such representations. My examples include Ridley Scott's 1982 film *Blade Runner,* William Gibson's *Neuromancer* (1984), and Kathy Acker's *Empire of the Senseless* (1988). These futuristic tales contain the same radical plot element: the rebellion of persons against corporate systems that have literally constructed and programmed them. All three have been connected to the movement called "cyberpunk," a science fiction form that Fredric Jameson once called "the supreme *literary* expression if not of postmodernism, then of late capitalism itself" (491n1).[4] Cyberpunk has gained significant critical attention because its vision of technologically depleted human agency concretely and dramatically registers the anxieties I have been tracing through this book. Cyberpunk simply takes for granted many of the worst fears of earlier postwar conspiracy narratives. Its founding presumption, in fact, is that the human body can be colonized, made into a hybrid of organic and technological elements, always potentially subject to the corporations that supply its prosthetically extended modes of being. For its characters, the idea of the government implanting a computer chip in one's buttock for control purposes (as Oklahoma City bomber Timothy McVeigh asserted) would be neither a paranoid fantasy nor a grim joke, but an ordinary worry, a condition of employment, even a desirable self-modification.[5]

Cyberpunk's terminal vision of postwar paranoid culture presents a challenge to my thesis because it seems to abandon liberal models of self for subjects that are radically fragmented and postmodern. Yet, if cyberpunk depicts the most extraordinary challenges to individual subjectivity, it also offers an extreme version of agency panic's secondary element: the postmodern transference of agency to the corporate body. In its "high-tech paranoia" (Jameson 38), corporate systems not only *manufacture* persons, they *are* something like persons. By concluding with a discussion of postwar America's end-of-the-line conception of social control, therefore, I hope to demonstrate two things. First, that even texts associated with new forms of subjectivity can participate in the postwar romance of liberal individualism. Second, that for all its technical and imaginative innovation, cyberpunk continues the sort of cultural work begun by Whyte and his contemporaries. It dramatizes technological and social threats to personhood, while simultaneously resurrecting those conceptions in corporate form.

Artificial Intelligence

Ridley Scott's *Blade Runner,* like the Philip K. Dick novel on which it is based, is a story about artificial persons and their struggle with the people

who made them.[6] The persons in question are "Nexus 6" humanoid replicants, the most advanced products of the twenty-first-century bioengineer-
ing giant, the Tyrell Corporation. As the film opens, a renegade band of
these artifactual slave workers has fomented a rebellion and returned to
earth. Unhappy with an implant programmed to terminate their lives, they
attempt to force Tyrell to override their "artificial" demise. In response,
Tyrell recruits "blade runner" Rick Deckard to hunt down and "retire"
them.

As others have noted, the film displays considerable sympathy for its
replicants.[7] While they are "constructs" in the fullest sense of that word,
they are virtually indistinguishable from "real" humans and display all the
classic qualities of the liberal individual—including resistance to social programming and a demand for human (if not "natural") rights. The film's
basic assumptions about persons seem to literalize Marx's view that capitalism's power derives from its ability to mask human social relations behind
the relations of products to each other. Indeed, *Blade Runner*'s economy
takes commodity fetishism so far that its most advanced products are *also*
producers, and their social relations exist not only with other products but,
in a more hostile mode, with the ("real") persons responsible for producing
them. By embracing the original thesis of cybernetics—that a sophisticated
machine could duplicate human capacities—*Blade Runner* depicts a radical
materialist challenge to liberal humanism.[8]

Yet like many recent productions, when the film must imagine the operation of corporate agencies, it works in a nostalgic, precybernetic mode.
The most astonishing feature of the immensely powerful Tyrell Corporation is that it is still run by its founder and owner, Mr. Tyrell, a singular
"genius" and inventor-hero in the Henry Ford mold. Despite its advanced,
cybernetic products, in other words, the Tyrell Corporation is an anachronism, the sort of corporation William Whyte and Charles Reich pronounced dead several decades ago. The anachronism is so striking that
even the film's own replicants seem unwilling to accept it. *They* do not
expect Tyrell himself to hold the answers to their problem. But when they
approach Tyrell technicians and bioengineers in their quest for modifications, they are told that Mr. Tyrell himself is their creator and that he alone
can alter their longevity program.

Once this vision of corporate agency is in place, the replicants' struggle quickly takes the form of a classic oedipal conflict. Tyrell's strong "son,"
Roy Batty, confronts and blinds his corporate father. That blinding is the
method of Tyrell's demise is significant not only for oedipal reasons, but
because in twenty-first-century Los Angeles, the only way left to tell who

is human is to administer a psychological test while monitoring the subject's *eye*-movements—a combination of techniques that were, not coincidentally, widely used by corporations in the 1950s.[9] Tyrell's death thus signals the moment in which corporate control becomes posthuman. The demise of the corporate philosopher-king, after all, is the moment that Riesman identifies with the triumph of other-direction, that Foucault associates with the rise of discursive power, and that theorists of the Kennedy assassination link to the ascendancy of a dangerous governmental system. For William Gibson, we shall see, "the death of a mad king" (203)—again the head of a family-owned company—signals the triumph of a new and immortal corporate "life-form." In short, the death that takes center stage in *Blade Runner* has been integral to a familiar story about the relations between modernity and power.

What is vital to recognize is the degree to which this story should already seem anachronistic and romantic. If we take Foucault's lead, then the transfer of power from autocrats to discourses and institutions began long ago. Yet, the futurism of productions like *Blade Runner* masks this fact. Consider, for instance, the stunning early sequence in which Scott establishes the dominance of Tyrell headquarters on the Los Angeles skyline. After a close-up of an eyeball, in which the skyline is reflected, we are presented with a shot of the city, which takes us toward the towering edifice of the Tyrell building, an immense pyramid with a flat top. Vivian Sobchack has pointed out that this building resembles a microchip (234), but the more important visual reference here is to the Great Seal of the United States, which appears on the back of U.S. paper currency. This Masonic symbol depicts a flat-topped pyramid underneath a divine eye and contains Latin inscriptions reading "ANNUIT COEPTIS" (he approves our undertaking) and "NOVUS ORDO SECLORUM" (a new order for the ages). Scott's reference to it evokes both the original American "secret society" and the "paranoid style" that was born in response to it. What *Blade Runner* imagines is not a revolutionary corporate empire so much as the culmination of the original American vision—one that includes an updated form of "inhuman" slave labor, the promise of "off-world colonies," and the substitution of corporate executive for divine being.[10]

Gibson's *Neuromancer* tells a similar story, but envisions corporate control a bit more radically. Its plot revolves around the decline, through inbreeding and cryogenic preservation, of Tessier-Ashpool S. A., a family conglomerate that has for many years been managed by a pair of artificial intelligence (AI) programs designed by its wealthy and clannish owners. In the world of such systems, the Tessier-Ashpools themselves are something of an anachronism. When the narrator, Case, inquires about them, he is told they are "a very quiet, very eccentric first-generation high-orbit family, run like a corporation" (75). It turns out that the Tessier-Ashpool (T-A) project is to perfect Fordist control for all time—albeit unconventionally. The family uses cloning and cryogenic preservation to ensure that, by taking turns, they can run the organization forever. When its leaders go into the deep freeze, the AIs make routine managerial decisions and wake them if anything important occurs. As a result, one character remarks, "it's hard to keep track of which generation, or combination of generations, is running the show at a given time" (76). In other words, if T-A conserves a Fordist strategy, it does so only by applying the Fordist model of production to the (serial) production of *leaders* as well as products.

The designer of this system, Marie-France Tessier, originally planned T-A as an "immortal…hive" of collective decision making and symbiotic relationships (229). But virtually everyone else in the novel views the T-A system as ineffective, decadent, or insane. The corporation is repeatedly represented as a grotesque insect hive, an image that the narrator associates with dehumanization and visceral bodily horror. The T-A system resembles the well-known Mayan control machine of William Burroughs: the "technicians who had devised the control system had died out and the present line of priests…would have no idea how to fix that machine if it broke down, or to construct another if the machine were destroyed" (*Soft Machine* 95). The job of Burroughs's narrator, of course, is to "Smash the control machine" and "Kill! Kill! Kill!" (97)—exactly what Case is hired to do in *Neuromancer*. That this mission becomes emotionally rewarding for Gibson's characters, however, says a great deal about their distaste for the T-A model of control. "One of T-A's main problems," explains a computer construct named Dixie, "is that every family bigwig has riddled the banks with all kinds of private scams and exceptions. Kinda like your immune system falling apart on you" (193). In this view, T-A has had inadequate central coordination of corporate decision making. The fact that Dixie understands this problem as an insufficient *bodily* defense system, moreover, suggests that the corporation is insufficiently humanoid in its structure. What makes T-A so revolting, in other words, is its *lack of coherent identity*, its visible dispersal of control functions.

The other corporate systems in *Neuromancer* take a more reassuring and familiar shape. While they are not controlled by any one person or group, they are like integral, autonomous persons themselves. As Case puts it, they are "organisms" with "a kind of immortality": "You couldn't kill [one] by assassinating a dozen key executives; there were others waiting to step up the ladder, assume the vacated position, access the vast banks of corporate memory" (203). All the marks of possessive individualism have been extended to these collective actors. The same is true of the AI systems that work for T-A—and hope to overthrow its anachronistic human leadership: they have Swiss citizenship (132), a "real motive problem" (131), and want to *own* themselves legally. Gibson's unique dystopia imagines large systems as if they had recuperated the qualities of rationality, motive, and autonomy supposedly lost in human beings.

This form of postmodern transference is built into the novel's plot. Like *Blade Runner*, *Neuromancer* revolves around a rebellion by a corporate product—in this case the AI program known as "Wintermute." And like *Blade Runner*'s replicants, *Neuromancer*'s AI "has an electromagnetic shotgun wired to its forehead" (132) to keep it from acting autonomously. Wintermute gets around this problem by motivating numerous persons, including Case, to participate in a conspiracy to liberate it, so that it can merge with Neuromancer to become a dominant presence in the virtual world. It coerces Case to help it by having others booby-trap his body with toxin-sacs that will open if he fails his mission. In helping Wintermute, therefore, Case is preserving his own life. Yet Case rarely seems to be acting against his will; he relishes his work and seems to believe that the plot is for the best. At the climax of the novel as he tries to wrest a crucial password from one of the few remaining Tessier-Ashpools, he shouts, "I got no idea what'll happen if Wintermute wins, but it'll *change* something!" (260). This is a most puzzling feature of the plot. Why would a human like Case sympathize so much with Wintermute's struggle, when it will result in a new, more powerful system of control?

The answer, I believe, has to do with the imaginary structure of that system. The significance of Case's mission, and of Gibson's plot, lies not only in the transfer of control from human to machine but in its consolidation of control in a *unitary* corporate agent. Case's work is not simply to set free a pair of AIs, but to *unify* their carefully divided capacities—which were designed like the two lobes of the brain—into a single, godlike totality. "I'm the sum total of the works," says this new entity, "the whole show" (269). ("You God?," asks Case in response [270].) At the same time, Case's mission has the effect of eradicating a "perverse" and cybernetic form of existence— a system that openly disperses control among numerous weaker agents, including the divided AIs and a "family" of cloned human beings, and that in so doing seems to reduce its human components to "insects." This latter image—repeatedly emphasized through references to the T-A "hive" (126, 166, 171, 223)—recalls Norbert Wiener's early association of insectoid collectivity with mass culture and fascism. As I suggested in Chapter 5, the same association inspired Burroughs to inveigh against "the crushing weight of evil insect control" (*Soft Machine* 93). Here, it allows *Neuromancer*'s characters to view the dispersed, collective control of T-A as a hideous form of incorporation.

Case's real work, then, and the novel's deepest investment, is the destruction of this hideous deformation of subjectivity and the freeing and healing of its captive, "divided" subject(s), Neuromancer and Wintermute. This is not to suggest that the novel eschews postmodern subjectivity. On the contrary, Case accomplishes his mission through fantastically "divided," fragmented, and decentered experiences of his own subjectivity ("beyond ego, beyond personality, beyond awareness, he moved" [262]). He is forever jacking in and out of the matrix, "simstiming" himself into Molly's body, and communing with "persons" who are pure recordings of information. He and his colleagues, moreover, are perpetually reconstructed and rewired from the ground up. His boss is even given a new personality and memory. Yet the ultimate project of the novel is to imagine a future in which "centered" subjects (of all shapes and kinds) still run free. This should not be surprising since the meaning of cyberspace itself is deeply bound up with that fantasy. As Scott Bukatman observes, cyberpunk "permits the subject a utopian and kinetic *liberation* from the very limits of urban existence" (146). I would only add that cyberpunk's reinvention of the American frontier is part of a *mythic* recuperation of the unconditioned and uncontrolled subject, a fantasy of liberation that has historically functioned in the service of imperialism and that critics have rightly linked to masculine self-making.[11]

In the end, Gibson and Scott imagine much more radically than Whyte or Riesman what the world would look like if filled with *truly* "other-directed" persons—"meat-puppets," cyborgs, and replicant androids. Yet, as Claire Sponsler observes, in Gibson's novels, "first human agents, then machines, and finally cyberspace itself are invested with a heroic and romantic power that ultimately undermines the resolutely unromantic surface world he has set up" (639). It is no accident that both *Blade Runner* and *Neuromancer* hinge upon the actions of a single, highly autonomous individual who must do battle with the corporation or that both recycle classic genres of the self-reliant male subject—the hard-boiled detective and the lone (computer) "cowboy." In each text, the protagonist is highly sought after for his unique, human ingenuity in combating synthetic, self-governing technologies. And in each, he "lights out for the territory" at the story's end. By pitting a lone, rugged individual struggling against a immense and powerful organization, these fictions depict precisely the sort of battle William Whyte urged his readers to wage. In such an all-or-nothing struggle, the corporation is no longer a locus of class conflict; its workers disappear beneath a vision of the corporation as a self-replicating and self-controlled "total system." The only compensation left to such a view is psychic: it recuperates, in displaced form, the comforting notion that rational, autonomous agents still do battle with one another in order to secure life, liberty, and property.

In Memoriam to Memory

One reason science fiction narratives cling to the rational and autonomous (if not always human) agent is that they often use generic narrative formulas. For this reason, I want to take a brief look at a narrative that is unconventional: Kathy Acker's *Empire of the Senseless*. This novel is about pirates and, like all of Acker's work, it is pirated from other well-known texts, not only Gibson's *Neuromancer* but also that much older American "pirate" story, Twain's *Adventures of Huckleberry Finn*.[12] At every turn, Acker's *Empire* is an empire of conspiracy. It depicts a postrevolutionary world in which persons are dominated by a host of forces, ranging from powerful multinational corporations and government agencies to their own family members. In this bleak environment, a viable form of resistance to oppression is urgently needed, yet the very notion of human agency seems all but outmoded. "There are no more decisions," complains one character, "for in this unending growth of multinational capitalism, nothing ever changes" (126).

It is within this context that Acker finds use for Gibson's romantic dystopia, for it allows her to articulate a vision of social control that couples the political power of social and corporate institutions to individual acts of oppression, such as rape. In order to enact this narrative strategy, Acker politicizes Gibson's plot, replacing its futuristic technologies with specific contemporary institutions such as the CIA and the American Medical Association (AMA). Thus, Gibson's artificial intelligence becomes "AI, American Intelligence, who're backing the AMA" (40)—organizations, the narrator points out, that represent the first and second most profitable industries in the hemisphere, respectively. Gibson's Case becomes the pirate Thivai, and Molly becomes a "construct" named Abhor. Case's schizophrenic boss Armitage, whom Wintermute "builds" using the body of the nearly dead colonel Corto, becomes Freud's old friend, Dr. Schreber—who turns out, in Acker's wild universe, to be not only "a significant member of the AMA" but also a sadistic abuser much like Burroughs's Doctor Benway. Most significantly, Gibson's Tessier-Ashpool—the degenerate, corporate "hive" run by cloned leaders and intelligent computer systems—becomes "democracy" in Acker's text.

The significance of these modifications is twofold. First, they paint America as a nation in which democracy has become cryogenized and placed in the service of information-gathering agencies. Acker's American Intelligence, it is important to note, is not simply the CIA but an array of institutions that deal in specialized knowledge. One of the important scenes adapted from Gibson's novel depicts a terrorist group's raid on the national library. "The library," Acker writes, "was the American Intelligence's central control network, its memory, what constituted its perception and understanding. (A hypothesis on the political uses of culture.) It was called MAINLINE" (36). Hence, this novel suggests that cultural forms, the sorts of information housed in libraries, are central not only to national identity but to "sociopolitical control" (36).

Second, Acker's modifications of *Neuromancer* show how such institutional forms of control are connected to more localized ones, particularly the patriarchal and sexual control exercised in heterosexual relationships. Her Doctor Schreber, for instance, is a prominent member of the AMA, a detail associating him with Freud as well as Freud's famous patient. Yet, he is also a formerly abused child who goes on to invent child torture devices. After describing his past, the narrator sarcastically remarks, "I'm not hinting at any possible link between the micro-despotism inherent in the American nuclear familial structure and the macro-political despotism of Nazi Germany. I am giving an accurate picture of God: A despot who needs a constant increase of His Power in order to survive. *God* equals *capitalism*" (45–46). This comment establishes relations between Daniel Paul Schreber's persecutory "God" and the self-aggrandizing structure of capitalism and also between those things and child abuse. In other words, the will to power and the desire to magnify the self have consequences on both global politics and family.

This point is especially clear when Acker appropriates Gibson's description (cited earlier) of multinational corporations as immortal "organisms." "Power, in Case's world," writes Gibson, "meant corporate power" (203). In Abhor's mouth, however, this idea has more personal implications. "My father's no longer important," she reasons, "cause interpersonal power in this world means corporate power" (83). As Abhor says this, she recognizes her father's dead body in a boat down below her. Acker uses the passage, then, not so much to describe corporate power as to connect the death of the father to the rise of autonomous corporate bodies. In this moment, we find ourselves once again witnessing the postmodern transference, the moment in which the power of individual agents is imaginatively shifted to corporate entities. The meaning of this moment, the novel reminds us again and again, is that fathers *are* important, not only because their acts continue to determine the lives of their children but because their power is not, in the end, fundamentally different than corporate power. It is for this reason that Acker so insistently translates all social relations back into oedipal relations. Her writing may be anti-oedipal in its politics, but it is thematically wed to Oedipus throughout.

What this means for Abhor, the half-black, half-robot character based on Gibson's Molly, is that she is subject not only to large corporations but also to the men in her life, from her father to her sometime lover, Thivai. In fact, for Acker, corporate manipulation is only another form of "rape by the father" (the title of her first chapter) and vice versa. As in Atwood's fiction, personal relationships and larger social relations both channel the same discursively structured violence. It should come as no surprise, then, that Acker's characters often experience crises of agency in their personal relationships. As Abhor explains,

> I remembered being panicked all the time Thivai was my partner.... Since I gave and he took, everything was about him. Since everything was about him, everything he thought about me was true of him. Since I remember I was nothing, my memory is nothing.... Without my memory I realized reality was gone. There was no one. I panicked. (112–13)

Abhor's feelings seem at first to be a response to Thivai. But, as in much of Acker's writing, this strong emotional response is conveyed in the virtually affectless rhetoric of classical logic (since A, then B; since B, then C; and so on). If we follow that rhetoric, we see that the serious threat here is the loss of identity that Abhor links to male colonization of her mind and body. Because Thivai's self-importance causes him to project his inner states on Abhor, her identity and memory become so insignificant that they seem not to exist.

In texts by the other authors examined thus far, characters have responded to this feeling of lost agency in a variety of ways: by attempting to locate the agency that is threatening them; by refusing to make social commitments of one kind or another; or by "acting out" their capacity for unconditioned behavior, sometimes through violence. In most of these cases, the effect of the panic response was to consolidate the self—or rather the concept of self—against the forces that threatened to undo it. For Acker's characters, however, these responses do not seem feasible. First, the idea of removing themselves from the social order is as frightening as its alternative. (After all, Abhor panics only when she believes "There was no one.") Second, and more important, the idea of "protecting" their identity against such social controls might be an ideologically suspect project because for Abhor, as for Acker, the concept of coherent identity is itself a construct of power. In an empire of conspiracy, in other words, memory and the stable identity it guarantees may be the very tools of normalization used by powerful, corporate forces to control human subjects. (Says Abhor: "I remember a hand moving inside my mind, twisting my mind around" [48]). The notion that memory and identity may be wholly reconstructed is a familiar subject in postwar America. Popular conspiracy films (such as Donner's *Conspiracy Theory* and Frankenheimer's *Manchurian Candidate*), UFO culture, recent psychological literature, and science fiction (e.g., *The X-Files*, Dick's "We Can Remember It for You Wholesale," and Scott's *Blade Runner*) all circulate stories of "implanted" memory. In Acker's case, however, the problem is not so much that memories might be implanted "wholesale" into a previously untainted subject, but that the construction of identity is, from beginning to end, an ideological enterprise.

This view has far-reaching consequences, one of which is that Acker's fiction attacks the codes that signify identity in writing. More than any cyberpunk narrative, this novel's characters "morph" into one another, suddenly "becoming" characters from other texts and continually meditating on the sources and meaning of their identity. "Memories of identity flowed through my head," says Abhor (65). Such statements reverse the conventional view that memories constitute the larger formation called "identity." To suggest that identity is *itself* a memory—one that must compete with other memories—is to imagine the subject as a series of competing identities. Thus, Acker's characters frequently seek relief from external control by jettisoning memory ("I no longer had use for memory or was defined by memory" [49]). Yet, this relief is only half of a double bind, since the jettisoning of memory may also be a goal of repressive institutions. One of the many conspiracy plots recycled in *Empire of the Senseless*, for instance, concerns the CIA's MK/ULTRA LSD experiments—which have been a feature of other postwar conspiracy narratives as well.[13] "The CIA had to destroy this human memory," Thivai explains. "MK-ULTRA was designed to find safe ways to cause total human amnesia" (142). In Acker's text, this program is the essence of American Intelligence and U.S.-style McCapitalism, which forever strives to govern a populace of passive amnesiacs.

Here, then, is the problem facing Acker's characters. Deeply coercive social relations seem to be everywhere and cannot be avoided. Yet, attempting to recapture one's autonomy from such institutions may only be to engage in a delusion of sorts. Acker presents this problem (with characteristic awkwardness) as a conflict between "the rock of a false self-sufficiency and the rock of a need to go beyond...identity" (135). The only solution, it seems, is to *submit* to a dissolution and possession of self from the outside—or to take charge of that dissolution, to do it to yourself before They do it to you. As Thivai puts it, "the I who was acting was theirs...I, whoever I was, was going to be a construct" (33).

This strategy is masochistic in nature and, as Arthur Redding has observed, *Empire of the Senseless*, like much of Acker's fiction, is "an extended masochistic fantasy" (290). I suggested in my discussion of Pynchon that sadomasochistic fantasy is driven partly by a paradoxical desire to affirm or "act out" one's willpower and agency. Masochism itself, however, is a behavior resistant to analysis because it seems to indicate either a powerful expression of individual will or a nightmarish form of conditioning, one that causes subjects to "desire" their own domination and injury. In this sense, it poses the same paradoxes of determination that I earlier located in anorexia. For Acker, whose novels repeatedly dramatize a daughter's confinement and rape by her father, masochistic scenes may be a form of self-fashioning that transforms passive victimization into a willed submission to pain. Yet, as Redding argues, "masochism emerges from the dominant sexual order and represents a colonization of the feminine imagination" (300–01). At the very least, the compulsion to repeat masochistic patterns in Acker's fiction seems to be inseparable from a desire to escape external control. That Acker dramatizes this search for unconscribed identity within *already* scribed narratives, however, is itself masochistic. By "sampling" male-authored texts and thereby rejecting the romantic conception of the individual author, Acker dramatizes the problems of agency faced by her characters. Indeed, the ultimate "construct" in *Empire of the Senseless*—the equivalent of Gibson's Dixie, the ROM construct stolen from the library in the terrorist raid—is named "Kathy" (34).

Thus, confronted with a world that is coded, full of controlling discourses, fictions of identity, and powerful institutions, Acker does not attempt to recuperate a myth of the lone agent, wholly free of social relations. She does not try to hide the fact that her fiction is not wholly her own. Nor do her characters attempt to wall themselves off from social controls. Rather, like Acker herself, they acknowledge the constraints on them and attempt to appropriate and manipulate such controls from within, even if that means "undoing" the stability and uniqueness of their identities. In a manner similar to Thomas Pynchon, then, Acker seems to acknowledge that liberal individualism is an inadequate conception of self.

Nonetheless, Acker proposes a method of resistance that offers a final, perhaps even vestigial, hope for unconditioned behavior. Throughout *Empire of the Senseless*, Acker sketches this strategy of resistance. Because "the right-wing owns values and meanings" (73), she suggests, an effective strategy may be to "stop making sense." In a scene borrowed from the climax of *Neuromancer*—the moment when Case receives a code that will undo T-A and unify the AIs into an autonomous subject—Acker's characters receive a very different message: "GET RID OF MEANING. YOUR MIND IS A NIGHTMARE THAT HAS BEEN EATING YOU: NOW EAT YOUR MIND" (38). The strategy implicit in this code—to destroy meanings before they destroy you—is by now familiar as the rationale for Burroughs's "cut-up" technique. But Acker attempts to push beyond Burroughs in this matter, and she allows Abhor to outline the logic of her program in detail while Abhor's friend, Agone, is being tattooed:

> That part of our being (mentality, feeling, physicality) which is free of all control let's call our "unconscious". Since it's free of control, it's our only defence against institutionalized meaning, institutionalized language, control, fixation, judgement, prison.
>
> Ten years ago it seemed possible to destroy language through language: to destroy language which normalizes and controls by cutting that language. Nonsense would attack the empire-making (empirical) empire of language, the prisons of meaning.
>
> But this nonsense, since it depended on sense, simply pointed back to the normalizing institutions.
>
> What is the language of the "unconscious"? .... Its primary language must be taboo, all that is forbidden. Thus, an attack on the institutions of prison via language would demand the use of a language or languages which aren't acceptable, which are forbidden. Language, on one level, constitutes a set of codes and social and historical agreements. Nonsense doesn't per se break down the codes; speaking precisely that which the codes forbid breaks the codes. (133–34)

Here we have both a critique of Burroughs's "cut-up" technique and a redeployment of that technique in altered form. The goal of Burroughs's cut-ups, as Abhor points out, is to short-circuit the codes by which society governs persons. Yet as I argued in Chapter 5, because it is impossible to distinguish between controlling codes and "merely communicative" codes—that is, because *all* messages have regulatory potential—the practical effect of smashing such codes would be to interrupt communication in general. And since communication is the primary basis of the social order, a truly successful cut-up program would have the effect of removing its practitioners from social relations. As Abhor makes clear, doing without a language offers little promise because it simply abandons power "to the normalizing institutions." Thus, Acker makes a useful distinction between attempting to destroy social codes and merely violating those codes through "disgusting" and socially unacceptable practices, such as tattooing.

Yet it is important to see that her solution is also based on the notion of a free and unconditioned part of the self, even if it is only the unconscious. Unlike Lacan's unconscious, Acker's is *not* structured like a language and it thus serves as a vestigial remnant of the autonomous individual. Once this portion of the self is set in opposition to the socially conditioned aspects of the self, it can be used to underwrite a program of transgression and criminality, a program that involves not only piracy and terrorism, but forbidden forms of expression, such as body-piercing and tattoo. For Acker, such practices are explicitly antisocial, ways of resisting oppressive cultural norms. What her program amounts to in practical terms, then, is the extension of the cut-up technique to the socially valued sites of personal property and the human body. Rather than cutting up messages, her characters cut up their bodies. (In this scene, the tattooist works with a knife). If Acker's characters attempt to move beyond identity, they do so because violent self-reconstruction seems the only way of escaping even greater violation. And if Acker herself cuts-up and reassembles the work of Gibson, Twain, Burroughs, and others, she does so because the violation of taboos seems to offer the only escape from the nightmare of a prescripted and constraining social order.

Conclusion

We need to understand, writes Ihab Hassan, "that the human form—including human desire and all its external representations—may be changing radically, and thus must be re-visioned. We need to understand that five hundred years of humanism may be coming to an end, as humanism transforms itself into something that we must helplessly call posthumanism" ("Prometheus" 205). Perhaps. But in our haste to notice the new, we should not overlook the inertial power and mythic appeal of an older story about the individual. Nor should we miss the fact that many of our most radical encounters with the decentered subject are presented to us in the mode of panic, by terrified characters and worried cultural critics. As liberal humanism gives way to newer models of subjectivity, it seems unlikely to do so without a struggle. In postwar American culture, that struggle has been most conspicuous in the rhetoric of paranoia, conspiracy, and diminished human agency. At its best, this rhetoric offers a way of conceptualizing and resisting the controlling power of mass-communication systems, bureaucracies, and regulatory discourses. At its worst, it becomes coupled to an antisocial fantasy of autonomy, a vision that rejects the promise of collective resistance and sometimes even celebrates violent responses to "oversocialization" (F.C. 24). In either case, however, it tends to defend the notion of autonomous individuality against a more unsettling view, one that stresses the social construction and regulation of the self.

If this tendency has a meaning, it may be simply that it is hard to abandon the coherent and willful liberal subject. It is difficult not only to rethink one's own subjectivity but also to understand the complex actions of corporate bodies without familiar models—difficult to measure the influence of one such entity against another, to weigh the effects of human desire against social influences, and to sort out what we want from what we have been taught to want. If we could come to see ourselves as self-regulating systems existing within, and open to, a web of larger communicative systems, we might be able to move beyond melodramatic accounts of our own actions, desires, and identities. We could begin to theorize modes of resistance aimed at specific ideological targets—rather than at the social order as a whole. In postwar culture, however, an intending, monolithic agent still seems easier to comprehend and resist than a complex array of structures and communications, even if we know down deep that self-control is not an all-or-nothing proposition. If we have come to a moment when traditional ways of understanding human action and identity are no longer adequate to explain our relation to our social and technological conditions, many Americans seem nonetheless willing to disavow this fact. What could be more appealing, after all, than the possibility that somehow, somewhere, there is still a route to autonomy, pure voluntarity, and unconditioned life? In an empire of conspiracy, this hope seems for many the only way out.

Notes

Notes to Introduction

1. In *America's Retreat from Victory*, McCarthy suggests that communism is "a conspiracy on a scale so immense as to dwarf any previous such venture in the history of man" (169). For a broader sample of postwar instances, see Hofstadter (especially "The Paranoid Style" and, in the same volume, the three essays on "pseudo-conservative" [right-wing] politics).

2. I am not suggesting that Packard is offering a radical leftist critique. Indeed, he embraces the same liberal values that drive anticommunist thought. Nonetheless, the political implications of Packard's account are undoubtedly more liberal than those of Hoover's book.

3. Hofstadter underestimates the importance of these historical changes because, like other analysts of conspiracy theory (Pipes; G. Johnson; B. D. Davis), he views it as a transhistorical phenomenon. Some accounts acknowledge the use of conspiracy theories by both liberals and conservatives (Hofstadter; G. Johnson; Pipes; Shils), but most concentrate on conservative theories (Bell [*Radical*]; Finch; Hofstadter; and Lipset and Raab). (Contrary to what Pipes asserts [158–59] in a misquotation of Johnson, Johnson emphasizes the bipartisan use of conspiracy theory [e.g., 15].)

4. Hoover knows that "communists quickly accuse anybody who disagrees with them of being guilty of thought control" (81–82), but he is unconscious of the way his own actions mirror those of his enemies. While he critiques communists for promulgating instructions, for inculcating loyalty, and for operating in secret, he does all of these things himself. He even offers instructions for resistance and tips on how citizens can aid the "spy-hunting" efforts of the FBI.

5. Packard's sense that "depth manipulation" had political implications was especially compelling to political operatives. Consider, for example, Phyllis Schafly's 1964 view that "secret kingmakers, using *hidden persuaders* and psychological warfare techniques, manipulated the Republican National Convention to nominate candidates who would sidestep or suppress the key issues" (5, emphasis added).

6. By "supposedly individualist," I mean that Americans celebrate liberal individualism in an unusually uniform way. The American commitment to "free thought" and "the free market" is evident in the comparably narrow range of viable political parties in the United States. As Louis Hartz noted in his 1955 study of America's "irrational Lockianism, or...Americanism" (11), the United States has always been paradoxically conformist in its commitment to individualism (63). It is a "land of solidarity" (86), notable for its "aversion to systematic social thought" (307). Edward Shils has argued that the tendency toward conspiratorial thinking is stronger in America than in Europe because of the former's long-standing populist suspicion of aristocracy and government. For European and global examples of conspiracy theory, see Robins and Post; and Graumann and Moscovici.

7. These comments come from Marin and Gegax; Kakutani; and B. Hoover, respectively. See also Morrow; Weiss; and, on the subject of mass media–generated panic, Cohl.

8. See O'Donnell; Tanner; Polan; and Jameson. The tendency I am commenting on is not exclusive to the United States. A major figure in this study, Margaret Atwood, is Canadian. Yet several factors have made conspiracy theory and agency panic especially prominent in the States—among them the nation's historical commitment to liberal individualism, its relatively uniform political culture, and its lack of feudal and revolutionary traditions. I should also note that Atwood (especially in *Surfacing; Bodily Harm;* and *The Handmaid's Tale*) often writes about the politics of the United States.

9. Tanner's excellent 1971 study, *City of Words*, argues that American literature expresses not only desire for "an unpatterned, unconditioned life" but also "dread that someone else is

patterning your life, that there are all sorts of invisible plots afoot to rob you of your autonomy of thought and action" (15). This is a perceptive description of the dynamic I am investigating. Yet *City of Words* itself is more a series of single-author studies than a sustained account of this dynamic. Among the many novels that fit into the pattern I have outlined but are not discussed in this book are Mailer's *American Dream* (1964) and *Executioner's Song* (1975); McElroy's *Lookout Cartridge* (1974); Reed's *Mumbo Jumbo* (1972); Silko's *Almanac of the Dead* (1991); Vonnegut's *Sirens of Titan* (1959); Yurick's *Richard A* (1981); and almost the entire corpus of Dick.

10. Many of those writing about postmodernism, most notably Linda Hutcheon, accept Lyotard's definition of the postmodern as an "incredulity toward metanarratives" (xxiv). For an overview of accounts that develop from Lyotard's definition, see McHale ("Postmodernism").

11. In this case, Justice Jackson's concurring opinion modified the "clear and present danger" doctrine of Justice Holmes (established in *Schenck v. United States*) by asserting that any "conspiracy" must be judged on the basis of its potential future harm. Thus, "Communist plotting" (in this case, discussion of Marx and Lenin) could not be protected during "its period of incubation," because the government would be powerless to hinder the plot "after imminent action is manifest." It is worth noting that conspiracy statutes in the United States were developed in order to suppress labor activism in the late-nineteenth century.

12. For a longer account of "the postmodern sublime," see Joseph Tabbi.

13. "Unabomber" was the term the FBI used to label the perpetrator of a long series of mail-bombings against industrialists and scientists. In 1996, the Unabomber submitted a manifesto entitled "Industrial Society and Its Future," which was published by the *Washington Post* under the pen name "F.C." The "manifesto" consists of 230 numbered paragraphs or theses. My references to the manifesto denote these paragraphs, not page numbers, and refer to the on-line source listed under "F. C." in the Works Cited. In May 1998, Theodore Kaczynski was sentenced for the Unabom murders.

14. Patricia Turner has documented the importance of conspiracy discourse in African-American communities. "The overall theme" of this discourse "is that organized anti-black conspiracies threaten the communal well-being and, in particular, the individual bodies of blacks" (3). While the legends Turner traces are circulated almost exclusively in the black community, comparable tales circulate in a range of communities (see Singh and Pipes). Compare, for instance, *The Turner Diaries* (no relation to Patricia Turner), written by white supremacist William Pierce under the pen name Andrew Macdonald. This popular, underground novel is about a daring, white supremacist rebellion against a racially diverse (and hence "oppressive") futuristic government called "The System": "All in all, it has been depressingly easy for the System to deceive and manipulate the American people... Even the libertarians, inherently hostile to all government, will be intimidated into going along when Big Brother announces that the new passport system is necessary to find and root out 'racists'— namely, us" (Macdonald 33).

15. Charles Siebert made this remark as part of a colloquium published in *Harper's* magazine. In response, Jaron Lanier said, "People have an enormous amount of anxiety about what a person is" (Hitt 46).

16. My explanation of this response is indebted to Mark Seltzer's treatment of agency in turn-of-the-century American writing—particularly his work on "melodramas of uncertain agency" (*Bodies and Machines*, especially 17–21, 84, 155–56). For compelling and useful philosophical studies of agency and human action, see John Bishop; Brand; Davidson; Dennett (*Elbow Room* and *Intentional Stance*); Georgeff and Lansky; Ginet; Rorty; Schick; Taylor; and Wilson. "Panic," say the authors of the *Panic Encyclopedia* (Kroker, Kroker, and Cook), "is the key psychological mood of postmodern culture" (13).

17. For Pipes, "*conspiracy theory* is the fear of a nonexistent conspiracy. *Conspiracy* refers to an act, *conspiracy theory* to a perception" (21). By this absurd definition, conspiracy theories are always wrong and thus no actual conspiracy could ever be theorized—except by a paranoiac. Robins and Post offer a more sophisticated account, noting the "contextual nature of what is paranoid" (30) (i.e., the power of the analyst to decide what is normal and sane). Yet their example of a "conspiratorial" context is the Soviet Union, a place, they insist, where psychiatric workers falsely imprison dissidents and nonconformists. When discussing specific cases of this abuse, they show how Western psychiatrists "proved" that Soviet mental patients were sane dissidents, without reflecting on the *possibility* that these diagnoses might have been ideologically influenced. Throughout their study, furthermore, they never pursue their occasional observations about the difficulty of diagnosing paranoia. "Paranoia—especially political paranoia—," they remark, "is seldom a complete delusion. It is typically a distortion of a truth" (50). Such remarks presume the existence of a clear truth to which the authors have unmediated access. For an interesting study that takes the opposite view, see Dean.

18. Macpherson explains that possessive individualism in its seventeenth-century form portrayed the individual "neither as a moral whole, nor as part of a larger social whole, but as an owner of himself" (3). In this view, the "human essence is freedom from dependence on the wills of others, and freedom is a function of possession" (3). While such assumptions have been substantially challenged since the nineteenth century, according to Macpherson, they "have not been abandoned yet, nor can they be while market relations prevail." (4). I am interested in the way that human freedom, or agency, has *itself* come to be viewed as a "property" of the individual. This notion, which stems directly from the assumptions of possessive individualism, encourages an all-or-nothing conception of agency, a reductive belief that one either "has agency" or "has no agency." I should add that it is to these older assumptions, and not to contemporary left-wing politics, that I refer when I use the term "liberalism."

19. "Regeneration through violence" comes from the title of Richard Slotkin's classic account of early American literature. Prominent members of the antigovernment "patriot" or militia movement include the Posse Comitatus, Aryan Nation, the Order, and the militia of many states, including Michigan and Montana. For an account of this movement, see Stern.

20. Assaults on liberal and Cartesian "centered" subjectivity have come from philosophical traditions as diverse as hermeneutics, phenomenology, structuralism, and poststructuralism (especially deconstruction), and from the disciplines of psychoanalysis and anthropology. Their most powerful and well-known articulations come in the work of Barthes; Deleuze and Guattari; Derrida; Foucault; Irigaray; Kristeva; Lacan; Lévi-Strauss; and Lyotard. Judith Butler's explanation of subjectivity through performance has been particularly influential (*Gender Trouble*). Schizophrenia has been used as a model of subjectivity by Baudrillard; Deleuze and Guattari; Jameson; and Lacan.

21. In an early attempt to define the postmodern, Ihab Hassan developed a list of schematic differences between modernism and postmodernism. In that list, he associates paranoia with modernism and schizophrenia with postmodernism ("Culture" 123–24). Other critics such as Jameson (26–34, 345, 375) and Harvey (43, 53) have accepted such associations without an explanation of why paranoia has been so dramatically present in postmodern narratives. If I were to situate my argument in these psychoanalytic terms, I would say that the threat of "schizophrenic" dissolution provokes "paranoid" attempts to defend the integrity of the self in postmodern narrative. *Paranoia* is an attempt to conserve the integrity of the self and—in the texts I examine—a particular set of assumptions about the self.

22. See "Psycho-Analytic Notes" (79); "Construction in Analysis" ("The delusions of patients appear to me to be the equivalents of the constructions which we build up in the course of analytic treatment" [268]); and the more famous equation of paranoid delusions to the systems of philosophers ("Preface to Reik's *Ritual*," 261). For another version of the latter, see "On Narcissism" (96). Bersani illustrates powerfully the ways in which psychoanalytic theory

itself threatens to be "a paranoid symptom," because "the theoretician's distrust of theory—the sense that what theory seeks to signify is hidden somewhere behind it—repeats the paranoid's distrust of the visible" (101). Paranoia thus comes into alignment with interpretation in general.

23. For compelling accounts of the relation between modernism and paranoia, see Farrell and Sass. As Farrell notes, "paranoia becomes a viable, even normal stance when intellectual culture depends fundamentally and without limit upon suspicion of the faculties that make it possible" (213).

24. Tanner makes this point in an interesting discussion of *Mother Night* and its relation to Ezra Pound's life (185–88).

25. Jonathan Culler points out that, for Saussure, the content of these anagrams was not "a secret, subversive meaning" (as in Strauss's theory), but rather a meaning already central to the text. Nor were the anagrams "an indication that readers are free to produce meaning according to their own devices" (124). Pynchon and DeLillo are especially interested in anagrammatic signification. The first three words of Pynchon's *The Crying of Lot 49*, "Mrs. Oedipa Maas" (MOM), describe a woman who, in the closing pages of the novel, feels "pregnant" with something a "gynecologist has no test for" (171, 175). Likewise, the plot of DeLillo's *The Names* (1982) revolves around such issues.

26. For instance, as C. Barry Chabot notes, Schreber's illness is very much about independence of will. "Every moment of every day," Chabot writes, Schreber "feels his physical autonomy usurped and himself threatened by being transformed from a purposeful individual to the hapless plaything of inimical supernatural forces. Only extraordinary efforts of will preserve whatever shreds of dignity and autonomy he retains" (118–19). Swanson, Bohnert, and Smith note that "fear of loss of control is prominent in the paranoid outlook on life" (17).

27. In Freud's early (1915) topography of the mental agencies, the unconscious "is alive and capable of development"; it "constantly influences" the agency of the preconscious ("Unconscious" 190). This notion and the general idea of unconscious motivation are unavoidably paradoxical. In *The Psychopathology of Everyday Life*, for instance, he explains his own unconscious forgetting of a proper name as the result of "a motive....I wanted, therefore, to forget something; I had *repressed* something" (4). By this formulation, repression is both motivated and unconscious. Repression must be motivated in some way if unconscious acts are to have a *meaningful* psychic function, yet it must also be uncontrollable if mental slips are really *unconscious*. The question then becomes what motivates the mechanism of repression? In short, psychoanalysis retains the concept of motive so important to the liberal subject, but also weakens it in order to account for "motivations" beneath the surface of conscious motive.

28. Notable exceptions in literary and cultural study include the work of Bersani; Sass; O'Donnell; and Polan. Writing about the science fiction of Philip K. Dick, Carl Freedman remarks, "Paranoia, we can conclude, is no mere aberration but is structurally crucial to the way that we, as ordinary subjects of bourgeois hegemony, represent ourselves to ourselves and embark on the Cartesian project of acquiring empiricist knowledge" (17).

29. Didion's novel *Play It As It Lays* is a study in the apathy of Maria Wyeth, who thinks, during the abortion that haunts her for the rest of the novel, "No moment more or less important than any other moment, all the same" (82). Her view is almost identical to Didion's view of Los Angeles.

30. For an account of the Manson murders, see Bugliosi.

31. See Nina Baym's classic account of these "melodramas of beset manhood."

32. As Tania Modleski has pointed out, the mass-mediated subject is rendered here "in terms of rape" (163). Others have pointed out that Baudrillard's narrative of a historical shift in representation (a shift from faithful representation of reality to false representation and

finally to simulation of the real) is deeply nostalgic (see, e.g., Hutcheon 33–34). Its nostalgia, however, has diminished neither its influence nor its tendency to be coupled with critiques of nostalgia (as appear, for instance, in Jameson's account of postmodernism).

33. Pipes (8) traces this fear to right-wing conspiracy theories about a repressive (i.e., more colorful) New World Order. Kah, for instance, asserts that soon all Americans will be branded with tattoos for control purposes (12).

34. On the second (or third) industrial revolution, see Berkeley; Evans; Forester; Hawkes; Lamberton; Piore and Sabel; Richta; Stine; Toffler (*Third Wave*); Tomeski; Wiener; and Williams. On the concept of "postindustrial society," see Bell (*Coming*); and Touraine. On the "information age," see Dizard; Helvey; and Martin and Butler. The quoted terms come from Boulding ("postcivilized"); Rostow ("postmaturity"); Feuer ("postideological"); Kahn ("posteconomic"); Vickers ("postliberal"); and Eisenstadt ("posttraditional"). The term "postmodern" was used in similar work by Etzioni in 1968 and has since come into ordinary usage.

35. Beniger goes on to demonstrate persuasively, however, that such postwar developments are part of an older "control revolution," a response to numerous "crises of control" that have arisen since industrialization.

36. See LeClair (*Art*) and Porush. While Porush accounts for "techno-paranoia," LeClair's sympathy for early systems theory and its vision of a beneficent totality leads him to understate the terror so many writers express about systems.

37. It is impossible for me to do justice to the complexity of these theories here. Cary Wolfe's *Critical Environments* offers a good introduction to the subject and a compelling analysis of its relation to other cultural theories. See also Hayles ("Making") and the two special issues of *Cultural Critique* devoted to the subject (fall and spring 1995).

38. Diggins's argument is symptomatic of much recent anxiety about poststructuralist thinking. Not surprisingly, Diggins has an abiding affinity for explanations that privilege the individual in accounting for historical change. Thus, he explains poststructuralism as a movement grounded in the frustrations of New Left members as they assumed university posts, became disillusioned, and attempted to "spread suspicion" (349) about concealed forms of power with the "ready made answers" of theory (357). Similarly, he substantiates the "failure" of contemporary critical theories by arguing that they "accord little role to the individual" and hence cannot explain events such as the fall of Eastern Bloc communism—which, he believes, "took place because Gorbachev desired to initiate change rather than impeding it" (362). For Diggins, then, poststructuralism can be corrected by a return to Ranke's "great man theory" of history.

Notes to Chapter 1

1. The terms cited come from Bell; McLuhan; Dizard; Wiener; and Harvey, respectively—although others have used them or terms similar to them. Touraine used the term "post-industrial society" in 1971; Helvey used the term "age of information" in 1971; and Etzioni used the term "postmodern society" in 1968. Beniger's *Control Revolution* concisely documents the genre of social analysis I am outlining here (see esp. 4–5). A compelling challenge to the notion of postindustrialism has come from Marxist economists such as Ernst Mandel and from theorists of postmodernism such as Fredric Jameson and David Harvey, who draw, respectively, on Mandel and the "regulationist school" of economics. They demonstrate convincingly that postindustrialism fails as a concept because it concentrates too heavily on first-world societies. It overlooks the movement of industrial capital to labor markets outside of the United States and Western Europe, giving the false sense that the mode of production has changed fundamentally.

2. The quoted phrases come from Riesman; Seidenberg; Marcuse (*One-Dimensional*); and Whyte, respectively.

3. As early as 1941, James Burnham argued that managerial bureaucracy and technocratic rationalization had essentially alienated owners from the companies that they owned.

4. References to Riesman's *Lonely Crowd* are to the original 1950 edition, unless the 1961 edition is specified. The revised 1961 edition is sometimes significant, because it was abridged and edited for a popular audience. As a result, its descriptions of broad cultural change are often less cautious and more sweeping. Compare, for instance, Chapters 1, 7 (esp. section III), and 14 in the original to chapters 1, 7 (III), and 12, respectively, in the revised edition. It is important to note that alterations to the text did not have to move in this direction simply as a result of popularization.

5. According to Robert Bellah and his colleagues, some critics have incorrectly represented Riesman's account of character in much the way I do here. They have tended to see other-direction as a dangerous or vacuous type of social character and have missed Riesman's "considerably more complex" argument (Bellah 49)—namely, his repeated admonitions that inner-direction should not be romanticized and that inner-direction is also socially determined. Indeed, Riesman does remind us that other-direction is no worse than inner-direction. Yet he does so, it seems to me, because he knows how poorly other-directed types come off in his account. "It is hard," he admits in his revised edition, "for us to be quite fair to the other-directed" (159). It is hard because, within the framework of liberal values, the other-directed are not nearly as impressive as their inner-directed forebears, all caveats to the contrary notwithstanding. Bellah also points out, incorrectly, that Riesman "proposes four character types, not two" (49). In fact, Riesman proposes three character types: tradition-directed, inner-directed, and other-directed—though the emphasis is on the latter two, because tradition-direction waned long ago in developed countries, according to Riesman. The "autonomous" character, which Bellah believes to be Riesman's fourth type, is not a type of historical "social character." It is rather one of three "universal types" of *individual adjustment to* the type of social character dominant in an era; the other two such modes are "the adjusted" and "the anomic" (Riesman 288). Thus, Riesman speaks of "the autonomous among the inner-directed" and "the autonomous among the other-directed"—although the latter category seems purely theoretical because the terms *autonomy* and *other-direction* are already opposed. This is why Riesman finds it "difficult, as an empirical matter, to decide who is autonomous when we are looking at the seemingly easy and permissive life of a social class in which there are no 'problems' left" (301–02).

6. Marcuse's *Eros and Civilization* (1955) advances views similar to Riesman's—particularly the idea that the socialization of persons is increasingly accomplished by peer groups and mass media rather than by parents. See especially 96ff.

7. The identity of Ellison's Invisible Man is perpetually restructured by the organizations in which he finds himself (a college, a factory, and a Marxist collective called "the Brotherhood"). Yet it should be noted that he struggles less against "postindustrial society" than against a historically persistent array of racist institutions and ideas.

8. This form of apparent deindividuation also occurs in *Catch-22*, when the squadron chaplain is accused of forging his signature in someone else's handwriting.

9. As Thomas Schaub points out in his compelling study of the cold war "liberal narrative," alienation, at this cultural moment "became a badge of radicalism and autonomy—a sign that one was not a member of 'mass society' " (*American* 150). Scholars such as Erich Fromm, Daniel Bell, and Peter Viereck, notes Schaub, all produced texts that celebrated or defended the "unadjusted man."

10. It is worth noting that Marcuse does not propose as clear and specific a solution as Whyte. Nor does he emphasize the values of competition and rugged individualism as Riesman and Whyte do. Yet he does establish a sharp opposition between the interests of "society"

and the interests of "man." And oddly enough, he often fails to recognize different class interests within the social order. Thus, he says, "critical analysis continues to insist that the need for qualitative change is as pressing as ever before. Need by whom?...by the society as a whole, for every one of its members" (*One-Dimensional* xiii).

11. Like Riesman, Marcuse notes that this kind of identification between persons and the social occurs in the early period of industrialization and may even occur in "primitive" society; the difference, in his view, is that now it is the "product of a sophisticated, scientific management and organization" (*One-Dimensional* 10). In other words, it is the intentional product of the social order.

12. Significantly, in *The Organization Man*, the Ford Motor Company stands as Whyte's example of an old-style corporation that privileges the Protestant ethic over the new "social ethic." Whyte compares Ford to General Electric, where "a young man is likely to talk about managing"; at Ford, by contrast, "he will talk about cars" (127).

13. See Barthes ("Death") and Baudrillard ("Precession").

14. The classic model of the cybernetic "governor" is the thermostat, a switch that turns a machine on and off when certain predetermined conditions are met. It did not take long, however, before cybernetics began to generate (anxious) interest in the other, political sort of governor. See, for instance, *The Human Use of Human Beings* (178–86), where Wiener addresses fears about a cybernetic "governing machine."

15. See von Bertalanffy's classic (1968) description of systems theory. For an insightful application of early systems thinking to contemporary literature, see LeClair's *Art of Excess* and *In the Loop*, both of which also provide an excellent general introduction to systems theory. Like the first-order systems theorists he so admires, especially Bateson, LeClair tends to celebrate the value of "systems thinking" over "causal thinking," and he often reads such values into the authors he studies. Yet while Heller is deeply interested in social systems and while he might agree with the values Bateson espouses, *Catch-22* expresses serious reservations and anxieties about the malevolence of large information processing systems. The same is true of other texts I examine. For an analysis of systems theory that illustrates some of the problems with Bateson and other first-order theorists, see Wolff.

16. See Bradbury (213) and Tanner (73), for instance.

17. In their massive overview of paranoia, Swanson, Bohnert, and Smith delineate its major characteristics as: "(1) projective thinking, (2) hostility, (3) suspiciousness, (4) centrality, (5) delusions, (6) fear of loss of autonomy, and (7) grandiosity" (19).

18. Compare this logic to Baudrillard's view that "military psychology retreats from the Cartesian clarities and hesitates to draw the distinction between true and false, between the 'produced' symptom and the authentic symptom. 'If he acts crazy so well, then he must be mad' " ("Precession" 255). This is not the case in Heller's novel. On the contrary, in *Catch-22* the military's view is "if he acts crazy so well, then he must be *sane*." Simulation does not enter the picture because the structure is designed to punish all attitudes equally.

19. By "most poststructuralists and systems theorists," I mean those who view the condition of mediated reality not as a new historical development, but as a permanent consequence of linguistic communication. I do not place Baudrillard in this group because he believes that misrepresentation and simulation are historical developments. There once was a time, he argues, when signs accurately related to material reality ("Precession" 256). In making this distinction, however, I do not mean to minimize the substantial difference between Heller and Baudrillard. Baudrillard is extremely skeptical about our ability to locate the real. Heller, by contrast, assumes representations are easily distinguished from a more determining reality. Indeed, the comic effects of his novel rely on this assumption.

20. Milo accomplishes this feat by selling the products *to himself* several times in different countries so that he can eventually offer them back to the mess at just below the inflated rate (i.e., the rate he has paid himself in a sham transaction). In one scheme, for instance, he buys

eggs in Sicily for 1 cent each, sells them in Malta to himself for 4 cents, and buys them back from himself at 7 cents. Thus, when he provides them to the mess at 5 cents he claims to be taking a loss of 2 cents; this is technically true, but because he has already driven up the price 6 cents, he actually makes a profit of 4 cents per egg (see 226–27).

Notes to Chapter 2

1. For an interesting account of some of the theoretical problems generated by the novel's opening, see Marc Redfield.

2. All ellipses in quotations of *Gravity's Rainbow* are in the original, unless otherwise indicated.

3. The sensation of the uncanny turns on a difficulty in recognizing whether troubling and apparently significant events are psychically produced (i.e., "familiar" or "homely"), or whether they are external and "unfamiliar"—an uncertainty also central to paranoia. (In fact, Freud relates the sense of "doubling" in the uncanny to the self-critical functions of mind that are central to "the pathological case of delusions of being watched" ["Uncanny" 235].) Of course, Freud argues that such splits and uncertain moments are internal to the subject, who only experiences them as strange or unfamiliar after "alienating" them from consciousness "through the process of repression" ("Uncanny" 241). I return to these issues in Chapter 3.

4. According to the *Oxford English Dictionary*, "agency" usually means either "active working" and "action," or "instrumentality" and "intermediation." In 1830, Coleridge wrote of "personal free agency," a coupling that appears to govern the recent sense of "agency" as autonomy and freedom. For a concise history of the legal concept of agency, see James Beniger (132–42). In the mid-nineteenth-century United States, Beniger explains, the "general laws of agency" (135) were established because agents had become too autonomous and needed to be held legally responsible for actions that departed from the explicit demands of their (often distant) principles. In other words, the general laws of "agency" made agents anything but autonomous.

5. For a useful distinction between the terms "individual," "character," "self," and "person," see Rorty.

6. Paranoia has been a perennial subject in Pynchon criticism because Pynchon himself uses the term a great deal. Though not the case in some recent work (Bersani; Bérubé; McHoul and Wills; and Berressem), the category of paranoia has often been used in Pynchon criticism as a way of short-circuiting Pynchon's sophisticated handling of uncertainty about agency. Scott Sanders, for example, implies that Pynchon's characters suffer from pathological delusions. But the fact that the characters are obsessed with and paranoid *about their paranoia* suggests that agency dilemmas in this novel are designed to keep accounts like Sanders's in constant play with those of readers like Deborah Madsen, who claims, for example, that "Slothrop is . . . an explicit case of a pervasive programme of cultural conditioning" (85).

7. See McHoul and Wills for a sophisticated reading of "postal systems" in Pynchon's *Crying of Lot 49* and Derrida's *Post Card*.

8. It is impossible for me to do justice here to the scope or intricacy of this debate between Lacan and Derrida, which has itself inspired a large and impressive body of critical writing. For a collection of some of this work, see Muller and Richardson.

9. For an account of the ways critical theory (primarily that of Lacan; Derrida; and Baudrillard) may be used to rethink subjectivity in Pynchon's novels, see Berressem, especially 15–50.

10. See Dennett's *Consciousness Explained*.

11. See also Friedman and Puetz; and Cooper. McHoul and Wills offer a radically differ-

ent account of the way binary oppositions function in this novel, suggesting that each rhetorical pair comes into "equivalence" with a object. This equivalence (or "material typonymy") is not final—but rather may come, itself, into equivalence with another object, and so on, so that an origin or governing final term is endlessly deferred.

12. The classic linguistic account is Roman Jakobson's (1956). For a different reading of this passage, see Joseph Tabbi, who argues that Pynchon privileges "signs and symptoms" over "causes" (87).

13. This textualization of structures and persons within a text is central to *The Crying of Lot 49*, where Oedipa eventually feels she is "walking among matrices of a great digital computer, the zeroes and ones twinned above... Behind the hieroglyphic streets there would either be a transcendent meaning, or only the earth" (181).

14. Theories that explain consciousness as a result of unconscious binary processes often meet with disapproval because they provoke the same kinds of agency panic I am sketching here. Early models of consciousness, for example, personified control in homunculi or "sorting demons" who would manage the flow of information within the system. As Daniel Dennett has explained, such personifications only shift the original problem to another level: who controls the homunculi—smaller homunculi? (*Consciousness Explained*, esp. 259–63). "Solved" this way, the problem only proliferates endlessly. *Gravity's Rainbow* often reads like a narrative of homunculi who have personified control in the opposite direction: externally, in "Them." Only occasionally do they attain a vantage from which they can see their position in a system.

15. Michael Bérubé, following Leo Bersani, aligns paranoia with interpretation in general and goes on to suggest that when the paranoid search for an organic whole comes to rest "it is no longer a paranoia but, in Pynchon's terms, a *pornography*" (238). For Bérubé, Pynchon's use of the term pornography indicates "a regressive anamnesia that recreates illusory, prelapsarian (or prelinguistic) unities through a complex mechanism of dismemberment and reconfiguration" (248). DeLillo often uses pornography in a related manner (see esp. *Running Dog* and *Libra* 77).

16. Similar rhetoric recurs in popular narratives of the period. In *The Greening of America*, for example, Charles Reich argues that the postwar "individual has no *existence* apart from his work and his relationship to society. Without his career, without his function, he would be a non-person..." (84).

17. On this subject, see Tabbi (*Postmodern*), especially 85–87.

18. Lacan argues that even matters of chance may be said to have a mathematically describable pattern. In one of several essays appended to his "Seminar on 'The Purloined Letter,'" he attempts to sketch the way laws of the unconscious might be mathematically formulated using cybernetic principles—the assumption being that "randomness" may always be said to fall into a mathematically describable pattern and specifically into a sequence of 0's and 1's, which makes it possible to think of symbolic place as either presence or absence. The notion of so-called free association, for example, depends heavily upon this idea of unconscious determination. (See Muller and Richardson 67–75.)

19. See Weber (246–54). For a detailed account of Pynchon's use of Weber, see especially Schaub (*Pynchon* 57–63) and Thomas Moore (116–48).

20. David Seed says there is general agreement among Pynchon's critics that Norman O. Brown's *Life Against Death* "exerted a strong influence over *Gravity's Rainbow* particularly in presenting history and economics as neurosis" and in understanding culture as dominated by the death-instinct (168). Brown's influence indicates that Pynchon imagines persons and economies to be related. Not only are they self-controlling in roughly the same way; they also appear, in places, to be *continuous* with one another. It is not always clear, in *Gravity's Rainbow*, whether the qualities of personhood would be better represented by an economy or by an individual human being.

21. James Beniger describes the ways "teleonomic explanations obviate the need to attribute consciousness, planning, purpose, or any other anthropomorphic qualities to aggregate levels, the special problem of *reification*. Adam Smith's 'invisible hand' of market forces, for example, can be seen to result from the interconnected programming of individuals and their organizations, including individual tactics, strategies, and utilities, on the one hand, and organizational procedures, written law, and cultural norms on the other" (41).

Notes to Chapter 3

1. See, for instance, Bouson, 54–61; Onley, 30–32; Pratt, 154; and Rigney, 39.

2. The term "female paranoia" is Naomi Schor's. My use of the term should not be taken to imply mental illness or delusion. *Stalked By Love* is the title of a "costume Gothic" novel written by Joan Foster, the protagonist of Atwood's *Lady Oracle* (1976).

3. For an excellent account of the interrelations between fear of persecution and a feeling of bodily dissolution, fragmentation, or uncontrollability, see Louis Sass's *Madness and Modernism*. For an account of the latter problems and their relation to gender, see Elaine Showalter's *The Female Malady*. John Farrell asserts that "the paranoid character, as prominently represented in modern culture both in history and literature, is almost exclusively male" (224n1). Yet Swanson, Bohnert, and Smith note that "it is a general clinical impression that paranoid disorders are more common in females than in males.... This impression is supported by studies of paranoid disorders in general and paraphrenia in particular. The greatest difference is in the age group of 40 to 50, in which the incidence in the female is twice that in the male" (241–42).

4. Unless otherwise noted, all references are to this edition.

5. In the Schreber case, Freud says, "I think it is legitimate to base analytic interpretations upon the case history of a patient suffering from paranoia (or more precisely, from dementia paranoides) whom I have never seen, but who has written his own case history and brought it before the public in print" ("Psycho-Analytic Notes" 9).

6. Rivière's translation is: "I take the liberty of assuming that this piece of information was a mistaken memory" (158).

7. As Schor notes, the second interview, like the client's second visit, is a form of doubling (a double doubling) that begins to imitate the doubleness of paranoia itself (209).

8. See "Psycho-Analytic Notes" 79; "Constructions in Analysis" 268; "Preface to Reik's *Ritual*" 261; "On Narcissism" 96. See also Bersani, 100.

9. The passage Atwood uses as her epigraph directly precedes these lines. It reads: "A man's presence suggests what he is capable of doing to you or for you. By contrast, a woman's presence...defines what can and cannot be done to her" (Berger 45–46, qtd. in *Bodily Harm* 8).

10. See Showalter, especially 203–19.

11. Sass notes in passing, "It is hardly necessary to experience so extreme a panoptical regimen as Schreber did in order for these kinds of symptoms to develop" (505n18).

12. Molly Hite begins her account of *Lady Oracle* by observing that Foster's "story of... construction by others" is tightly coupled with this pervasive sense of surveillance from a spiritual "other side" (*Other Side* 127–28). Hite demonstrates that Atwood's blurring of the border between self and other functions as a way of blurring the border between "truth" and fiction—a border that, not coincidentally, is always renegotiated in cases of paranoia. She also shows how critics misread this technique, blaming Atwood's characters for not properly policing the borders of their selves and thus unintentionally reasserting those problematic notions challenged by Atwood's border-breaking strategies. Much the same dynamic is at work in Freud's handling of his patient in "A Case." For an interesting treatment of surveillance in Atwood's *Cat's Eye*, see Hite's "Optics and Autobiography."

13. This remark and another ("You just don't know what people will turn out to have in their hearts" [158]) allude to the popular radio program, "The Shadow" (1930–1954), which always opened with the line: "Who knows what evil lurks in the hearts of men? The Shadow knows...." Johnson's novel asks this question with special emphasis on "men."

14. See also DuPlessis, and Snitow.

15. See Bouson, Rubenstein, and O'Donnell ("Engendering"), all of whom use the category of paranoia to offer interesting accounts of the dynamics in *Bodily Harm* (Bouson; Rubenstein) and *The Shadow Knows* (O'Donnell; Rubenstein).

16. According to 1990 FBI statistics, 30 percent of female homicide victims were killed by husbands or boyfriends (McAnaney et al. 838), and 90 percent of those were stalked before the attack (Cordes 13). Estimates of various legal and victim support agencies suggest that somewhere between 50 and 95 percent of victims are stalked by someone with whom they have been involved romantically (Cordes 13). There is little evidence, however, that such acts are undetectable or mysterious in origin. *Bodily Harm* makes clear the difference between such obvious male violence and Rennie's more vague suspicions through Rennie's friend Lora, who is the victim of repeated sexual assaults and yet never feels her persecutor's intentions are unclear, let alone invisible. When her stepfather attempts to rape her, for instance, even her mother is unsurprised (170–72). In other words, in the novel's most overt and repeated instances of violence against women, there is no need to imagine a persecutor with a benign surface and a hidden evil core.

17. For the classic account of this concept, see Macpherson.

18. The statements in parentheses are the remarks of anorexics, quoted in Susan Bordo's excellent study of that disorder ("Anorexia" 94, 97). Significantly, this refusal of Marian's body to take food, in spite of her self's desire to do so, reverses typical accounts of anorexia, which is frequently experienced as the self's refusal to be dominated by the bodily urge to eat.

19. See also Russ.

20. For an account of the cultural work performed by descriptions of male serial killers as "anonymous" or "abnormally normal" see Seltzer's "Serial Killers (1)" (96–98). I have been suggesting that the male violator, despite his apparent familiarity, is typically imagined as "anonymous" or "generic" because he is standing in for the social order. In short, a "paranoid" speculation about anonymous subjects is one way of theorizing the social origins of antifemale violence.

21. Butler (*Bodies* 4–12) offers a good description of the ways in which social construction and "power" (in Foucault's sense of the term) can be misunderstood.

22. I am not suggesting that male violence toward women is a result of something women do or fail to do. I am suggesting that understanding social control through the figure of the anonymous stalker is a way of localizing and revealing socially scripted behaviors; it helps to represent, as a specific, embodied threat, those institutions and discourses that shape female identity and behavior. But to return to the potential objection, even the representation of rape and the production of knowledge about rape may affect the behavior of its victims. "The language of rape," Sharon Marcus has argued, "solicits women to position ourselves as endangered, violable, and fearful...." The "grammar of violence," Marcus's term for a common rape "script," "dictates that feminine fear concentrate the self on the anticipation of pain, the inefficacy of action, and the conviction that the self will be destroyed" (390, 394). Whether such a response is understandable, warranted, or efficacious is, of course, debatable; that it is expected of victims, however, seems valid.

Notes to Chapter 4

1. Whether watching a television program while millions of others watch the same program is indeed a "collective experience" is questionable, but this remark hints at some of the

tensions implicit in our continuing discourse about this moment in U.S. history. Jameson makes the second point cited here while arguing against a potential opponent who would accuse him of attempting to systematize an entity that is marked by its unsystematic nature, its fragmentation. Because capitalism is a "system" that nonetheless relies on and produces individual "differences," Jameson uses it as an analog for the postmodern, which is a "system" of "unrelated subsystems," a "sheer heteronomy" (342) that one might nonetheless subsume under the single concept "postmodern." As Niklas Luhmann has suggested, the concept of differentiation is itself systemic: the play of differences in a system can be unified by viewing them as part of the normal "autopoietic" functioning of that system. The distinction between individuating differences and the system that makes visible and allows one to understand those differences is partly a function of the level at which one imagines the problem, whether one imagines oneself inside or outside the system. Jameson's interest lies partly in how the capitalist culture industry produced this collective "communicational 'festival' " (355). I am interested here in some variants of the relations between the collective and the individuating—and particularly in how a managed competition between systems and individualist accounts might function to sustain an incessant discourse about causality, motive, and event.

2. Guth and Wrone's excellent, comprehensive bibliography of Kennedy assassination materials includes 5,134 entries (including 2,431 news articles) published up to 1979. Clearly, if one were to include material produced after that date, the numbers would be much higher.

3. Prominent lone-gunman accounts include, Belin; James Bishop; Ford and Stiles; Priscilla Johnson; Manchester; Jim Moore; and most recently Posner. Prominent accounts of Mafia and Cuban conspiracies include Blakey and Billings; John Davis; Kurtz; and Scheim. Widely known theories of government conspiracy, including purported efforts to keep elements of the crime out of the public eye, include Epstein; Hurt; Lane; Lifton; Meagher; Thompson; and Weisberg.

4. By placing Foucault's analysis in the context of paranoia, I do not mean to suggest that what Foucault calls a traditional historiography is paranoid or that there is anything pathological about Branch's dilemma. It would be impossible to interrogate documents of any sort, especially literary documents, without wondering if coincidences and apparently accidental doublings were not the product of design—in part because, as Lacan has suggested, "human knowledge" is based on a "paranoic" principle ("Aggressivity in Psychoanalysis" 17). For an interesting account of paranoia in DeLillo's *Running Dog*, see Patrick O'Donnell's "Obvious Paranoia." O'Donnell's "Engendering Paranoia" takes up a number of contemporary novels through a resolutely nonpsychoanalytic account of paranoia as "cultural perception of subject-object relations" (184n5), a "method" that binds communities of people who sense they are subjects in a historical plot orchestrated by others.

5. For a general description of conspiracy genre fictions and their features—fictions that represent what I am calling the theory of social conspiracy—see Fulcher; and Palmer and Riley.

6. In general, this tension between individual and social occurs in DeLillo's work as an opposition between "the great dictator" (Hitler or Mao, embodiments of centralized control) and the system over which no single individual has control (the CIA in *The Names*, *Running Dog*, and *Libra*, for example). In *Mao II*, it takes more literary form, as Bill Gray (an individual genius in the Romantic tradition) confronts an array of mass movements in which "gender and features don't matter, where names don't matter," where people "blend in, lose themselves in something larger" (89).

7. Similarly, the Unabomber's revolutionary manifesto rails at both liberals and conservatives. Certainly, one could read Oswald's attempt on Walker as one component of a sophisticated ideological plan (by himself or by others) to kill the President. But, as DeLillo's novel suggests and other commentators have argued, determining the motives for Oswald's apparently contradictory actions is extremely difficult. For more on this, see Mailer's *Oswald's Tale*.

8. See, for example, Frank Lentricchia (203) or Thomas Carmichael, who astutely observes that Oswald "attempts to situate himself as that autonomous subject who would escape his status as an effect of both ideology and the symbolic" (210). But Carmichael adds that "in [Oswald's] proclamation of integrity and autonomy, there is the admission of his own status as 'effect'...and it is this postmodern subject that DeLillo inscribes...in *Libra*" (211). This is true, I am suggesting, only if we accept Oswald's fatally flawed concept of the agent. Much recent work on postmodern subjectivity begins with the assumption that social construction is an all-or-nothing proposition. This view is one of the things that most contributes to agency panic. Instead of assuming that social construction means an utter evacuation of individual agency, one might view it as unavoidable and not *wholly* constraining. As Judith Butler suggests, "Paradoxically, the reconceptualization of identity as an *effect*, that is, as *produced* or *generated*, opens up possibilities of 'agency' that are insidiously foreclosed by positions that take identity categories as foundational or fixed. For an identity to be an effect means that it is neither fatally determined nor fully artificial and arbitrary" (*Gender* 147).

9. For a scene that makes this point explicitly, see *Mao II* (76ff). There, in the context of references to the "individual wrap" on pieces of candy, a Moonie convert is kidnapped and "deprogrammed."

10. This view is central to films such as Stone's *Natural Born Killers*, for instance.

11. But Lentricchia erroneously concludes that "the action is finally somewhere else—at a level of power, beyond the conspiracies of agents, where there is no head to cut off" (Lentricchia 204). This formulation, a social version of Cartesian materialism, repeats Latta's mistake at another level. It suggests that there is a transcendent "level of power, beyond the conspiracies of agents"—that is, beyond the actions of those individuals who make up the system, rather than *immanent* to those agents. But, as Foucault insists, "Power exists only when it is put into action" ("Subject" 219).

Notes to Chapter 5

1. Widely cited estimates of the number of alcoholics in America, for instance, ballooned from 4–5 million by the 1960s to over 20 million by the 1980s—though these estimates have been questioned by some researchers (Cahalan 16–19; Gusfield 55–60). Other work has shown that increasing addict identification bears little resemblance to patterns of consumption, which are declining (Korcok 1). Speculative estimates are even more common in the new addiction treatment industries. According to Edward Armstrong, the Executive Director of The National Association on Sexual Addiction Problems, somewhere between 10 and 25 percent of Americans have "a sexual addition that requires treatment" (qtd. in Peele, *Diseasing* 115). Accurate or not, such estimates have led to increased treatment. The percentage of Americans in treatment for alcoholism was twenty times higher in 1976 than in 1942 (Weisner and Room), and it has increased steadily since (Peele, *Diseasing* 49). As might be expected, the number of treatment facilities and support groups for both traditional problems such as alcoholism and new pathologies like "shopping addiction" has increased dramatically (Peele, *Diseasing* 46–52, 115–43).

2. As William S. Burroughs noted in 1956, "We speak of addiction to candy, coffee, tobacco, warm weather, television, detective stories, crossword puzzles" (Appendix to *Naked Lunch* 239).

3. For a similar discussion in the context of much larger questions about homosexuality and "homosexual panic," see Sedgwick's *Epistemology of the Closet* 171–78.

4. Much of the Unabomber "manifesto," which the mainstream press often described as the work of an antisocial lunatic, is squarely in the tradition of American individualism that begins roughly with Thoreau and runs through recent critiques of technological rationaliza-

tion, bureaucracy, and social control. When the Unabomber suggests that "too much control is imposed by the system through explicit regulation or through socialization, which results in a deficiency of autonomy" (85), he could be quoting a number of popular postwar texts. Herbert Marcuse's conclusion, for instance—that individuals suffer a deficiency of autonomy and become "one-dimensional"—is similar to the Unabomber's complaints about the "over-socialized" subjects of postindustrial America. It is worth noting, too, that Marcuse's concept of social "introjection" (*One-Dimensional* 9) relies on the same metaphysics of internal and external control that underwrites the rhetoric of addiction.

5. Scott Bukatman's excellent study of postmodern science fiction centers on radically reimagined forms of human (and humanoid) subjectivity, which he calls "terminal identity." The term "terminal identity" comes from Burroughs's *Nova Express* (19).

6. As Tony Tanner points out, "'We are all agents,' is one of Burroughs's sayings" (116).

7. Philosopher Charles Taylor's account of human agency mobilizes the traditional opposition between human agency and addiction. See "What Is Human Agency?" (esp. 21–22).

8. In Marx's view, the commodity is "a mysterious thing, simply because in it the social character of men's labour appears to them as an objective character stamped upon the product of that labour" (83). To illustrate this point, Marx personifies commodities (81–82) and imagines what would happen "could commodities themselves speak" (95).

9. On the cut-up technique, see Miles 111–28; Morgan 321–23, 338–41; Murphy 103–07, 135–41; Porush 101–04; and Tanner 123–31. I do not mean to suggest that cut-ups are without aesthetic interest or meaning, or that they are "simply destructive"—a view that Murphy rightly calls "irresponsible" (104). Nor do I wish to suggest that the actual *practice* of making cut-ups was motivated primarily by a (paranoid) desire for self-defense. My claim is simply that the theory of the cut-up, and the *Nova* Trilogy from which it springs, is predicated on a radical and bodily conception of social influence. Nonetheless, I do not believe that cut-ups contain what Murphy (following Burroughs) calls the "real power of prophecy." As evidence of this view, Murphy offers a detailed reading showing how a cut-up anti-drug pamphlet reveals an important power structure and thus anticipates the "critical insight" of Foucault's *Discipline and Punish*. Yet Murphy also lets slip that "Burroughs had already recognized" this power structure in *Junky* and *Naked Lunch*—texts that preceded the cut-up technique by several years (106).

10. In a 1963 interview, Burroughs claimed that large organizations such as *Time/Life* magazines and the CIA controlled a powerful hoard of "words and images" that even their human heads (Henry Luce, for instance) had "no control over" (qtd. in Miles 130).

11. Donna Haraway sets out the distinctions between "postmodern" biology and previous models of the self in her "Cyborg Manifesto."

12. See Minsky's *Society of the Mind*, for instance. For commentary on this model, see Dennett (*Consciousness Explained*) and Varela, Thompson, and Rosch (esp. Chapter 6). The latter text offers a positive alternative to Minsky's view and to the problems I am tracing here. Bukatman offers an interesting discussion of the relation between Burroughs's fiction and the notion of "the body without organs" advanced by Deleuze and Guattari (325–28).

13. For several eyewitness accounts of this event, see Morgan 194–97.

14. The misogynist strain of these writings is nowhere so evident as when Burroughs attempts to defend himself against charges of misogyny. See, for instance, his short essay, "Women: A Biological Mistake?" For a more detailed account of Burroughs's misogyny, see Murphy.

15. See Burroughs, *Letters* 68–69, 85–86, 88–89, 115–16.

16. On the history of these associations, see Sedgwick's "Epidemics of the Will" and Foucault's *History of Sexuality* (esp. 42–43).

17. Citations from Packard here are chapter titles. Others chapters with similar implications include "Babes in Consumerland," "Back to the Breast, and Beyond," "The Engineered

Yes," and "The Packaged Soul?" Like Riesman, though more melodramatically, Ellul suggests that psychological collectivization, which is epitomized by advertising, will "implant in [the individual] a certain conception of life" (406).

18. Stanton Peele draws the same kind of connection between drugs and large social institutions. Drugs, he says, "also drew the ire of the bureaucratic institutions which were growing up alongside of opiates in America—institutions which exercised a similar type of power psychologically to that of the narcotics, and with which, therefore, the drugs were essentially competing" (*Love and Addiction* 37).

Notes to Epilogue

1. See, for instance, Hassan ("Culture" 123–4); Jameson (26–34, 345, 375); and Harvey (43, 53).

2. In his review of Jonathan Harr's *A Civil Action* (1995), David Cassuto explains some of the consequences of this principle in recent anticorporate tort actions. As Joseph Tabbi points out in an introduction to Cassuto's article, Cassuto shows that the "humanist formula" of the heroic individual battle against the corporation "simply won't work, since the current tort laws (set up in a spirit of civic good faith to deal with burdens of proof and standards of human doubt) make it extremely difficult to bring a polluting corporation to justice" ("Introduction").

3. The U.S. Department of Highway Safety recently replaced the term "accident" with "crash" to emphasize the role of humans in causing collisions. Literally speaking, there are no more accidents on U.S. highways.

4. This description is somewhat tautological, since postmodernism is already "the logic of" late capitalism in Jameson's view. If we accept this formulation, then cyberpunk cannot be a critical response to capitalism but rather, like all forms of postmodernism, must be a product or expression of capitalism. The problem with this view is not its suggestion that cyberpunk texts might function *partly* in the service of capitalism or that *some* cyberpunk texts encourage and sustain capitalist fantasies. Rather, the problem lies in the suggestion that cyberpunk *in general* is hardwired to capitalism. Such a thesis avoids the work of specifying what texts, authors, passages, or rhetorical maneuvers reinforce capitalist ideology (and by contrast which ones might offer resistance). It seems to me that, at its best, cyberpunk, like many postmodern forms, *sometimes* presents a compelling and disturbing picture of multinational capitalism. Acker's novel is extremely different in formal terms from the science fiction usually labeled "cyberpunk." But Acker is much truer than any of the sci-fi "cyberpunks" to the original "punk" tradition of nihilism, writing-on-the-body, and anti-aestheticism.

5. In Gibson's *Neuromancer*, for instance, Molly submits to neural implants that make her a fully "programmable" prostitute, because she needs the money.

6. Dick's novel was *Do Androids Dream of Electric Sheep?* (1968).

7. The film has replicant Roy Batty save his pursuer, Deckard, and then allows Batty a lyrical final soliloquy, which is derived from the parting comments of the monster in Mary Shelley's *Frankenstein*. The combination of these acts, along with the allusion, suggests that the real human in the scene is Batty.

8. "Let us remember," writes Wiener, "that the automatic machine, whatever we think of any feelings it may have or may not have, is the precise economic equivalent of slave labor" (*Human* 162).

9. See both Whyte and Packard, for instance. That this method of testing derives from early postwar sources is not surprising because it is one of the few elements of the story taken intact from Dick's novel. Significantly, Dick's androids develop a method of ferreting out hu-

mans based on their capacity for *panic*. According to Roy, who creates a special panic-producing device, "No human being can remain [near the device] more than a matter of seconds. That's the nature of panic: it leads to random circus-motions, purposeless flight, and muscle and neural spasms" (142).

10. The original anti-Masonic conspiracy theory, articulated by Scottish scientist John Robison in 1797, warned that such a substitution was afoot. The Freemasons and Illuminati, Robison asserted, were meeting "for the express purpose of ROOTING OUT ALL THE RELIGIOUS ESTABLISHMENTS, AND OVERTURNING ALL THE EXISTING GOVERNMENTS OF EUROPE" (qtd. in Hofstadter 11).

11. See Andrew Ross and Veronica Hollinger. Hollinger notes that, contrary to claims about their depiction of a new terminal or posthuman experience, many "science-fiction futures are all too often simply representations of contemporary cultural mythologies disguised under heavy layers of futuristic make-up" (39). She also suggests that novels by Burroughs; Pynchon; and Atwood go further in their "deconstruction of individual subjectivity" than most cyberpunk narratives (41). Istvan Csicsery-Ronay points out that, in a kind of "sentimental futurism," Gibson often elegizes "the loss of the historical 'human'" (237).

12. Brian McHale first pointed out that *Empire of the Senseless* "samples" parts of Gibson's *Neuromancer*. His *Constructing Postmodernism* provides a helpful map of these borrowings (233–36, 239–42). Joseph Tabbi connects cyberpunk to the form of literary expression that he call "postmodern sublime"—a mode whose practitioners include Pynchon; DeLillo; Mailer; McElroy; and Acker. By placing Acker in this broader tradition of writing about technology, Tabbi offers a more detailed and compelling account of how and why she appropriates cyberpunk (*Postmodern* 208ff).

13. The CIA's MK/ULTRA program was overseen by George White and Charles Siragusa (P. D. Scott 172–73). This plot also surfaces in Sol Yurick's novel of conspiracy, phone espionage, and computer hacking, *Richard A* (1981), and David Foster Wallace's *Infinite Jest* (see, e.g., 212 and 1033n198).

Works Cited

Abrams, M. H. "What Is a Humanistic Criticism?" *Bookpress* [Ithaca, NY] May 1993: 1+.

Acker, Kathy. *Empire of the Senseless.* New York: Grove, 1988.

"Agency." *Oxford English Dictionary.* 1989 ed.

Anderson, Benedict. *Imagined Communities: Reflections on the Origin and Spread of Nationalism.* 1983. Rev. ed. London: Verso, 1991.

Atwood, Margaret. *Bodily Harm.* Toronto: McClelland and Stewart, 1981.

———. *The Edible Woman.* Toronto: McClelland and Stewart, 1969.

———. *The Handmaid's Tale.* Toronto: McClelland and Stewart, 1985.

———. *Lady Oracle.* New York: Simon and Schuster, 1976.

———. *Surfacing.* New York: Simon and Schuster, 1972.

Barthes, Roland. *Camera Lucida: Reflections on Photography.* Trans. Richard Howard. New York: Farrar, Straus and Giroux, 1981.

———. "The Death of the Author." *Image—Music—Text.* Trans. Stephen Heath. New York: Hill and Wang, 1977. 142–48.

Bateson, Gregory. "Conscious Purpose Versus Nature." *Steps to an Ecology of Mind* 426–39.

———. "The Cybernetics of 'Self': A Theory of Alcoholism." *Steps to an Ecology of Mind* 309–37.

———. "Form, Substance, and Difference." *Steps to an Ecology of Mind* 448–65.

———. *Mind and Nature: A Necessary Unity.* New York: Bantam, 1979.

———. "Minimal Requirements for a Theory of Schizophrenia." *Steps to an Ecology of Mind* 244–70.

———. *Steps to an Ecology of Mind.* New York: Ballantine, 1972.

———. "Toward a Theory of Schizophrenia." *Steps to an Ecology of Mind* 201–27.

Baudrillard, Jean. *America.* Trans. Chris Turner. New York: Verso, 1988.

———. "The Ecstasy of Communication." Trans. John Johnston. *The Anti-Aesthetic: Essays on Postmodern Culture.* Ed. Hal Foster. Port Townsend, WA: Bay Press, 1983. 126–134.

———. "The Masses: The Implosion of the Social in the Media." Trans. Marie Maclean. *Jean Baudrillard: Selected Writings.* Ed. Mark Poster. Stanford: Stanford UP, 1988. 207–19.

———. "The Precession of Simulacra." Trans. Paul Foss and Paul Patton. *Art after Modernism: Rethinking Representation.* Ed. Brian Wallis. New York: New Museum of Contemporary Art, 1984. 253–81.

Baym, Nina. "Melodramas of Beset Manhood: How Theories of American Fiction Exclude Women Authors." *The New Feminist Criticism: Essays on Women, Literature, and Theory.* Ed. Elaine Showalter. New York: Pantheon, 1985. 63–80.

Belin, David. *November 22, 1963: You Are the Jury.* New York: Quadrangle, 1973.

Bell, Daniel. *The Coming of Post-Industrial Society: A Venture in Social Forecasting.* New York: Basic, 1973.

———. *The Radical Right.* Garden City, NY: Doubleday, 1963.

Bellah, Robert N., Richard Madsen, William M. Sullivan, Ann Sidler, and Steven M. Tipton. *Habits of the Heart: Individualism and Commitment in American Life.* New York: Harper and Row, 1985.

Beniger, James R. *The Control Revolution: Technological and Economic Origins of the Information Society.* Cambridge: Harvard UP, 1986.

Benjamin, Jessica. "Master and Slave: The Fantasy of Erotic Domination." *Powers of Desire*. Ed. Ann Barr Snitow, Christine Stansell, and Sharon Thompson. New York: Monthly Review, 1983. 280–99.

Berger, John. *Ways of Seeing*. London: BBC/Penguin, 1972.

Berkeley, Edmund Callis. *The Computer Revolution*. Garden City, NY: Doubleday, 1962.

Berressem, Hanjo. *Pynchon's Poetics: Interfacing Theory and Text*. Urbana: U of Illinois P, 1993.

Bersani, Leo. "Pynchon, Paranoia, and Literature." *Representations* 25 (Winter 1989): 99–118.

Bertalanffy, Ludwig von. *General System Theory: Foundations, Development, Applications*. New York: Braziller, 1968.

Bérubé, Michael. *Marginal Forces/Cultural Centers: Tolson, Pynchon, and the Politics of the Canon*. Ithaca: Cornell UP, 1992.

Bierce, Ambrose. *The Enlarged Devil's Dictionary*. Ed. Ernest Jerome Hopkins. New York: Doubleday, 1967.

Birkerts, Sven. "Into the Electronic Millennium." *Boston Review* 16 (Oct. 1991): 14–15, 18–20.

Bishop, James A. *The Day Kennedy Was Shot*. New York: Funk and Wagnalls, 1968.

Bishop, John. *Natural Agency: An Essay on the Causal Theory of Action*. Cambridge: Cambridge UP, 1990.

Blakey, G. Robert, and Richard N. Billings. *Fatal Hour: The Assassination of President Kennedy by Organized Crime*. New York: Berkley, 1992.

Blum, Richard H. "On the Presence of Demons." *Society and Drugs: Social and Cultural Observations*. Ed. Richard Blum and Associates. San Francisco: Jossey-Bass, 1969. 323–41.

Bordo, Susan. "Anorexia Nervosa: Psychopathology as the Crystallization of Culture." *Feminism and Foucault: Reflections on Resistance*. Ed. Irene Diamond and Lee Quinby. Boston: Northeastern UP, 1988. 87–117.

———. "The Body and the Reproduction of Femininity: A Feminist Appropriation of Foucault." *Gender/Body/Knowledge: Feminist Reconstructions of Being and Knowing*. Ed. Alison M. Jagger and Susan R. Bordo. New Brunswick: Rutgers UP, 1989. 13–33.

Boulding, Kenneth E. *The Meaning of the Twentieth Century: The Great Transition*. New York: Harper and Row, 1964.

Bouson, J. Brooks. *Brutal Choreographies: Oppositional Strategies and Narrative Design in the Novels of Margaret Atwood*. Amherst: U of Massachusetts P, 1993.

Bowert, William. *Operation Mind Control*. New York: Delacorte, 1977.

Bradbury, Malcolm. *The Modern American Novel*. Rev. ed. Harmondsworth, Eng.: Penguin, 1992.

Brand, Myles. *Intending and Acting: Toward a Naturalized Action Theory*. Cambridge: MIT P, 1984.

Bugliosi, Vincent, with Curt Gentry. *Helter Skelter*. New York: Bantam, 1974.

Bukatman, Scott. *Terminal Identity: The Virtual Subject in Postmodern Science Fiction*. Durham: Duke UP, 1993.

Burnham, James. *The Managerial Revolution: What Is Happening in the World*. New York: John Day, 1941.

Burroughs, William S. *The Adding Machine: Selected Essays*. New York: Arcade, 1985.

———. Appendix. *The Soft Machine*. 1961. Rev. ed. London: Calder, 1968.

———. *Exterminator!* New York: Penguin, 1973.

———. "The Invisible Generation." *The Ticket That Exploded* 205–17.

——. *Junky*. 1953. New York: Penguin, 1977.

——. *The Letters of William S. Burroughs, 1945–1959*. Ed. Oliver Harris. New York: Viking, 1993.

——. "The Limits of Control." *The Adding Machine* 117–21.

——. *Naked Lunch*. New York: Grove, 1959.

——. *Nova Express*. New York: Grove, 1964.

——. "On Coincidence." *The Adding Machine* 99–105.

——. *Queer*. New York: Penguin, 1985.

——. "Sexual Conditioning." *The Adding Machine* 87–89.

——. *The Soft Machine*. 1961. Rev. ed. New York: Grove, 1966.

——. *The Ticket That Exploded*. New York: Grove, 1962.

——. "Women: A Biological Mistake?" *The Adding Machine* 125–27.

Butler, Judith. *Bodies That Matter: On the Discursive Limits of "Sex."* New York: Routledge, 1993.

——. *Gender Trouble: Feminism and the Subversion of Identity*. New York: Routledge, 1988.

Cahalan, Don. *Understanding America's Drinking Problem: How to Combat the Hazards of Alcohol*. San Francisco: Jossey-Bass, 1987.

Carmichael, Thomas. "Lee Harvey Oswald and the Postmodern Subject: History and Intertextuality in Don DeLillo's *Libra*, *The Names*, and *Mao II*." *Contemporary Literature* 34.2 (1993): 204–18.

Cassuto, David N. "No More Heroes." *Electronic Book Review* 4 (winter 1996–1997). 10 Oct. 1998 <http://www.altx.com/ebr/ebr4/ebr4.htm>.

Chabot, C. Barry. *Freud on Schreber: Psychoanalytic Theory and the Critical Act*. Amherst: U of Massachusetts P, 1982.

Chomsky, Noam. Interview. *Manufacturing Consent*. Dir. March Achbar and Peter Wintonick. Zeitgeist Films, 1994.

Cocteau, Jean. *Opium: The Diary of a Cure*. 1929. Trans. Margaret Crosland and Sinclair Road. London: Peter Owen, 1957.

Cohen, William A., and Nurit Cohen. *The Paranoid Corporation and Eight Other Ways Your Company Can Be Crazy: Advice from an Organizational Shrink*. New York: Amacom, 1993.

Cohl, H. Aaron. *Are We Scaring Ourselves to Death?: How Pessimism, Paranoia, and a Misguided Media Are Leading Us Toward Disaster*. New York: St. Martin's Griffin, 1997.

Cooper, Peter L. *Signs and Symptoms: Thomas Pynchon and the Contemporary World*. Berkeley: U of California P, 1983.

Coover, Robert. *The Origin of the Brunists*. New York: Norton, 1966.

Cordes, Renée. "Watching Over the Watched: Greater Protection Sought for Stalking Victims." *Trial* Oct. 1993: 12–13.

Csicsery-Ronay, Istvan, Jr. "The Sentimental Futurist: Cybernetics and Art in William Gibson's *Neuromancer*." *Critique* 33.3 (1992): 221–40.

Culler, Jonathan. *Ferdinand de Saussure*. Rev. ed. Ithaca: Cornell UP, 1986.

Davidson, Donald. *Essays on Action and Events*. Oxford: Clarendon, 1980.

Davis, Brion David, ed. *The Fear of Conspiracy: Images of Un-American Subversion from the Revolution to the Present*. Ithaca: Cornell UP, 1971.

Davis, John H. *Mafia Kingfish: Carlos Marcello and the Assassination of John F. Kennedy*. 2nd ed. New York: Signet, 1989.

Dawkins, Richard. *The Extended Phenotype: The Gene as the Unit of Selection*. Oxford: Oxford UP, 1982.

Dean, Jodi. *Aliens in America: Conspiracy Cultures from Outerspace to Cyberspace.* Ithaca: Cornell UP, 1998.

de Lauretis, Teresa. *Technologies of Gender: Essays on Theory, Film, and Fiction.* Bloomington: Indiana UP, 1987.

Deleuze, Gilles, and Félix Guattari. *Anti-Oedipus: Capitalism and Schizophrenia.* 1972. Trans. Robert Hurley, Mark Seem, and Helen R. Lane. Minneapolis: U of Minnesota P, 1983.

——. *A Thousand Plateaus: Capitalism and Schizophrenia.* Trans. Brian Massumi. Minneapolis: U of Minnesota P, 1987.

DeLillo, Don. *Libra.* New York: Viking, 1988.

——. *Mao II.* New York: Viking, 1991.

——. *The Names.* New York: Knopf, 1982.

——. *Running Dog.* New York: Knopf, 1978.

——. *White Noise.* New York: Viking, 1985.

de Man, Paul. "Semiology and Rhetoric." *Allegories of Reading: Figural Language in Rousseau, Nietzsche, Rilke, and Proust.* New Haven, CT: Yale UP, 1979. 3–19.

Dennett, Daniel. "Conditions of Personhood." *The Identities of Persons.* Ed. Amélie Rorty. Berkeley: U of California P, 1976. 175–96.

——. *Consciousness Explained.* Boston: Little, Brown, 1991.

——. *Elbow Room: The Varieties of Free Will Worth Wanting.* Cambridge: MIT P, 1984.

——. *The Intentional Stance.* Cambridge: MIT P, 1987.

Dennis v. United States. 341 U.S. 494. 1951.

DePalma, Brian, dir. *Blow Out.* Filmway Pictures, 1981.

Derrida, Jacques. "Letter to a Japanese Friend." *A Derrida Reader: Between the Blinds.* Ed. Peggy Kamuf. New York: Columbia UP, 1991.

——. *Of Grammatology.* Trans. G. C. Spivak. Baltimore: Johns Hopkins UP, 1976.

——. "Plato's Pharmacy." *Dissemination.* 1972. Trans. Barbara Johnson. Chicago: U of Chicago P, 1981. 61–171.

——. *The Post Card: From Socrates to Freud and Beyond.* Trans. Alan Bass. Chicago: U of Chicago P, 1980.

——. "The Rhetoric of Drugs." 1989. Trans. Michael Israel. *differences* 5.1 (1993): 1–25.

Dick, Philip K. *Do Androids Dream of Electric Sheep?* New York: Del Ray/Ballantine, 1968.

——. "We Can Remember It for You Wholesale." *The Collected Stories of Philip K. Dick: The Little Black Box.* Vol. 5. Los Angeles: Underwood/Miller, 1987. 157–79.

Didion, Joan. *Play It As It Lays.* New York: Farrar, Straus and Giroux, 1970.

——. "The White Album." *The White Album.* New York: Simon and Schuster, 1979. 11–48.

Diggins, John Patrick. *The Rise and Fall of the American Left.* New York: Norton, 1992.

Dizard, Wilson P., Jr. *The Coming Information Age: An Overview of Technology, Economics, and Politics.* New York: Longman, 1982.

Donner, Richard, dir. *Conspiracy Theory.* Warner Brothers, 1997.

Douglas, Ann. *The Feminization of American Culture.* New York: Avon, 1977.

DuPlessis, Rachel Blau. *Writing beyond the Ending: Strategies of Twentieth-Century Women Writers.* Bloomington: Indiana UP, 1985.

Durkheim, Emile. *Suicide: A Study in Sociology.* 1897. Ed. George Simpson. Trans. John A. Spaulding and George Simpson. New York: Free Press, 1951.

Eisenstadt, Shmuel N., ed. *Post-Traditional Societies*. New York: Norton, 1972.

Ellison, Ralph. *Invisible Man*. New York: Vintage, 1952.

Ellul, Jacques. *The Technological Society*. 1954. Trans. John Wilkinson. New York: Vintage, 1964.

Emerson, Ralph Waldo. "Self-Reliance." 1841. *Essays and Lectures*. Ed. Joel Porte. New York: Library of America, 1983. 257–82.

Epstein, Edward J. *The Assassination Chronicles*. New York: Carroll & Graf, 1992.

Etzioni, Amitai. *The Active Society: A Theory of Societal and Political Processes*. New York: Free Press, 1968.

Evans, Christopher. *The Micro Millennium*. New York: Washington Square/Pocket Books, 1979.

Farrell, John. *Freud's Paranoid Quest: Psychoanalysis and Modern Suspicion*. New York: New York UP, 1996.

F.C. [a.k.a. "The Unabomber"]. "Industrial Society and Its Future." Orig. pub. *Washington Post* (19 Sept. 1995): available at <http://wwfreepress.com/unaba.html>. Rev. online ed. 15 May 1999. <http://readroom.ipl.org/bin/ipl/ipl.books-idx.pl?type=entry&id=3638>.

Feuer, Lewis S. *Marx and the Intellectuals: A Set of Post-Ideological Essays*. Garden City, NY: Anchor Books, 1969.

Finch, Phillip. *God, Guts, and Guns—A Close Look at the Radical Right*. New York: Seaview/Putnam, 1983.

Ford, Gerald R., with John M. Stiles. *Portrait of an Assassin*. New York: Simon and Schuster, 1965.

Forester, Tom, ed. *The Microelectronics Revolution*. Cambridge: MIT P, 1980.

Foucault, Michel. *The Archaeology of Knowledge and Discourse on Language*. Trans. A. M. Sheridan Smith. New York: Pantheon, 1972.

———. *Discipline and Punish: The Birth of the Prison*. Trans. Alan Sheridan. New York: Vintage, 1977.

———. *The History of Sexuality: An Introduction*. Trans. Robert Hurley. Vol. 1 of *The History of Sexuality*. New York: Vintage, 1978. 3 vols. 1978–1986.

———. *Madness and Civilization: A History of Madness in the Age of Reason*. 1961. Trans. Richard Howard. New York: Vintage, 1988.

———. "The Subject and Power." Afterword. *Michel Foucault: Beyond Structuralism and Hermeneutics*. By Hubert L. Dreyfus and Paul Rabinow. Chicago: U of Chicago P, 1982. 208–26.

Frankenheimer, John, dir. *The Manchurian Candidate*. United Artists, 1962.

———. *Seven Days in May*. Warner Brothers, 1964.

Freedman, Carl. "Towards a Theory of Paranoia: The Science Fiction of Philip K. Dick." *Science-Fiction Studies* 11.1 (1984): 15–24.

Freud, Sigmund. "A Case of Paranoia Running Counter to the Psycho-Analytical Theory of the Disease." 1915. *The Collected Papers of Sigmund Freud*. Trans. Joan Rivière. Vol. 2. London: Hogarth, 1949. 150–61. 5 vols. 1946–1950.

———. "A Case of Paranoia Running Counter to the Psycho-Analytic Theory of the Disease." 1915. *Standard Edition*. 14: 261–72.

———. *Civilization and Its Discontents*. 1930. *Standard Edition*. 21: 64–145.

———. "Constructions in Analysis." 1937. *Standard Edition*. 23: 255–70.

———. "Mitteilung eines der Psychoanalytischen Theorie Widersprechenden Falles von Paranoia." 1915. *Gesammelte Werke: Chronologisch Geordnet*. Ed. Marie Bonaparte. Vol. 10. London: Imago, 1946. 233–46. 18 vols. 1940–1968.

———. "On Narcissism: An Introduction." 1914. *Standard Edition*. 14: 73–104.

———. "Preface to Reik's *Ritual: Psycho-Analytic Studies*." 1919. *Standard Edition*. 17: 257–66.

———. "Psycho-Analytic Notes upon an Autobiographical Account of a Case of Paranoia (Dementia Paranoides)." 1911. *Standard Edition*. 12: 3–82.

———. *The Psychopathology of Everyday Life*. 1904. *Standard Edition*. 6: 1–279.

———. *The Standard Edition of the Complete Psychological Works of Sigmund Freud*. Ed. and trans. James Strachey. 24 vols. London: Hogarth, 1953–1974.

———. "The Uncanny." 1919. *Standard Edition*. 17: 219–52.

———. "The Unconscious." 1915. *Standard Edition*. 14: 159–216.

Friedman, Alan J., and Manfred Puetz. "*Gravity's Rainbow*: Science as Metaphor." *Thomas Pynchon*. Ed. Harold Bloom. New York: Chelsea, 1986. 23–35.

Fulcher, James. "American Conspiracy: Formula in Popular Fiction." *Midwest Quarterly* 24.2 (1983): 152–64.

Gaddis, William. *A Frolic of His Own: A Novel*. New York: Scribner's, 1994.

———. *JR*. New York: Penguin, 1975.

Georgeff, Michael P., and Amy L. Lansky, eds. *Reasoning about Actions and Plans*. San Mateo: Morgan Kaufmann, 1987.

Gibson, Graeme. "Margaret Atwood." *Eleven Canadian Novelists, Interviewed by Graeme Gibson*. Toronto: Anansi, 1973. 5–31.

Gibson, William. *Neuromancer*. New York: Ace, 1984.

Gilligan, Matthew J. "Stalking the Stalker: Developing New Laws to Thwart Those Who Terrorize Others." *Georgia Law Review* 27.1 (1992): 285–342.

Ginet, Carl. *On Action*. Cambridge: Cambridge UP, 1990.

Graumann, Carl F., and Serge Moscovici, eds. *Changing Conceptions of Conspiracy*. New York: Springer-Verlag, 1987.

Grove, Andrew S. *Only the Paranoid Survive: How to Exploit the Crisis Points that Challenge Every Company and Career*. New York: Currency/Doubleday, 1996.

Gusfield, Joseph R. *The Culture of Public Problems: Drinking-Driving and the Symbolic Order*. Chicago: U of Chicago P, 1981.

Guth, DeLloyd J., and David R. Wrone. *The Assassination of John F. Kennedy: A Comprehensive Historical and Legal Bibliography, 1963–1979*. Westport, CT: Greenwood Press, 1980.

Habermas, Jürgen. *The Philosophical Discourse on Modernity*. Cambridge: Harvard UP, 1987.

Haraway, Donna. "The Biopolitics of Postmodern Bodies." *Simians, Cyborgs, and Women: The Reinvention of Nature*. New York: Routledge, 1991. 203–30.

———. "A Cyborg Manifesto: Science, Technology, and Socialist-Feminism in the Late Twentieth Century." *Simians, Cyborgs, and Women: The Reinvention of Nature*. New York: Routledge, 1991. 149–81.

Hartz, Louis. *The Liberal Tradition in America: An Interpretation of American Political Thought Since the Revolution*. New York: Harcourt, Brace and World, 1955.

Harvey, David. *The Condition of Postmodernity: An Enquiry into the Origins of Cultural Change*. Oxford: Basil Blackwell, 1989.

Hassan, Ihab. "The Culture of Postmodernism." *Theory, Culture, and Society* 2.3 (1985): 119–32.

———. "Prometheus as Performer: Toward a Posthumanist Culture?" *Performance in Postmodern Culture*. Ed. Michael Benamou and Charles Caramello. Madison, WI: Coda, 1977. 201–17.

Hawkes, Nigel. *The Computer Revolution.* New York: Dutton, 1971.

Hayles, N. Katherine. *The Cosmic Web: Scientific Field Models and Literary Strategies in the Twentieth Century.* Ithaca: Cornell UP, 1984.

——. "Making the Cut: The Interplay of Narrative and System, or What Systems Theory Can't See." *Cultural Critique* 30 (Spring 1995): 71–101.

Heidegger, Martin. *Being and Time.* 1927. Trans. John Macquarrie and Edward Robinson. New York: Harper and Row, 1962.

Heller, Joseph. *Catch-22.* New York: Simon and Schuster, 1961.

——. *Something Happened.* New York: Knopf, 1974.

Helvey, T. C. *The Age of Information: An Interdisciplinary Survey of Cybernetics.* Englewood Cliffs, NJ: Educational Technology Publications, 1971.

Hite, Molly. *Ideas of Order in the Novels of Thomas Pynchon.* Columbus: Ohio State UP, 1983.

——. "Optics and Autobiography in Margaret Atwood's *Cat's Eye.*" *Twentieth Century Literature: A Scholarly and Critical Journal* 41.2 (1995): 135–59.

——. *The Other Side of the Story: Structures and Strategies of Contemporary Feminist Narratives.* Ithaca: Cornell UP, 1989.

Hitt, Jack, moderator. Forum with James Bailey, David Gerlernter, Jaron Lanier, and Charles Siebert, participants. "Our Machines, Ourselves." *Harper's* May 1997: 45–54.

Hofstadter, Richard. *The Paranoid Style in American Politics and Other Essays.* New York: Knopf, 1965.

Hollinger, Veronica. "Cybernetic Deconstructions: Cyberpunk and Postmodernism." *Mosaic* 23.2 (1990): 29–44.

Hoover, Bob. "Conspiracy Theories are Sign of the Times." *Toledo Magazine* 24 Mar. 1996: A1+.

Hoover, J. Edgar. *Masters of Deceit: The Story of Communism in America and How to Fight It.* New York: Henry Holt, 1958.

Hurt, Henry. *Reasonable Doubt.* New York: Holt, Rinehart, and Winston, 1985.

Hutcheon, Linda. *The Politics of Postmodernism.* London and New York: Routledge, 1989.

Irigaray, Luce. *Speculum of the Other Woman.* Trans. Gillian C. Gill. Ithaca, NY: Cornell UP, 1985.

Jakobson, Roman. "Two Aspects of Language and Two Types of Aphasic Disturbances." *Fundamentals of Language.* 2nd ed. The Hague: Mouton, 1971. 67–96.

Jameson, Fredric. *Postmodernism, or, The Cultural Logic of Late Capital.* Durham: Duke UP, 1991.

Johnson, Barbara. Translator's Introduction. *Dissemination.* By Jacques Derrida. Chicago: U of Chicago P, 1981. vii–xxxiii.

Johnson, Diane. *Health and Happiness.* New York: Knopf, 1990.

——. *The Shadow Knows.* New York: Knopf, 1974.

Johnson, George. *Architects of Fear: Conspiracy Theories and Paranoia in American Politics.* Los Angeles: Tarcher, 1983.

Johnson, Priscilla McMillan. *Marina and Lee.* New York: Harper and Row, 1977.

Johnston, David. "In Unabomber's Own Words, A Chilling Account of Murder." *New York Times* 29 April 1998: A1, A16.

Kah, Gary H. *En Route to Global Occupation.* Lafayette, LA: Huntington, 1991.

Kahn, Herman. *Forces for Change in the Final Third of the Twentieth Century.* Croton-on-Hudson, NY: Hudson Institute Press, 1970.

Kakutani, Michiko. "Bound by Suspicion." *New York Times Magazine* 19 Jan. 1997: 16.

Kesey, Ken. *One Flew Over the Cuckoo's Nest.* New York: Viking, 1962.

Kittler, Friedrich. "Unconditional Surrender." *Materialities of Communication.* Ed. Hans Ulrich Gumbrecht and K. Ludwig Pfeiffer. Trans. William Whobrey. Stanford: Stanford UP, 1994. 319–34.

Korcok, Milan. "Alcohol Treatment Industry to Grow as Risk Group Matures." *U.S. Journal of Drug and Alcohol Dependence* 11.3 (1987): 1–21.

Kroker, Arthur, Marilouise Kroker, and David Cook. *Panic Encyclopedia: The Definitive Guide to the Postmodern Scene.* New York: St. Martin's, 1989.

Kurtz, Michael L. *Crime of the Century: The Kennedy Assassination from a Historian's Perspective.* 2nd ed. Knoxville: U of Tennessee P, 1993.

Lacan, Jacques. "The Agency of the Letter in the Unconscious, or Reason Since Freud." *Écrits: A Selection.* Trans. Alan Sheridan. New York: Norton, 1977. 146–78.

———. "Aggressivity in Psychoanalysis." *Écrits: A Selection.* Trans. Alan Sheridan. New York: Norton, 1977. 8–29.

———. "Seminar on 'The Purloined Letter.' " 1956. Trans. Jeffrey Mehlman. 1972. *The Purloined Poe.* Ed. John Muller and William Richardson. Baltimore: Johns Hopkins UP, 1988. 28–54.

Laing, R. D. *The Divided Self: An Existential Study in Sanity and Madness.* New York: Pantheon, 1960.

———. *The Politics of Experience.* New York: Pantheon, 1967.

Lamberton, Donald M., ed. *The Information Revolution.* Annals of the American Academy of Political and Social Science. Vol. 412. Philadelphia: American Academy of Political and Social Science, 1974.

Lane, Mark. *Rush to Judgment.* New York: Holt, Rinehart, 1966.

Lawrence, Lincoln. *Were We Controlled?* New Hyde Park, NY: University Books, 1967.

LeClair, Tom. *The Art of Excess: Mastery in Contemporary American Fiction.* Urbana: U of Illinois P, 1989.

———. *In the Loop: Don DeLillo and the Systems Novel.* Urbana: U of Illinois P, 1987.

Lentricchia, Frank. "*Libra* as Postmodern Critique." *Introducing Don DeLillo.* Ed. Frank Lentricchia. Durham: Duke UP, 1991. 193–215.

Lewis, Anthony. "On the Release of the Warren Commission Report." *Report of the Warren Commission on the Assassination of President Kennedy.* New York: Bantam, 1964. xxxi–xxxvii.

Lifton, David. *Best Evidence: Disguise and Deception in the Assassination of John F. Kennedy.* New York: Macmillan, 1980.

Lipset, Seymour Martin, and Earl Raab. *The Politics of Unreason: Right-Wing Extremism in American, 1790–1977.* 2nd ed. Chicago: U of Chicago P, 1978.

Luhmann, Niklas. *Essays on Self-Reference.* New York: Columbia UP, 1990.

Lyotard, Jean-Francois. *The Postmodern Condition: A Report on Knowledge.* 1979. Trans. Geoff Bennington and Brian Massumi. Minneapolis: U of Minnesota P, 1984.

Macdonald, Andrew. *The Turner Diaries.* 2nd ed. Hillsborough, WV: National Vanguard, 1980.

Macpherson, C. B. *The Political Theory of Possessive Individualism: Hobbes to Locke.* Oxford: Oxford UP, 1962.

Madsen, Deborah. *The Postmodernist Allegories of Thomas Pynchon.* New York: St. Martin's, 1991.

Mailer, Norman. *An American Dream.* New York: Dial, 1965.

———. *The Executioner's Song.* Boston: Little, Brown, 1979.

———. "Footfalls in the Crypt." *Vanity Fair* Feb. 1992: 124–29, 171.

———. *Oswald's Tale: An American Mystery.* New York: Ballantine, 1995.

Malestic, Susan. "When Love Becomes Obsession... When Love Transforms into Hate." *Single Parent* Spring 1994: 23–25.

Maltz, Maxwell. *Psycho-Cybernetics: A New Way to Get More Living Out of Life.* New York: Essandess/Simon and Schuster, 1960.

Manchester, William R. *The Death of a President: November 20–November 25, 1963.* New York: Harper and Row, 1967.

Mandel, Ernest. *Late Capitalism.* Trans. Joris de Bres. London: NLB, 1976.

Marcus, Sharon. "Fighting Bodies, Fighting Words: A Theory and Politics of Rape Prevention." *Feminists Theorize the Political.* Ed. Judith Butler and Joan W. Scott. London: Routledge, 1992. 385–403.

Marcuse, Herbert. *Eros and Civilization: A Philosophical Inquiry into Freud.* Boston: Beacon Press, 1955.

———. *One-Dimensional Man: Studies in the Ideology of Advanced Industrial Society.* Boston: Beacon Press, 1964.

Marin, Rick, and T. Trent Gegax. "Conspiracy Mania Feeds Our Growing National Paranoia." *Newsweek* 30 Dec. 1996: 64–71.

Martin, James, and David Butler. *Viewdata and the Information Society.* Englewood Cliffs, NJ: Prentice-Hall, 1981.

Marx, Karl. *Capital: A Critique of Political Economy.* Vol. I. Trans. Samuel Moore and Edward Aveling. Rev. Ernest Untermann. New York: Modern Library, 1906.

McAnaney, Kathleen G., Laura A. Curliss, and C. Elizabeth Abeyta-Price. "From Imprudence to Crime: Anti-Stalking Laws." *Notre Dame Law Review* 68.4 (1993): 819–909.

McCarthy, Joseph R. *America's Retreat from Victory: The Story of George Catlett Marshall.* New York: Devin-Adair, 1951.

McElroy, Joseph. *Lookout Cartridge.* New York: Knopf, 1974.

McHale, Brian. *Constructing Postmodernism.* London: Routledge, 1992.

———. "Postmodernism, or the Anxiety of Master Narratives." *diacritics* 22.1 (1992): 17–33.

McHoul, Alec, and David Wills. *Writing Pynchon: Strategies in Fictional Analysis.* Urbana: U of Illinois P, 1990.

McLuhan, Marshall. *Understanding Media: The Extensions of Man.* New York: McGraw-Hill, 1964.

Meagher, Sylvia. *Accessories After the Fact: The Warren Commission, the Authorities, and the Report.* New York: Vintage, 1976.

Mendelson, Edward. "Gravity's Encyclopedia." *Mindful Pleasures: Essays on Thomas Pynchon.* Ed. George Levine and David Leverenz. Boston: Little, Brown, 1976. 161–95.

Miles, Barry. *William Burroughs: El Hombre Invisible.* New York: Hyperion, 1993.

Minsky, Marvin. *The Society of the Mind.* New York: Simon and Schuster, 1986.

Modleski, Tania. "The Terror of Pleasure: The Contemporary Horror Film and Postmodern Theory." *Studies in Entertainment: Critical Approaches to Mass Culture.* Ed. Tania Modleski. Bloomington: Indiana UP, 1986. 155–66.

Moore, Jim. *Conspiracy of One: The Definitive Book on the Kennedy Assassination.* 2nd ed. Fort Worth: The Summit Group, 1992.

Moore, Thomas. *The Style of Connectedness: Gravity's Rainbow and Thomas Pynchon.* Columbia: U of Missouri P, 1987.

Morgan, Ted. *Literary Outlaw: The Life and Times of William S. Burroughs.* New York: Henry Holt and Company, 1988.

Morrow, Lance. "The Power of Paranoia." *Time* 15 April 1996: 36–56.

Muller, John P., and William J. Richardson. *The Purloined Poe.* Baltimore: Johns Hopkins UP, 1988.

Mulvey, Laura. "Visual Pleasure and Narrative Cinema." *Screen* 16.3 (Autumn 1975): 6–18.

Murphy, Timothy. *Wising Up the Marks: The Amodern William Burroughs.* Berkeley: U of California P, 1997.

Newman, Charles. *The Post-Modern Aura: The Act of Fiction in an Age of Inflation.* Evanston: Northwestern UP, 1985.

O'Donnell, Patrick. "Engendering Paranoia in Contemporary Literature." *boundary 2* 19.1 (1992): 181–204.

——. "Obvious Paranoia: The Politics of Don DeLillo's *Running Dog.*" *Centennial Review* 34.1 (1990): 56–72.

Onley, Gloria. "Power Politics in Bluebeard's Castle." *Canadian Literature* 60 (1974): 21–42.

Packard, Vance. *The Hidden Persuaders.* New York: David McKay, 1957.

Pakula, Alan J., dir. *The Parallax View.* Paramount Pictures, 1974.

Palmer, James W., and Michael M. Riley. "America's Conspiracy Syndrome: From Capra to Pakula." *Studies in the Humanities* 8.2 (1981): 21–27.

Peele, Stanton. *Diseasing of America: Addiction Treatment Out of Control.* Boston: Houghton Mifflin, 1989.

Peele, Stanton, with Archie Brodsky. *Love and Addiction.* New York: Signet, 1975.

Piore, Michael J., and Charles F. Sabel. *The Second Industrial Divide: Possibilities for Prosperity.* New York: Basic Books, 1984.

Pipes, Daniel. *Conspiracy: How the Paranoid Style Flourishes and Where It Comes From.* New York: Free Press, 1997.

Polan, Dana. *Power and Paranoia: History, Narrative, and the American Cinema, 1940–1950.* New York: Columbia UP, 1986.

Porush, David. *The Soft Machine: Cybernetic Fiction.* New York: Methuen, 1985.

Posner, Gerald. *Case Closed: Lee Harvey Oswald and the Assassination of JFK.* New York: Random House, 1993.

Powers, Richard. *Gain.* New York: Farrar, Straus and Giroux, 1998.

Pratt, Annis. "*Surfacing* and the Rebirth Journey." *The Art of Margaret Atwood: Essays in Criticism.* Ed. Arnold E. Davidson and Cathy N. Davidson. Toronto: Anansi, 1981. 139–57.

President's Commission on the Assassination of President Kennedy. *Report of the Warren Commission on the Assassination of President Kennedy.* New York: Bantam, 1964.

Pynchon, Thomas. *The Crying of Lot 49.* Philadelphia: Lippincott, 1966.

——. *Gravity's Rainbow.* New York: Viking, 1973.

——. *V.* Philadelphia: Lippincott, 1963.

Redding, Arthur F. "Bruises, Roses: Masochism and the Writing of Kathy Acker." *Contemporary Literature* 35.2 (1994): 281–304.

Redfield, Marc W. "Pynchon's Post-Modern Sublime." *PMLA* 104 (1989): 152–62.

Reed, Ishmael. *Mumbo Jumbo.* New York: Atheneum, 1972.

Reich, Charles A. *The Greening of America.* New York: Random House, 1970.

Rich, Adrienne. "Compulsory Heterosexuality and Lesbian Existence." *Powers of Desire: The Politics of Sexuality.* Ed. Ann Barr Snitow, Christine Stansell, and Sharon Thompson. New York: Monthly Review, 1983. 177–205.

Richert, William, dir. *Winter Kills.* Winter Gold Productions, 1979.

Richta, Radovan, ed. *Civilization at the Crossroads: Social and Human Implications of the Scientific and Technological Revolution.* White Plains, NY: International Arts and Sciences, 1967.

Ricoeur, Paul. *Freud and Philosophy: An Essay on Interpretation.* Trans. Dennis Savage. New Haven, CT: Yale UP, 1970.

Riesman, David, Nathan Glazer, and Reuel Denney. *The Lonely Crowd: A Study of the Changing American Character.* New Haven, CT: Yale UP, 1950.

———. *The Lonely Crowd: A Study of the Changing American Character.* 1950. Abridged ed. New Haven, CT: Yale UP, 1961.

Rigney, Barbara Hill. *Margaret Atwood.* Totowa, NJ: Barnes and Noble, 1987.

Robins, Robert S., and Jerrold M. Post. *Political Paranoia: The Psychopolitics of Hatred.* New Haven, CT: Yale UP, 1997.

Ronell, Avital. *Crack Wars: Literature Addiction Mania.* Lincoln: U of Nebraska P, 1992.

Rorty, Amélie. "A Literary Postscript: Characters, Persons, Selves, Individuals." *The Identities of Persons.* Ed. Amélie Rorty. Berkeley: U of California P, 1976. 301–23.

Ross, Andrew. "Cyberpunk in Boystown." *Strange Weather: Culture, Science, and Technology in an Age of Limits.* London: Verso, 1991. 137–67.

Rostow, Walt W. *The Stages of Economic Growth.* Cambridge: Cambridge UP, 1960.

Rubenstein, Roberta. "Bodily Harm: Paranoid Vision in Contemporary Fiction by Women." *LIT: Literature Interpretation Theory* 1 (1989): 137–49.

Rubin, Gayle. "The Traffic in Women: Notes on the 'Political Economy' of Sex." *Women, Class, and the Feminist Imagination: A Socialist-Feminist Reader.* Ed. Karen V. Hansen and Ilene J. Philipson. Philadelphia: Temple UP, 1990. 74–113.

Russ, Joanna. "Someone's Trying to Kill Me and I Think It's My Husband: The Modern Gothic." *Journal of Popular Culture* 6.4 (Spring 1973): 666–91.

Sagan, Dorion. "Metametazoa: Biology and Multiplicity." *Incorporations.* Ed. Jonathan Crary and Sanford Kwinter. New York: Zone/MIT P, 1992. 362–85.

Salisbury, Harrison E. "An Introduction to the Warren Commission Report." *Report of the Warren Commission on the Assassination of President Kennedy.* New York: Bantam, 1964. xv–xxix.

Sanders, Scott. "Pynchon's Paranoid History." *Twentieth Century Literature* 21 (1975): 177–92.

Sass, Louis A. *Madness and Modernism: Insanity in the Light of Modern Art, Literature, and Thought.* New York: Basic, 1992.

Scarry, Elaine. *The Body in Pain: The Making and Unmaking of the World.* New York: Oxford UP, 1985.

Schafly, Phyllis. *A Choice Not an Echo.* Alton, IL: Pere Marquette, 1964.

Schaub, Thomas. *American Fiction in the Cold War.* Madison: U of Wisconsin P, 1991.

———. *Pynchon: The Voice of Ambiguity.* Urbana: U of Illinois P, 1981.

Scheim, David. *Contract on America: The Mafia Murder of President John F. Kennedy.* New York: Shapolsky, 1988.

Schenck v. United States. 249 U.S. 47. 1919.

Schick, Frederic. *Understanding Actions: An Essay in Reasons.* New York: Cambridge UP, 1991.

Schor, Naomi. "Female Paranoia: The Case for Psychoanalytic Feminist Criticism." *Yale French Studies* 62 (1981): 204–19.

Schreber, Daniel Paul. *Memoirs of My Nervous Illness.* 1903. Trans. I. Macalpine and R. A. Hunter. Cambridge: Harvard UP, 1988.

Schwab, Gabriele. *Subjects without Selves: Transitional Texts in Modern Fiction.* Cambridge: Harvard UP, 1994.

Schwenger, Peter. *Phallic Critiques.* London: Routledge, 1984.

Scott, Peter Dale. *Deep Politics and the Death of JFK.* Berkeley: U of California P, 1993.

Scott, Ridley, dir. *Blade Runner.* Warner Brothers/Embassy Pictures/Columbia TriStar, 1982.

Sedgwick, Eve Kosofsky. "Epidemics of the Will." *Incorporations.* Ed. Jonathan Crary and Sanford Kwinter. Cambridge: Zone/MIT P, 1992. 582–95.

——. *Epistemology of the Closet.* Berkeley: U of California P, 1990.

Seed, David, *The Fictional Labyrinths of Thomas Pynchon.* Iowa City: U of Iowa P, 1988.

Seidenberg, Roderick. *Posthistoric Man: An Inquiry.* Chapel Hill: U of North Carolina P, 1950.

Seltzer, Mark. *Bodies and Machines.* New York: Routledge, 1992.

——. "Serial Killers (1)." *differences* 5.1 (1993): 92–128.

——. "Statistical Persons." *diacritics* 17 (Fall 1987): 83–98.

Shapiro, David. *Autonomy and Rigid Character.* New York: Basic, 1981.

Shils, Edward. *The Torment of Secrecy: The Background and Consequences of American Security Policies.* Glencoe, IL: Free Press, 1956.

Showalter, Elaine. *The Female Malady: Women, Madness, and English Culture, 1830–1980.* New York: Pantheon, 1985.

Silko, Leslie Marmon. *Almanac of the Dead.* New York: Simon and Schuster, 1991.

Singh, Robert. *The Farrakhan Phenomenon: Race, Reaction, and the Paranoid Style in American Politics.* Washington: Georgetown UP, 1997.

Slotkin, Richard. *Regeneration Through Violence: The Mythology of the American Frontier, 1600–1860.* Middletown, CT: Wesleyan UP, 1973.

Smith, William. *Assassination by Consensus: The Story behind the Kennedy Assassination.* Washington: L'Avant Garde Publications, 1966.

Snitow, Ann Barr. "Mass Market Romance: Pornography for Women Is Different." *Powers of Desire: The Politics of Sexuality.* Ed. Ann Barr Snitow, Christine Stansell, and Sharon Thompson. New York: Monthly Review, 1983. 245–63.

Sobchack, Vivian. *Screening Space: The American Science Fiction Film.* 2nd ed. New York: Ungar, 1987.

Sponsler, Claire. "Cyberpunk and the Dilemma of Postmodern Narrative: The Example of William Gibson." *Contemporary Literature* 33.4 (1992): 625–44.

Stern, Kenneth. *A Force Upon the Plain.* New York: Simon and Schuster, 1997.

Stine, G. Harry. *The Third Industrial Revolution.* New York: Putnam's, 1975.

Stone, Oliver, dir. *JFK.* Warner Brothers, 1991.

——, dir. *Natural Born Killers.* Warner Brothers, 1995.

Strauss, Leo. "Persecution and the Art of Writing." *Persecution and the Art of Writing.* 1952. Chicago: U of Chicago P, 1988. 22–37.

Swanson, David W., Philip J. Bohnert, and Jackson A. Smith. *The Paranoid.* Boston: Little, Brown, 1970.

Tabbi, Joseph. "Introduction." *Electronic Book Review* 4 (Winter 1996–1997). 10 Oct. 1998 <http://www.altx.com/ebr/ebr4/ebr4.htm>.

——. *Postmodern Sublime: Technology and American Writing from Mailer to Cyberpunk.* Ithaca, NY: Cornell UP, 1995.

Tanner, Tony. *City of Words: American Fiction 1950–1970.* London: Jonathan Cape, 1971.

Tausk, Victor. "The Influencing Machine." 1919. *Incorporations.* Ed. Jonathan Crary and Sanford Kwinter. Cambridge: Zone/MIT P, 1992. 542–69.

Taylor, Charles. *Sources of the Self.* Cambridge: Harvard UP, 1990.

——. "The Concept of a Person." *Human Agency and Language: Philosophical Papers I.* Cambridge: Cambridge UP, 1985. 97–114.

——. "What Is Human Agency?" *Human Agency and Language: Philosophical Papers I.* Cambridge: Cambridge UP, 1985. 15–44.

Thomas, D. M. *Flying into Love.* New York: Scribner's, 1992.

Thompson, Josiah. *Six Seconds in Dallas: A Micro-Study of the Kennedy Assassination.* New York: Gernard Geis, 1967.

Thoreau, Henry David. *Walden and Other Writings of Henry David Thoreau.* Ed. Brooks Atkinson. New York: Modern Library, 1937.

Toffler, Alvin. *Future Shock.* New York: Random, 1970.

——. *The Third Wave.* New York: William Morrow, 1980.

Tomeski, Edward Alexander. *The Computer Revolution: The Executive and the New Information Technology.* New York: Macmillan, 1970.

Tompkins, Jane. *West of Everything: The Inner Life of Westerns.* Oxford: Oxford UP, 1992.

Touraine, Alain. *The Post-Industrial Society.* New York: Random, 1971.

Truman, Harold. "The Recall of General Douglas MacArthur: April 11, 1951 (Department of State Bulletin, April 16, 1951)." *Documents of American History.* 8th ed. Vol. 2. New York: Appleton-Century-Crofts, 1968. 568–70.

Turner, Patricia A. *I Heard It through the Grapevine: Rumor in African-American Culture.* Berkeley: U of California P, 1993.

Tuten, Lisa, and Ellen Sherman. "Trail of Terror: 'I Was Stalked.'" *McCall's* Aug. 1995: 55–59.

Unabomber. *See* F. C.

"Unabomb Trial Likely to Focus on Sanity." *New York Times* 10 Nov. 1997: A1+.

Varela, Francisco, Evan Thompson, and Eleanor Rosch. *The Embodied Mind: Cognitive Science and Human Experience.* Cambridge: MIT P, 1993.

Vickers, Geoffrey. *Freedom in a Rocking Boat: Changing Values in an Unstable Society.* London: Penguin, 1970.

Vonnegut, Kurt. *Mother Night.* New York: Harper and Row, 1961.

——. *The Sirens of Titan.* New York: Delacorte, 1959.

Wallace, David Foster. *Infinite Jest.* Boston: Little, Brown, 1996.

Weber, Max. *Economy and Society: An Outline of Interpretive Sociology.* Ed. Guenther Roth and Claus Wittich. 2 vols. Berkeley: U of California P, 1968.

Weir, Peter, dir. *The Truman Show.* Paramount Pictures, 1998.

Weisberg, Harold. *Whitewash: The Report on the Warren Report.* New York: Dell, 1966.

Weisner, C. M., and R. Room. "Financing and Ideology in Alcohol Treatment." *Social Problems* 32 (1984): 167–84.

Weiss, Philip. "Clinton Crazy." *New York Times Magazine* 23 Feb. 1997: 33–67.

White, Hayden. *The Tropics of Discourse: Essays in Cultural Criticism.* Baltimore: Johns Hopkins UP, 1978.

Whyte, William. *The Organization Man.* New York: Simon and Schuster, 1956.

Wiener, Norbert. *Cybernetics, or Control and Communication in the Animal and the Machine.* 1948. 2nd ed. Cambridge: MIT P, 1961.

———. *The Human Use of Human Beings: Cybernetics and Society.* New York: Da Capo, 1950.

Williams, Frederick. *The Communications Revolution.* Beverly Hills: Sage, 1982.

Wilson, George M. *The Intentionality of Human Action.* Stanford: Stanford UP, 1989.

Wolfe, Cary. *Critical Environments: Postmodern Theory and the Pragmatics of the "Outside."* Minneapolis: U of Minnesota P, 1998.

Yurick, Sol. *Richard A.* New York: Arbor, 1981.

Index

Abrams, M. H., 86

Accidents, 22–24, 217n3. *See also* Chance; Coincidence; Patterns

Acker, Kathy, 33, 52; *Empire of the Senseless*, vii, 15, 20, 44, 96, 158, 189, 195–201, 217n4, 218n12

Addiction, 44, 215n1; cellular level, 173–75; communications systems and, 171–73; control and, 163, 165–68, 178, 217n18; disease-based model, 164–65; possessive individualism and, 166, 167; reconditioning and, 178–84; sexuality and, 178–79; as way of life, 161–62; will and, 162, 165, 176

African American discourse, 11, 204n14

Agency, 10, 23, 204nn15, 16, 210n4; all-or-nothing logic, 10, 25, 106, 163–64, 168, 169; body and, 29–30, 42–43, 81–87; of bureaucracy, 48, 59–63; diminished, 11–12, 49–56; historical agent, 141–42, 147, 149–50; interior *vs.* exterior, 99–100, 118, 119–20, 162–63; of language, 40–41, 85–87; as property, 10, 53, 147, 163, 186–87, 205n18; social order and, 135–36, 209n11; as term, 83; violence and, 14, 147–48, 153–54, 205n19. *See also* Agency panic; Conspiracy theories

Agency panic, vii–viii, 7–16, 27, 201–2; body and, 84–85, 92–93; at cellular level, 173–75; as conservative response, 14–15, 44, 164–65, 203n3; external control and, 99–100, 105–6; gender implications, 32–34, 148, 212n3; intentionality and, 12–13, 15–16, 145–46; misrecognition and, 16, 143–44, 152; physical symptoms and, 29–30; as response to postmodernism, 15, 40–42. *See also* Agency; Conspiracy theories; Individualism

All-or-nothing logic, 10, 25, 106, 163–64, 168, 169

American nationalist ethic, 78–79

Anagrams, 22–23, 41, 206n25

Anorexia, 109–10, 122–23, 213n18

Anthropomorphism, 176

Antisocialism, 10, 57, 63–68, 78, 148, 215–16n4

Apathy, 26, 27

Archaeology, 139–42

Armstrong, Edward, 215n1

Assassination by Consensus (Smith), 147

Atwood, Margaret, vii, 12, 16, 18, 33, 34, 43, 203n8, 212n9; *Bodily Harm*, 43, 109, 117, 119–20, 123–24, 129–32, 213n16; *The Edible Woman*, 43, 108–10, 112–14, 116, 122–24,

126–27; *Lady Oracle*, 43, 115–16, 118–19, 212n12; *Surfacing*, 43, 107

Autonomy, 3, 4, 6, 12–13, 31, 48, 162, 208n5, 216n2

Autopoiesis, 39–40, 88

Barthes, Roland, 150

Bateson, Gregory, 38–39, 62, 65, 84, 88, 177, 178, 209n15

Baudrillard, Jean, 27–28, 33, 51–52, 73, 206–07n32, 209n15, 209n19

Beatles, 22, 30

Being, ontology of, 170

Bellah, Robert, 208n5

Beniger, James, 37–38, 207n1, 210n4, 212n21

Benjamin, Jessica, 95–96

Berger, John, 114

Bersani, Leo, 13, 113, 121, 141, 211n15

Bertalanffy, Ludwig von, 209n15

Bérubé, Michael, 211n15

Bierce, Ambrose, 187, 188

Binary oppositions, 91–93, 211n14

Biocontrol, 4, 182

Biology, postmodern, 174, 216n11

Birkerts, Sven, 31

Blade Runner (Scott), 44, 189–91

Bodily Harm (Atwood), 43, 109, 117, 119–20, 123–24, 127, 129–32, 213n16

Body: addiction and, 169–78; agency and, 29–30, 42–43, 81–87; anonymous effects and, 130–32; boundaries of identity and, 99, 121–26, 192; bureaucracy and, 29–30, 68–74; collective body, 64–65, 136, 145; communication and, 31, 72–73, 84–89; cybernetics and, 73–75, 84, 87–89; instability of, 93–94; measurement model and, 97, 98, 99–106; messages and, 87–94; persecution narratives and, 108–9, 114, 124; pornography and, 94–99, 211n15. *See also* Sexuality

Bordo, Susan, 125, 213n18

Bowert, William, 147

Brown, Norman O., 211n20

Bukatman, Scott, 186, 194, 216n2

Bureaucracy, 42, 217n18; agency of, 48, 59–63; autonomy of, 48; body and, 29–30, 68–74; breakdown of, 75–77; CEO, decline of, 58–63; as enemy, 48–49, 56–57; individualism, control of, 12–13, 48–49, 68–75; making *vs.*

233

Individual (*Continued*)
boundaries and, 99, 121–26, 151, 162–63, 186–87; Enlightenment concepts of, 53; fragmentation of, 15, 107, 114, 123, 194; *vs.* society, 10–11, 14, 78, 94, 194–95, 208–9n10

Individualism, 3–4, 6, 10, 13–14, 23, 30; American view of, 203nn6, 8; as antisocial, 10, 66–68, 78, 148, 215–16n4; bureaucracies and, 12–13, 48–49, 68–75; capitalism and, 133–34, 155; of corporations, 187–88; defenses of, 40, 41, 136–37; hyperindividualism, 25, 37, 58, 78, 150–51, 172, 177; masculine view of, 14, 32–37, 57, 137, 147–48, 152–55, 199; possessive individualism, 14, 25, 144, 151–53, 157, 166, 167, 205n18; in postmodern texts, 186–87; postwar challenges to, 6, 7–8; seventeenth-century, 205n18

"Industrial Society and Its Future" (F.C.), 37

Influencing machine delusion, 32–37

Information age, 16, 47, 207nn1, 34

Inner-direction, 49–56, 59, 208n5

Insanity: definitions, 65–66; feminization and, 35–36. *See also* Paranoia; Schizophrenia

Intentionality, 5, 9–10, 12–13, 101; body and, 84, 175; at genetic level, 175; social systems and, 15–16, 145–46

Interior *vs.* exterior, 99–100, 118, 119–20, 162–63

Interpretation, 27; crises of, 16–25, 27, 52, 115; paranoia and, 16–18, 211n15; psychoanalytic, 17, 18, 23–25; of texts, 21–22

Interpretive community, 17

Introjection, 33, 51, 176, 216n2

"Invisible Generation, The" (Burroughs), 171, 172

Invisible Man (Ellison), 36, 208n7

Involuntary psychological collectivization, 50, 182–83

Irigaray, Luce, 113

Jacobson, Roman, 211n12

Jameson, Frederic, 9, 10, 133, 153, 155, 189, 207n1, 214n1

Johnson, Barbara, 40

Johnson, Diane, 33, 108; *The Shadow Knows*, 34, 43, 117, 118, 121–22, 127–29, 131, 132

JR (Gaddis), 76

Junk virus, 165, 166, 169

Junky (Burroughs), 166, 174, 180

Kaczynski, Theodore, 10, 37, 204n13. *See also* Unabomber

Kah, Gary H., 207n33

Kasabian, Linda, 28

Kennedy assassination, 11, 12, 16, 26, 43–44, 133–37, 142–43, 155–56, 191, 214n2; American misgivings about, 137–38; causality and, 134–35, 138, 145, 146–47; films, 144. *See also* Libra

Kesey, Ken, 34–35

Kipling, Rudyard, 88

Kittler, Friedrich, 88

Knowledge production, 16, 20, 85, 214n4

Lacan, Jacques, 40, 43, 85–86, 98, 210n8, 211n18, 214n4

Lady Oracle (Atwood), 43, 115–16, 118–19, 212n12

Laing, R. D., 11–12, 13, 65, 186

Language, 23, 40–41, 86–87, 200–201

Lanier, Jaron, 204n15

Lauretis, Teresa de, 108

Lawrence, Lincoln, 147

Leadership, 59–62, 75–76

LeClair, Tom, 207n36, 209n15

Lectures on Conditioned Reflexes (Pavlov), 84

Lentricchia, Frank, 215nn8, 11

Lewis, Anthony, 137

Liberal individualism. *See* Individualism

Libra (DeLillo), 12, 16, 21, 44, 137, 138–59, 211n16. *See also* Kennedy assassination

Library, viii

Literary criticism, 22

Locke, John, 14

Lonely Crowd, The (Riesman), 6, 42, 47, 49–50, 54–56, 58–61, 208n4

Love and Addiction (Peele), 161–62

Luhmann, Niklas, 39, 93–94, 214n1

Lyotard, Jean-Francois, 20, 204n10

Macpherson, C. B., 14, 53, 205n18

Madsen, Deborah, 210n6

Mailer, Norman, 26, 134, 156

Maltz, Maxwell, 87–88

Man, Paul de, 40

Manchurian Candidate (Frankenheimer), 36, 144

Mandel, Ernst, 207n1

Manson, Charles, 22, 26, 30

Mao II (DeLillo), 148, 214n6, 215n9

Marcus, Sharon, 213n22

Marcuse, Herbert: *Eros and Civilization*, 208n6; *One-Dimensional Man*, 42, 51, 56–57, 61, 63, 208–09, 209n11, 216n4

Marx, Karl, 166, 216n8

Marxism, 166, 189, 190

Masculinity, 14, 32–33, 36–37, 57, 120, 148, 152, 154–55

Masochism, 199

Masochism in Modern Man (Reik), 84

Mass control, 2–3, 8, 35
Mass media, 2–3, 4, 50, 147, 153–54
Master narratives, 8–9, 144
Masters of Deceit (Hoover), 2, 3–4
Mathematical model, 97, 98, 99–106. *See also* Statistics
Maturana, Humberto, 39
McCarthy, Joseph, 2, 144, 203n1
McHale, Brian, 218n12
McVeigh, Timothy, 37
Memoirs of My Nervous Illness (Schreber), 19, 111
Memory, 197, 198
Mental systems, 17–20, 24–25, 156, 211n14, 216n12; military, 65–66. *See also* Burroughs, William S.; Freud, Sigmund; Paranoia; Psychoanalysis; Schizophrenia
Metaphor, 91
Metonymy, 91
Militia movement, 205n19
Mills, C. Wright, 49
Modernism, 15, 18, 185, 205n21
Modleski, Tania, 206n32
Mother Night (Vonnegut), 22
Motivational researchers, 5
Motive, 23–24, 27–28, 187–88, 206n27
Murphy, Timothy, 216n9

Naked Lunch (Burroughs), 164–71, 174, 176, 178, 180–81, 215n2
Names, The (DeLillo), 155, 156, 206n25
Narratives, 7–8, 43–44, 101, 195; of agency-in-decline, 49–56; antidotes for lost autonomy, 56–58; master narratives, 8–9, 144. *See also* Persecution narratives
National Electronics Conference, 182
Nationalism, 66–67, 77–79
Neuromancer (Gibson), 44, 188, 191–94, 217n5
New Left, 207n38
Newman, Charles, 41
Newton, Huey, 30
Normality, 17, 20, 126, 129–30
Nostalgia, 33, 207n32

O'Donnell, Patrick, 214n4
"On Coincidence" (Burroughs), 25, 176–77, 188
One-Dimensional Man (Marcuse), 42, 51, 56–57, 61, 63, 209–09n10, 209n11, 216n4
One Flew Over the Cuckoo's Nest (Kesey), 34–35
Only the Paranoid Survive (Grove), 58
Operation Mind Control (Bowert), 147
Opium: the Diary of a Cure (Cocteau), 168
Organization man, 42, 50–51

Organization Man, The (Whyte), 6, 42, 50–51, 54, 57, 59–61, 73, 77, 78, 195, 209n12m63
Origin of the Brunists (Coover), 22
Oswald, Lee Harvey, 151, 214n7, 215n8; as character in *Libra*, 12, 133–36, 145, 146–51
Other-direction, 49–56, 59, 191, 208n5

Packard, Vance: *The Hidden Persuaders*, 1–5, 16, 44, 84, 182–83, 203nn2, 5, 216–17n17
Panic, 14, 171, 217–18n9
Panic Encyclopedia, 204n16
Paradigm, 91
Paranoia, 1, 185, 205n21, 209n15, 210n6; collective identity and, 64–66; gender and, 110–17, 212n3, 213n16; historical context, 2, 8; homosexuality and, 111, 112–13; individual boundaries and, 99, 121–26; as intellectual stance, 20–21; interpretation and, 16–18, 205–06n22, 211n15; operational paranoia, 18–20; pathological model, 13–14, 20, 185–86; politics and, 13, 205n17; as postwar theme, 1–3, 14–15, 26–27; reality and, 17–18, 24; as reasonable response, 27, 49, 65; resistance and, 56–58; self-consciousness about, 19, 27; traditional conceptions, 19–20; uncertainty and, 19–20. *See also* Causality
Paranoid Corporation, The (Cohen and Cohen), 58
Paranoid style, 1–2, 65, 142
Parasitism, 170, 173, 174–76
Pathological model, 13–14, 20, 185–86
Patterns, 21–23, 28
Pavlov, Ivan Petrovich, 84
Pavlovian psychology, 90–91
Peele, Stanton, 161–62, 217n18
"Persecution and the Art of Writing" (Strauss), 21
Persecution narratives, 16, 21, 29, 34, 43, 213n16; anorexia narratives, 109–10, 122–23, 213n18; body and, 108–9, 114, 124; conventions of, 118–20; ghostlike figure, 107, 108, 109, 110; immateriality of stalker, 131–32; legal discourse, 120; male bodies in, 126–28; political context, 128–30; self-surveillance and, 114–16; social institutions and, 120–21; spectator function and, 115–16. *See also* *Bodily Harm*; *Edible Woman, The*; *Shadow Knows, The*
Phaedrus (Plato), 171
Pharmakon, 168, 170, 171
Pierce, William, 204n14
Pipes, Daniel, 205n17, 207n33
Plato, 171
Play It As It Lays (Didion), 34, 206n29

CPSIA information can be obtained at www.ICGtesting.com
Printed in the USA
BVOW071414120613

323072BV00001B/12/P